Welfare of Disadvantaged

About the Editors

Asok Kumar Sarkar, an alumnus of Tata Institute of Social Sciences and Jawaharlal Nehru University, is Professor and former Head of Department of Social Work, Visva-Bharati, Sriniketan. Before joining the present position, he served in Institute of Health Management, Pachod; Department of Social Work, Assam University, Silchar; and School of Social Work, IGNOU, New Delhi in different capacities. He has authored and edited books including NGOs: The New Lexicon of Health Care (Concept), NGOs and Globalization: Developmental and Organizational Facets (Rawat) and contributed papers in many academic and peer reviewed journals. He has been serving as editor of Journal of Social Work and Social Development since 2010. His areas of research interests include maternal morbidity, reproductive health, health care, NGOs and social development.

Prasanta Kumar Ghosh is a Professor and former Head of the Department of Social Work, Visva-Bharati. He is a proactive social work educator, researcher and activist. He has served as Reader in the Department of Personnel Management & Industrial Relations at Tata Institute of Social Sciences, Mumbai and Principal of Institute of Rural Reconstruction, Visva-Bharati. He is a Fulbright Fellow on Academic Administration. He has been a Visiting Professor at the School of Social Work, of the University of Illinois, Urbana-Campaign and Dominican University, Chicago, USA. He has published articles in books, journals in the area of social welfare and social development at the national and international levels. He has also published number of research papers and attended a number of national and international seminars and conferences. Apart from his academic activities he has been engaged in promoting rural entrepreneurship for livelihood development since last three decades.

Welfare of Disadvantaged

Exploring Community Development Approach

Editors
Asok Kumar Sarkar
Prasanta Kumar Ghosh

CONCEPT PUBLISHING COMPANY PVT. LTD.
NEW DELHI-110059

ISBN-13: 978-93-86682-21-5

First Published 2018

Published and Printed by

Concept Publishing Company Pvt. Ltd.
A/15-16, Commercial Block, Mohan Garden
New Delhi-110059 (India)
T: 25351460, 25351794, *F*: 091-11-25357109
E: publishing@conceptpub.com, W: www.conceptpub.com

Cataloging in Publication Data—Courtesy: D.K. Agencies (P) Ltd. <docinfo@dkagencies.com>

Asok Kumar Sarkar, Prasanta Kumar Ghosh.
Welfare of Disadvantaged : exploring community development approach/editors,
pages cm
Includes bibliographical references and index.
ISBN 9789386682215

1. Community development—India. 2. People with disabilities—Government policy—India. 3. Women—Government policy—India. I. Sarkar, Asok Kumar, 1971- editor. II. Ghosh, Prasanta Kumar (Professor of social work), editor.

LCC HV393.W45 2018 DDC 361.60954 23

Preface

'Welfare' or 'common good', which is beneficial to a particular group or all in the society, cannot be done through one person. It needs collective action or collective decision to initiate work. In ancient time, Greek philosophers Plato (427-347 BCE) and Aristotle (384-322 BCE) had spoken much on the 'public good' or 'common good' and established their doctrines. In ancient India, Kautilya's (350-275 BCE) *Arthashastra* discussed in detail the justification or means or ways of social welfare. The issue of 'common good' became very prominent in the modern Europe. Several thinkers like John Locke (1632-1704), David Hume (1711-1776), Rousseau (1712-1778), Adam Smith (1723-1790), etc. being political thinkers debated to a great extent on this issue. Thus, the *Social Choice Theory* or *Collective Decision Rules* emerged, which tried to understand the process of common good. In the contemporary era, Professor Amartya Sen, winner of the Nobel Prize in economics and great thinker, has developed authority on the issue of "collective choice and social welfare" through his path-breaking work. Thus, it is well understood or evident that 'common good' needs plurality in approach.

The present book offers a plural view. It insists on collective interventions, i.e. initiatives of the state, non-profit and voluntary sector, and corporate bodies, towards the welfare of disadvantaged in Indian context. There are different approaches and those could be institutional or community-based. This book focuses only on community development approach. There are total twenty articles in the book. Five articles included here were submitted for the National Seminar on "*Community Development, Social Work and HIV/AIDS*" held in the Department of Social Work, Visva-Bharati,

Sriniketan, West Bengal. The remaining fifteen articles are invited for this book. The book has been divided into three sections. Section-I, entitled as *Community Development: Issues and Models,* ranging from Chapter 1 to Chapter 6, has discussed vividly various debates or emerging concerns and models of community development being practiced. Section-II, entitled as *Disadvantaged and Community Development,* includes Chapter 7 to Chapter 15, is on disadvantaged people such as financially poor and marginalized, scheduled tribes, persons with disabilities (PWDs), school going poor children, vulnerable or sexually abused children etc. Section-III on *Gender and Community Development* begins from Chapter 16 and incorporates the remaining articles. This section touches upon domestic violence issue, marital disputes, women's empowerment, women's health, women's contribution to environment etc.

There are many people who must be acknowledged for academic contribution, continuous support and inspiration to bring out this book. The idea to publish this book would not come if the national seminar as cited above would not have taken place. Professor Gracious Thomas, former Director of School of Social Work, Indira Gandhi National Open University (IGNOU), New Delhi collaborated with Professor Prasanta Kumar Ghosh, former Head, Department of Social Work, Visva-Bharati, Sriniketan, West Bengal to host the seminar at Sriniketan. I profusely thank to both of them for their initiatives that led the foundation stone for this gigantic task. I also extend thanks to Dr. Joseph Varghese and Mr. Neelmani Jayswal who initially shared some responsibilities but could not precede much due to very few articles. At the outset, we had only five to six papers based on the national seminar and it was just an impossible task to shape an edited book. Therefore, many authors such as Professor Partha Sarathi De, Dr. Paramita Roy, Dr. Sujit Kumar Paul, Dr. Tarun Bikash Sukai, Dr. Rakesh Dwivedi, Dr. Rupa Biswas, Dr. Swapan Shaw, Mrs. Moumita Laha, Ms. Srenwantee Bhattacharjee, Mr. Subhrasil Basu and Mr. Indranil Sarkar were invited to kindly contribute papers for this book. We are really indebted to all of them. As several papers were lying with us for long time, a few authors' continuous pressure and persuasion forced us to finally materialize this work. Mr. Indranil

Sarkar, one of the invited authors and our student, assisted us at the last moment in typing and clerical work. Mr. Ashok Kumar Mittal, Managing Director, Concept Publishing Company (P) Ltd., New Delhi personally met us, continuously persuaded and encouraged to complete this long pending work. We are thankful to him also. The book would be valuable and more useful for the master degree students, research scholars and teachers in the disciplines such as social work, sociology, rural development and development studies. Hope readers will find the volume constructive, informative and very timely in today's context.

Asok Kumar Sarkar
Prasanta Kumar Ghosh

Contents

SECTION-II
Disadvantaged and Community Development

List of Contributors

Prof. Asok Kumar Sarkar, Professor, Department of Social Work, Visva-Bharati, Sriniketan, West Bengal.
Email: *asoksarkar2001@yahoo.co.uk*

Dr. Ankur Saxena, Associate Professor, Faculty of Social Work, M.S. University, Baroda, Gujarat.
Email: *ankur.a. saxena@gmail.com*

Dr. Amit Bhowmick, Assistant Professor, Department of Sociology, Noor Mohammad Smriti Mahavidyalaya, Dhulian, Murshidabad, West Bengal.
Email: *partha_de2006@yahoo. co.in*

Indranil Sarkar, Research Scholar, Department of Social Work, Visva-Bharati, Sriniketan, West Bengal.
Email: *indranilsarkar@gmail.com*

Dr. Jaimon Varghese, Assistant Professor, CSRD Institute of Social Work and Research, Ahmednagar, Maharashtra.
Email: *jaimonbobby@gmail.com*

Dr. Kakali Paul Mitra, Assistant Professor, Purnidevi Chowdhury Girls' College, Bolpur, Birbhum, West Bengal.
Email: *skpaulrd@gmail.com*

Kaushalendra Pratap Singh, Research and Teaching Assistant (RTA), School of Social Work, IGNOU, New Delhi.
Email: *gaur.kpsingh@gmail.com*

Dr. Moumita Laha, Assistant Professor, Department of Social Work, Visva-Bharati, Santiniketan, West Bengal.
Email: *moumi.laha@gmail.com*

Dr. Paramita Roy, Associate Professor, Department of Social Work, Visva-Bharati, Sriniketan, West Bengal.
Email: *proy669@gmail.com*

Prof. Partha Sarathi De, Professor, Department of Sociology, University of Kalyani, Kalyani, Nadia, West Bengal. Email: *partha_de2006@yahoo.co.in*

P.J. Kochurani, Ph.D. Scholar, Nirmala Sadan, Muvattupuzha, Kerala. Email: *sr.ranijose@yahoo.in*

Prof. Prasanta Kumar Ghosh, Professor, Department of Social Work, Visva-Bharati, Sriniketan, West Bengal. Email: *prasanta1958@gmail.com*

Dr. Rakesh Dwivedi, Assistant Professor, Department of Social Work, University of Lucknow, Lucknow, Uttar Pradesh. Email: *dr.rakeshdwivedi@gmail.com*

Dr. Ram Prasad Das, Associate Professor, Department of Social Work, Visva-Bharati, Sriniketan, West Bengal. Email: *dasramprasad66@gmail.com*

Dr. Rupa Biswas, Assistant Professor and In-charge, Department of Social Work, Durgapur Law College, Durgapur, West Bengal. Email: *rupabiswas13@rediffmail.com*

Dr. Rupa Ghosh, Assistant Professor, Loreto College, Kolkata, West Bengal. Email: *rupaghosh21@gmail.com*

Sekhar Sain, Research Scholar, Department of Social Work, Visva-Bharati, Sriniketan, West Bengal. Email: *sekhsain@ gmail.com*

Srenwantee Bhattacharjee, Research Scholar, Department of Social Work, Visva-Bharati, Sriniketan, West Bengal. Email: *srenwantee11b@gmail.com*

Subhrasil Basu, State Agricultural Management & Extension Training Institute (SAMETI), Ramakrishna Mission Ashrama, Narendrapur, Kolkata, West Bengal. Email: *sbasu3010@ gmail.com*

Dr. Sudeshna Lahiri, Assistant Professor, Department of Education, University of Calcutta, Kolkata, West Bengal. Email: *sudeshna.lahiri@gmail.com*

Dr. Sujit Kumar Paul, Associate Professor, Department of Lifelong Learning and Extension, Visva-Bharati, Sriniketan, Birbhum, West Bengal. Email: *skpaulrd@gmail.com*

Suvashree Roy Chowdhury, Junior Research Fellow-UGC, Department of Education, University of Calcutta, Kolkata, West Bengal. Email: *suvashreeroychowdhury@gmail.com*

Swapan Shaw, Welfare Officer, Central Social Welfare Board, New Delhi. Email: *swapanshawmsw@gmail.com*

Dr. Tarun Bikash Sukai, Assistant Professor, Department of Social Work, Assam University, Silchar, Assam.
Email: *tbsukai@gmail.com*

Introduction

The term 'Welfare' refers to a provision of services for assistance or a minimum well-being to the disadvantaged or needy individuals and families. It has been provided by the informal social groups, religious groups, charities and state for thousands of years. For instance, Augustus[1] (the founder of the Roman Empire) during 27 BC to 14 AD, the Song dynasty government[2] during 1000 AD in China, the medieval Roman Catholic Churches[3] during 11th to 15th Century and the English Poor Law[4] of 1601 in Europe made welfare provisions available for the disadvantaged citizens. More prominently organized system of welfare provisions under the state initiative emerged in the late nineteenth and early twentieth century. Otto von Bismarck's[5] welfare programmes for working class people in 1880s in Germany, welfare provisions during 1906–1914 under Liberal Prime Minister Herbert Asquith in Great Britain[6], President Franklin D. Roosevelt's[7] 'New Deal' in 1933 for relief, recovery and reform work in response to the Great Depression[8] in USA are very specific examples. After the World War II, the concept of 'Welfare State' appeared very strongly in the both developed and developing regions of the world.

The modern welfare states accentuated on the protection and promotion of the economic and social well-being of its citizens. It was understood that government had the responsibility for well-being of its citizens by ensuring a minimum standard of living to everyone. State's commitments were translated into provisions of universal and free education, universal medical care, insurance against disability, sickness, and unemployment, family allowances for income supplement, old age pensions etc. The concept of welfare state lasted very well for almost three decades, but it increased the burden of balance of payment in many countries. This situation brought the issue of 'Welfare Reform' throughout the world. Welfare reform was aligned with the neo-liberal policies that insisted role back of the state in social sector, lifting ban on foreign investments, prominent role of market and civil society organizations in provisioning of welfare services etc. The concept of welfare state, therefore, has been reconceptualised further and Danish sociologist Gosta Esping-Andersen[9] has classified three welfare state models in 1990s, i.e. Social-Democratic Welfare State model (based on the principle of Universalism that provides access to benefits and services based on citizenship), Christian-Democratic Welfare State model (based on the principle of subsidiary and the dominance of social insurance schemes), and Liberal model (based on market dominance and private provision; ideally, the state only interferes to ameliorate poverty and provide for basic needs, largely on a means-tested basis).

As stated above, it is clear that the neo-liberal policies brought the change in the formation or approach of welfare state. The onslaught of neo-liberalism today has caused social polarization in many developing countries including India. While the governments around the world are curtailing state expenditure fiercely and creating structural inequalities and marginalization, India stands out as a case of state intervention by following inclusive growth model[10], implementing the Right to Education Act, 2009, National Rural Employment Guarantee Act, 2005 (now MGNREGA), National Food Security Act, 2013 etc. In India, apart from the Government initiated welfare programmes, there are also many innovative projects being designed and implemented through NGOs and Corporate bodies. The stakeholders for welfare of the disadvantaged are many in India and also the approach is different. Approach could be institutional or community-based. The present book has made efforts to explore the community development approach in details. Few of the papers included here were submitted for the National Seminar on "Community Development, Social Work and HIV/AIDS" held in the Department of Social Work, Visva-Bharati, Sriniketan, West Bengal. The remaining papers are invited for this book. The book has been divided into three sections such as: (I) Community Development: Issues and Models, (II)

Disadvantaged and Community Development, and (III) Gender and Community Development. Each section incorporates several chapters. Brief ideas about these chapters are mentioned below:

The First section, ranging from Chapter 1 to Chapter 6, has discussed vividly various debates or emerging concerns and models of community development being practiced. Chapter 1, written by **Professor Asok Kumar Sarkar**, makes a starting with historical background. His chapter initially gives an overview of community development initiatives in modern India particularly since the beginning of twentieth century. He has epitomized how various landmarks became instrumental and various government sponsored programmes have come into effect. In the course of deliberation, few facets of community work such as approaches, beneficiary oriented development *versus* infrastructure or region oriented development, environmental concern, and impact of globalization have been analyzed logically. The last section of his chapter has brought out some emerging trends which the contemporary academia are observing, i.e., recent trend in the areas of intervention, how professional mingling is taking place, how theories are being authenticated, trend in financing to initiate work, and how 'community work research' has appeared as a 'welfare business'. Professor Sarkar concludes by saying that community development programmes in India are very diverse in nature and it has been flowing spontaneously with the passage of time or social order or social change.

In Chapter 2, **Professor Prasanta Kumar Ghosh**, has portrayed Tagore's experiment. Gurudev Rabindranath Tagore was not only a poet or writer who was awarded with the Nobel in Literature, but also a multi-faced creative genius as Philosopher, Artist, Music composer, Musician, Dramatist and above all, one of the great Humanists. He was concerned about the suffering of the people and the planet. He observed the plight of the rural mass with extreme poverty, illiteracy and ill health leading to poor quality of life. People lived with frustration and hopelessness and without self-respect and faith on their potential capacity. They tended to believe that suffering as a punishment from God and that is their fate as designed by him for the prevailing sufferings. They had no faith in their inner power which can easily be used to fulfil and sustain their all needs to live in a civil society with civic conditions of life. To him many of these social and economic obstacles could be dealt with its own mechanism inbuilt in the structure and norms of the Indian rural society with the participation and cooperation of each other and by using its own resources. The persons need to find their own strength and weakness and plan strategy, based on their own strength to overcome those at their endeavour. Rural organization for rural reconstruction was the basic principle he applied to cope with illiteracy, ill health and poverty. His dream of model village could have taken the çountry to a different social status than what we have today in about six lakh forty thousand villages in India. His providence towards the people and the planet is far reaching, e.g. the need for environmental education introduced by him in his '*Brahmacharya Ashrama*' during the first decade of the 20th century has ultimately been implemented by UGC as a compulsory course to be taught at the undergraduate level since last two decades of the same century. His thoughts and philosophy of rural reconstruction in India on self-help (mutual help, Cooperation) basis is the current concern in all social development projects being implemented in the country.

Chapter 3 of **Dr. Sudeshna Lahiri, Ms. Suvashree Roy Chowdhury** and **Mrs. Rupa Ghosh** has put forward the need for social work intervention for community development. They mention, Community Development (CD) is both an occupation (such as a community development worker in a local authority) and a way of working with communities. Its key purpose is to build communities based on justice, equality and mutual respect. In this regard, Social Work Intervention (SWI) is intended to aid clients in alleviating problems impeding their well-being. The interventions used by social workers are those that are identified as potentially helpful on the basis of the social worker's ongoing assessment of these seekers. Effectiveness of SWI depends on depth of knowledge, skill, gender and awareness of exact needs of the marginalized. A strategic planning is of utmost importance here not only for community's sustainable development, but also to intellectually prepare the underprivileged to seize the opportunities and turn them to their advantage. In our society social work often misunderstood as providing simple relief, direct aid and sometimes providing one time medical help. Also the deprivation affects men and women differently as women are more vulnerable to poverty, racial discrimination, sexual abuse, violence, negative attitudes etc. All these further deteriorate their ability to survive—physically and mentally. Social work interventionists need to be formed as specialized teams addressing the problems of men, women, youth, and children separately. The present study attempts to discuss the importance of Social Work Intervention for Community Development towards community and individual who are socially marginalized by virtue of its gender; physical disability and social exclusion. The chapter further analyses the required professional approach from the interventionists in the form of therapy through education and health improvement to make the weaker sections self-reliant and decision-maker in their life. This intervention would make them aware about their entitlements and rights and to equip them with ideas how to increase their asset building capacity.

Chapter 4 of **Dr. Rakesh Dwivedi** shows, social work is a profession derived from humanitarian as well democratic philosophy, based on scientific knowledge and technical skills for helping individuals or groups or community with the objective of creating equilibrium between their needs, capacities, resources and enhancement of social functions. It involves a deep understanding of power dynamics and social relations which help the community in achieving social justice and development through community participation. The methods of social work play a vital role in capacity building of people. The application of these methods leads to community development and results in improved quality of living in society. His chapter attempts to explore various dimensions of community development through social work practice.

There is connection between spirituality and sustainable development. Gandhi's vision of spiritualist philosophy has applicability towards this goal. Gandhi achieved in his life and advocated for others the principle of inclusive spirituality which is essential for establishing global peace, communal harmony and sustainable development. Gandhi's *Sarvodaya*, *Gramswaraj* and *Swadeshi* have similar goals with that of sustainable development goals endorsed by United Nations in 2015. Gandhian ideal of *Gramswaraj* has already been successfully demonstrated in various parts of the country. **Dr. Jaimon Varghese's** contribution, in Chapter 5, is based on a case study of two model villages such as Ralegon Siddhi and Hiware Bazar in Ahmednagar District of Maharashtra, which exhibits sustainable development strategy-based on Gandhian principles of *Gramswaraj*.

In Chapter 6, grassroots-level planning with holistic approach emphasizes a form of planning at lower institutional-levels of the block and village, where people from all sections of the society get together for the development of their own community. The 73rd Constitutional Amendment Act of 1992 ensures people's participation in the development process and role of the *Panchayat*. The vast scope of grassroots-level planning includes animal husbandry and dairy farming, minor irrigation, fishing, social forestry, small scale industries, rural housing, water supply, electricity and energy, education, public works, public health and sanitation, social welfare, poverty alleviation, development and welfare of scheduled castes and scheduled tribes, promotion of sports and cultural affairs, public distribution system, relief work during natural calamities etc. One of the unique features of democratic decentralisation is the involvement of all sections of the society in the planning and execution process. The weaker sections of the society are involved in decision-making process for community development and given legal right to be part of the grassroots-level planning. However, in recent time, owing to political nature of the PRI system economic benefit related activities are given more emphasis neglecting social sectors. Thus, the very purpose of grassroots-level planning is yet to produce good result in real sense. **Mr. Ram Prasad Das**, in this chapter, attempts to explore how grassroots-level planning is working at the village-level.

Section-II of the present book, includes Chapter 7 to Chapter 15, is on disadvantaged people such as financially poor and marginalized, scheduled tribes, persons with disabilities (PWDs), victims of domestic violence, school going poor children, vulnerable or sexually abused children etc. **Dr. Paromita Roy**, in Chapter 7, makes an attempt to explore community health insurance scheme. She feels health expenditures can be a major source of panic and distress to poor households. This often causes deterioration in the living standards of many families experiencing such health related shocks. Some community health insurance schemes have been successful in some places to provide protection against health hazards to people with a common context and without depending too much on external finances. This chapter studies two of these cases and tries to unearth the factors behind their success. The chapter particularly analyses whether these schemes have the potential to help in the process of providing health insurance to all the similarly vulnerable people who are unable to afford private health insurance as individuals.

Panchayati Raj Institutions (PRIs) would have always been considered a means of good governance and 73rd Constitutional Amendment was effected in the hope that it would lead to a good governance and political space to the disadvantaged section of the society like Scheduled Castes, Scheduled Tribes, and Women. **Mrs. Moumita Laha's** Chapter 8, indicates how the disadvantaged people like women, SCs and STs are participating in the electoral process as well as in the decision-making process of PRI. She mentions that reservation has emerged as an important motivator for participation in the local governance. But, in spite of that, the issues of surrogate participation and proxy participation are big challenges for real participation. Lack of awareness about the rights, lack of family support and illiteracy prevent the SCs, STs and women from performing duties of the newly elected members. Often it is influenced by power crisis and patriarchal society. Mrs. Laha proposes urgent need for capacity building programmes, clear mandate, performance monitoring, incentives, and transparent decision-making process for newly elected members' involvement in the effective democratic governance. Thus, these excluded communities would be empowered and would best utilize their reservation in the local governance process.

Chapter 9 of **Dr. Ankur Saxena** is on Pastoral Community. Kutch district of Gujarat is large and wide. Various communities like pastoral, slat workers, small marginal farmers, farm labourers and fisherman live there. Among all these communities, pastoral community depends on livestock for their livelihood. The Kutch district is drought prone area. People face draught situation in every second or third year. During that time, pastoral community migrates to other places with their family members in search of livelihood, water, food and fodder for their animals. Most of them live wandering life and the bad social customs have made their lives more miserable. Socio-economically, the pastoral community is very backward. The rate of education among them is very low and most of the women are illiterate. As a result, there are bad social customs, blind faith, bride price, child marriage and also the maximum expenditures are incurred on the religious occasions. Their main occupation is animal rearing and the main source of income is from the livestock such as the wool of the sheep and selling of the animals. But, during the draught and migration, they lose their animals for the want of grass/fodder and during the epidemics if any they tend to lose livestock in great number. Dr. Ankur Saxena's empirical study focuses on the right to livelihood of the pastoral community and the *modus operandi* adopted by them in the Kutch region. The study also focuses on the perceptions of the respondents on the existing condition and the coping strategies adopted by the pastoral community to sustain their existence and stop migration.

Ms. Kochurani, **P. J**. by dint of Chapter 10, bring to the fore that the magnitude of the problem of disability today is very vast and its impact is severe on the individual, families and the community. It is important that we should have accurate data regarding people with disability. In this context the researcher has made an effort to compare the data provided by the *panchayats* and data collected by door-to-door survey in 10 *panchayats* of Ernakulam district, Kerala. The researcher has also analysed the data in terms of gender, age and type of disability. The findings obtained shows that there exists a significant difference in the number of persons with disabilities when the two sets of data sets are compared. The data pertaining to door-to-door survey show that more number of males have disability than females and persons with orthopaedic disability outnumber all other disabilities. It could be due to the summation of congenital (cerebral palsy) and acquired disabilities (accidents and infections). The age-wise distribution of disability shows that maximum individuals with disability belong to adulthood and hence, the welfare and supportive strategies need to be planned, by giving priority to this population. So, finding out accurate data is necessary and it is a challenge for social workers who are involved in intervention programmes for PWDs. Detailed household surveys are required for social work intervention and social development programmes; however, it is expensive and time consuming.

Mr. Kaushalendra Pratap Singh, in Chapter 11, is of the opinion that the coverage of mid-day meal programme has steadily expanded during the last two years and cooked lunches are rapidly becoming part of the daily school routine across the country. The objectives of the Mid-Day Meal (MDM) programme are to increase the enrolment, retention and attendance of children in school leading to universalisation of primary education, impacting learning and simultaneously also improving the nutritional status of children. Studies of different social scientists have shown that children come to school on an empty stomach and the issue of 'classroom hunger' is extremely serious. Households run by women, widows and mothers who work through the day place a deep value on the free lunch provided in the school. The present study in three primary schools of district Lucknow has tried to evolve some strategies to strengthen MDM scheme for the upliftment of the community, to improve the primary education, and to improve nutritional status of children. The study also suggests social work intervention for implementing the evolved strategies. Structured questionnaire supported by focused group discussion and firsthand observation have formed the part of primary assessment. A wide range of secondary materials are also accessed, reviewed and analysed to support the study.

Economic development lies at the very root of a society. It is the watch-ward especially in the context of poverty alleviation and rural development. The rural poor especially the tribal people, who are too unorganized and powerless, cannot improve their lives without economic activities. Since independence, considering the general socio-economic backwardness of the tribal communities, Government of India has been planning and the Integrated Tribal Development Programme (ITDP) was launched in the year 1972. From the very beginning of tribal development, it was realized that no development activity could be of benefit to the tribal population unless their exploitation was prevented and an integrated credit-*cum*-marketing services developed in the sub-plan areas. The perception and attitude of the tribals should be changed for eradicating their poverty. Hence, elimination of exploitation was given priority in objectives of Tribal Sub-Plan. Priority was also given to do away with middlemen and the moneylenders. The field-level investigation of **Dr. Sujit Kumar Paul** and **Dr. Kakali Paul**, in Chapter 12, state that some beneficiaries carried out schemes successfully and in some cases schemes failed. They also noticed that the schemes could not make similar impact on the beneficiary households. The families with the same type of schemes could not have the same economic benefit. It involved activities and responsibilities of both - project functionaries and project beneficiaries. From this point of view, an attempt was made to study the perception and attitude of the tribal beneficiaries about the poverty alleviation schemes those were running under the project area. Efforts were also made to understand their own perception about their actual need. The present study was conducted in the Bolpur-Labhpur project area in the district of Birbhum, West Bengal. Total 264 households were identified. Four tribal groups such as the Santal, the Mahali, the Kora and the Oraon/Sardar were considered under the study.

Chapter 13 written by **Ms. Srenwantee Bhattacharjee** shows child sexual abuse is more than bruises and broken bones; it scars a child emotionally. Sexually abused children are tormented by shame and guilt which makes very difficult for children to come forward and talk about it. Children and adolescents who have been sexually abused often face a range of psychological and behavioural problems, from mild to severe, in both the short and long term. Her chapter looks at available work on sexual abuse of boys and highlights the problem that boys face in disclosing of sexual abuse. It also tries to get an understanding of the role of community as a factor affecting disclosure of sexual abuse among boys.

In Chapter 14, **Mr. Indranil Sarkar** states, in the 21st century, the world has witnessed various dimensions of development; still the children of the planet are at high risk and vulnerability. He has tried to bring into fore multiple types of child marginalization and vulnerability and also various factors that influence and create this difficult situation. In addition, the chapter has added different policies and constitutional articles which are creating an atmosphere to protect the children of India.

In Chapter 15, **Mr. Subhrasil Basu** observes that Indian indigenous people are abjectly deprived of basic requirements for their survival in the true sense of the term. Constitutional safeguards, Legislations and plenty of Schemes and Programmes could neither alleviate their acute hindrances nor elevate their socio-economic condition. On the contrary, available information in relation to social indicators of development viz. education, sex-ratio, health, economic condition, violence against their female members, provision of civic amenities, socio-economic empowerment taken place among them have exposed their disgraceful state of affairs. Apart from highlighting these issues, probable measures for their well-being with reference to the prevailing development approach and the writer's own practical exposure have also been focused in brief in his write-up.

Section-III on "Gender and Community Development" begins after the end of Chapter 15 and incorporates the remaining papers. The Chapter 16 of **Dr. Rupa Biswas** and **Professor Asok Kumar Sarkar** is an outcome of review of literature. Though women constitute nearly half of the total human population in India, their share in the fruits of development is abysmally low. The chapter attempts to portray an account of Indian women's journey towards gender equality at the threshold of the new millennium and the issues those women confront in their march towards equality. The article also reflects the efforts in terms of Government initiatives which are being made to address gender justice and tries to highlight on the policy framework needed for ensuring gender justice.

In 2005, National Rural Employment Guarantee Act was enacted and NREGS was launched subsequently as a comprehensive rural development programme towards alleviating poverty and uplifting the lifestyle of entire rural communities in India. It has objective of providing people 100 days of guaranteed employment and development of infrastructure base at and adjacent to communities. The scheme was launched in 2006 and renamed as Mahatma Gandhi National Rural Employment Guarantee

Scheme (MGNREGS) in 2009. **Mr. Sekhar Sain** and **Prof. Prasanta Kumar Ghosh** in Chapter 17 endeavours to focus upon the diverse way of intervention of this scheme for the socio-economic development of rural people. It shows, how far NREGS raised the income-level of the poor people leading to a better standard of living, the significant changes in the social and agrarian relations of the poor labour providing them bargaining power and economic freedom and increasing women's participation denoting their empowerment. The chapter tries to explore whether the expected level of empowerment of women had been brought about by NREGS or it could be implemented with meaningful outcomes deducting the adverse effects upon the society as well as the economy with better opportunity for women instead of mere numerical inclusion. Authors concluded with the latest transition declared by the new government to make the scheme most comprehensive and an effective tool towards community development in India.

Of late, linkages among the gender, poverty and environment are discussed widely. Literatures show, the causes of poverty and environmental degradation are structured by the uneven process of development operating *via* technologies, incentives, institutions and regulations which favour some. But much of the mainstream literatures on environmentally sustainable development have ignored the gender dimensions. Gender analysis, very recently is emerging as an important area because experiences of poverty and environmental change are gender-differentiated. There are significant differences between women's and men's experience of poverty and environmental change because of gender inequalities in access to environmental resources, command over labour, capacity to diversify livelihood strategies, and decision-making powers. This implies that there is a need to widen the range of choices available to poor men and women taking into consideration gendered differences in rights over land and resources to enhance environmentally sustainable development. Effective natural resources management requires participatory approaches that take into account the different activities of household members, the impact of their different uses of natural resources on the environment, and the gendered interests and incentives for natural resource management. **Dr. Tarun Bikash Sukai's** effort in Chapter 18 has attempted to make a gender analysis of environmentally sustainable development and poverty. It has also highlighted the policy implications.

Prof. Partha Sarathi De and **Dr. Amit Bhowmick,** in Chapter 19, feel reproductive health care practice of women is one of the major concerns in Indian society. It is the worry of the community where adequate services are not available. Diverse cultural practices are associated with or imposed upon them within the framework of community. This chapter primarily focuses upon the peculiar cultural practices performed by women and mothers during their reproductive phases. Though there have been landmark transformation occurred in human society, there have not been any significant changes in the case of cultural practices performed by the mothers in rural India. It is the fact that an inbuilt mechanism exists in the community setting. They adhere to those practices which were followed by their preceding generations. Most of the practices do not have any significant basis in modern situation. Those are the products of their long standing belief or faith, customs, folkways and mores and are associated with the community living and internalized for the betterment of their next generation.

There are growing instances of divorce, marital discord, demand for dowry, bride burning, violation of woman's dignity etc. In order to help couples with strained relations, marital discord and to provide the family a platform to discuss their problems and to find solutions, the scheme of Family Counselling Centres (FCCs) was launched by Government of India in 1983. It is being implemented by Central Social Welfare Board through voluntary organizations across the country. **Dr. Swapan Shaw's** attempt in Chapter 20 highlights the role of FCCs to provide preventive and rehabilitation services to women and families who are victims of atrocities, harassment and family mal-adjustments through crisis intervention and systematic counselling.

Notes

1. http://penelope.uchicago.edu/Thayer/E/Roman/Texts/secondary/SMIGRA*/Frumentariae_Leges.html
2. http://www.zhangzhiyong.cn/english/society_culture.htm
3. For details, please see: Jawad, R., 2009: *Social Welfare and Religion in the Middle East—A Lebanese Perspective*, UK: The Policy Press.
4. http://socialwelfare.library.vcu.edu/programs/poor-laws/
5. http://www.historyhome.co.uk/europe/bisdom.htm
6. https://www.gov.uk/government/history/past-prime-ministers/herbert-henry-asquith, for further details, please see: Orloff, A.S., 1993: *The Politics of Pensions—A Comparative Analysis of Britain, Canada, and the United States*, 1880-1940, London: The University of Wisconsin Press.
7. http://www.loc.gov/teachers/classroommaterials/presentationsandactivities/presentations/timeline/depwwii/newdeal/
8. http://www.history.com/topics/great-depression
9. For details, please see: Andersen, G.E., 1990: *The Three Worlds of Welfare Capitalism*, New Jersey: Princeton University Press.
10. https://www.imf.org/external/pubs/ft/wp/2014/wp1463.pdf

SECTION-I
Community Development Issues and Models

1

Community Development in India

Background, Dimensions and Emerging Issues

Asok Kumar Sarkar

Community Development initiatives have occurred time-to-time throughout the history. The significant landmarks, which are normally referred and have been propagated, took place after the Seventeenth century. For example, community initiatives during social reform movement in Britain and North America after 1750s[1]; Robert Owen's[2] community experiments in Scotland, UK and Indiana, USA respectively in 1825 and 1826; the Antigonish movement[3] started in 1920s in Nova Scotia, eastern Canada, that blended adult education, co-operatives, micro-finance and rural community development to improve socio-economic circumstances; community development proposals based on community planning to help local people with indirect assistance from colonial authorities during 1920s and 1930s in East Africa etc. The issue of community development gained momentum after the Second World War. The United Nations[4] in 1948 defined "Community Development is a process designed to create conditions of economic and social progress for the whole community with its active participation and fullest possible reliance upon the community's initiative." In fact, philosophers or activists or academicians have defined it differently. Community Development is understood sometimes as a movement, sometimes as a method, and sometimes as a process to promote social, economic and cultural conditions of communities with people's active participation. It increases choices to lead productive and creative lives. Community development from Indian perspective is the main thrust of this book. The present chapter has given an overview of community development experiences of India portraying and analysing various facts and issues in three different sections.

I. Background

Referring to the context of India, Mozumdar (1971) stated, "Community Development aims at self-engineered growth of the participating community. It sharpens the tools of self-development through integration of interests and voluntary joint efforts toward a common objective." One point is very clear from the above cited as well as Mozumdar's definitions of Community Development that *Social Consciousness* whether it occurs from the rational understanding or realization of each other's interest, is very important. The social consciousness for community development initiatives in the Twentieth Century India did not come automatically or considering the upheavals in the Indian villages. The powerful social reform movements and cultural renaissance of the Nineteenth Century provided impetus to raise social consciousness. People started realizing the situations in rural communities, i.e. poverty, illiteracy, orthodox beliefs, superstitions and casteism those were imposed by a few elites or Brahmins in every village and kept the villagers under deplorable conditions. Referring to Ambedker's the then view[5], "A village is a sink of localism, a den of ignorance, narrow-mindedness and communalism" the state of suffering can be experienced. Anyway, the social consciousness of the then intelligentsia or thinkers or national leaders (for instance, Rabindranath Tagore, M.K. Gandhi etc.) motivated to initiate community development activities in the Twentieth Century India.

Especially, the decade of 1920s is very remarkable for community development initiatives. Several rural experiments with unique approach for community development emerged. For instance, Dr. Spencer Hatch's Martandam[6] experiment in 1921, Sriniketan[7] Experiment of Gurudev Rabindranath Tagore in 1922, and Brayne's Gurgaon[8] experiment in 1927. A scheme of rural reconstruction under the enlightened Maharaja in Boroda[9] in 1932, which was led by Mr. V.T. Krishnamachari, covering various aspects of rural life and aiming at developing "will to live better" and a "capacity for self-help and self-reliance" was also amazing. M.K. Gandhi, the father of the nation, after returning to India permanently, joined the Indian National Congress (INC) and was introduced to Indian issues and politics. He became an active leader of INC and under his leadership, the Congress was reorganised with a new constitution and with the goal of *Swaraj*. Gandhian[10] strategy of rural community development was based on *Village Swaraj* and *Swadeshi Movement*. The basic principles of *Village Swaraj*, as outlined by him, were trusteeship, *swadeshi*, full employment, bread labour, self-sufficiency, decentralisation, equality, *Nai Talim* etc. Gandhiji started materialising this community development approach since April 1936 at 'Sevagram', 8 km from Wardha town, which was latter known as his experimental laboratory.

The provinces of India under the British rule were given autonomy as per the "Government of India Act, 1935". The same act incorporated rural development as an important programme for welfare of the people. The 'World War II' and the 'Bengal Famine of 1943' further provided the impetus for community development initiatives through state mechanisms. When India became free from British Raj in 1947, the issue of community development received further importance and therefore, a pilot community development project, called Etawah[11] projrct, in Uttar Pradesh under the leadership of Mr. Albert Mayer was initiated in 1948. On the basis of community development experiences during 1920s, 1930s and 1940s within the country as well as abroad and as per the recommendations of various committees formed by the Government, such as Fiscal Commission (1949), Grow More Food Enquiry Committee[12] (1952) etc. the Government of India launched Community Development Programme (CDP) on October 2, 1952 in 55 community projects. The CDP covered the entire country by 1964.

The CDP of 1952 had been debated from various perspectives and became a matter of controversy. Though some termed it as a 'salient revolution', critics left no stone unturned and gave a political colour. The CDP was started just after nine months of the first General Election of 1951. As the next election occurred in 1957, Congress party used it for achieving political mileage and the opponents wanted to prove government's failure to implement CDP (Nayar, 1960). Thus, political objective of the CDP became economic planning in general. The various components of the CDP such as improvement of agriculture, co-operatives, education, health and social welfare; establishment of *Panchayats* in rural areas; voluntary contribution of money and labour by the people etc. had been assumed by the opponents as means for gaining only economic prosperity. Critics highlighted, First Five Year Plan spent 460 million rupees for 77.5 million populations, i.e. less than rupees six per head. Some of the national newspapers, like *The Statesman* (Calcutta, 21 May, 1958), criticized it stating "Sprinkles on the Desert". In addition, it was argued that CDP could not yield desired results due to bureaucratic temper and failure of democracy to remove caste system. Dominant castes manipulated administrative machineries and their exploitative pressure marginalised the poor further (Neale, 1983). Lion's share of the programme was monopolised by the rich people.

Apart from Community Development Programme of 1952, Government of India started and made operational a series of programmes in the community. These include: Intensive Agricultural District Programme (IADP) 1960, Marginal Farmers and Agriculural Labourers Scheme (MFAL) 1970-71, Small Farmer Development Agency (SFDA) 1971-72, Rural Works Programme (RWP), 1971-72, Employment Guarantee Scheme (EGS) 1972-73, Drought Prone Area Programme (DPAP) 1973-74, Minimum Needs Programme (MNP) 1974-78, Twenty Point Programme (TPP) 1975, Food For Work Programme (FFWP) 1977, Desert Development Programme (DDP) 1977-78, Integrated Rural Development Programme (IRDP) 1978-79, Training of Rural Youth for Self-Employment (TRYSEM) 1979, National Rural Employment Programme (NREP) 1980, Development of Women and Children in Rural Areas (DWCRA) 1982, Rural Landless Employment Guarantee Programme (RLEGP) 1983, Jawahar Rojgar Yojana (JRY) 1989 (Merging NREP & RLEGP), Indira Awas Yojana (IAY) 1989, Integrated Wasteland Development

Programme (IWDP) 1989-90, Employment Assurance Scheme (EAS) 1993, National Social Assistance Programme (NSAP) 1995, Swarnajayanti Gram Swarojgar Yojana (SGSY) 1999, Annapurna Yojana 1999-2000, Antodyaya Anna Yojana (AAY) 2000, Pradhan Mantri Gram Sadak Yojana (PMGSY) 2000, Pradhan Mantri Gramodaya Yojana (PMGY) 2000-01, Sampoorna Grameen Rojgar Yojana (SGRY) 2001, National Common Minimum Programme (NCMP) 2004, National Food for Work Programme 2004-05, Mahatma Gandhi National Rural Employment Guarantee Scheme (MGNREGS) 2005, Aam Aadmi Bima Yojana 2007, Rajiv Awas Yojana 2009, Mahila Kisan Sashaktikaran Pariyojana (MKSP) 2010-11 etc. In addition, Modi Government after coming to the power has initiated a couple of programmes to improve socio-economic condition in the community. A few of those programmes include: Swachh Bharat Abhiyan (2014), INDRADANUSH (2014), MUDRA Bank Yojana (2015), Atal Pension Scheme (2015), HRIDAY (2015), Beti Bachao Beti Padhao Yojana (2015) etc.

In the preceding paragraph, efforts have been made to cite several popular and well known programmes. It is true that many more programmes are not included in the list. We can presume, in the same way, a large number of programmes will come in effect in future also especially to improve socio-economic condition, to remove poverty and to establish democracy. After almost seventy years of independence, we are not sure how many years more we need to remove poverty or to continue experiments. In fact, lack of political will and widespread corruption is instrumental for it and hence one after another programme is being conceived, millions of rupees are being poured and bulky performance reports of these programmes are flooding government offices. At the same time, no one will refute that development has taken place certainly. We are in a better position today than the previous time. The above cited programmes and experiments those were introduced in the community had impacted with varied results and therefore a few critical observations on those have been made in the following part.

II. Facets

The backdrop that has been portrayed here influence to assume a few facets of community development work in India. This may include: approach (practical or theoretical) to community development, beneficiary oriented development *versus* infrastructure or region oriented development, environmental concern in community development, and beginning of globalization as well as subsequent scenario. Of course, these facets are not very clear cut or very distinct or like water-tight departments. They may overlap to each other in terms of time, service sector, benefits received, and so on. The facets have been assumed or observed considering the programme implementation approach, nature of services, international treaty or global social policy, re-structuring of economic policy of government and its impact etc. Let us try to discuss these facets.

Approach to Community Development as an important facet needs elaboration. It has been noticed that the community development initiatives those appeared in the first half of the twentieth century, i.e. especially during 1920s or after had some ideological motive and experimental basis. Most of them had village development approach. For instance, the initiatives of Tagore, Brayne, Krishnamachari, and Gandhiji that tried to upgrade the villages. These experiments and ideologies led to form many voluntary organizations in rural areas and also became instrumental for theory development, i.e. highlighting the best practices or experiences that could be applied further in community development work. Mozumdar (1971) cited several beliefs for community work. Those beliefs were in fact authenticated in the experiments of 1920s (or after) and we study today those beliefs as theory in our books related to community organization and community development. The beliefs include: considering felt needs of the people, involvement of people or grassroots planning in fulfilling local needs, self-help approach and maximum utilization of local resources, state and welfare agencies should extend guiding hand, develop institutional base for sustaining development, keep your approach experimental and flexible, and finally community development as a continuous and educational process.

Theoretically, many more approaches are noticed. The systematic review of social work and community development journals identifies that "community development traditions" found on different parts of the globe have been thoroughly debated and analyzed. Each of these traditions follows a particular approach. The traditions are broadly classified into three groups, such as, geographical, methodological and intellectual traditions of community development (Westoby and Hope-Simpson, 2011). A specific strategy or movement or group of practices of community development linked to a specific region or culture comes under geographical tradition. For instance, the Antigonish Movement[13] inspired by Dr. Jimmy Tompkins and Dr. Moses Coady to improve the situation of farmers, fishers and miners in eastern Nova Scotia, Canada in 1920s and 1930s (MacAulay, 2001); and the Muintir na Tire[14, 15], a cooperative development movement based on the idea of self-help and neighbourliness, for socio-economic and cultural promotion of rural people of Ireland in 1930s (Cearbhaill and Varley, 1996). Methodological traditions generally incorporate different methods of social change such as the Alinksy tradition (Synzka, 2002), the Freirean tradition (Westoboy and Dowling, 2013), the Settlement House tradition (Koerin, 2003) etc. Intellectual traditions are basically ideological prescriptions for social change which have been developed comprehensively over a period of time, e.g., social guidance, social learning and social mobilization traditions (Campfens, 1997). Apart from these, Pawar (2010) cites a few approaches which theoretically have become very popular now-a-days, such as, community driven development, rights-based development, assets-based development, sustainable livelihoods approach, people-centred capacity building approach, etc.

The facet referring *beneficiary oriented development* versus *infrastructure* or *region oriented development* is well understood from the background. The need to develop an individual was major thrust of the cultural renaissance of the Nineteenth century. Social consciousness of the then people created a demand to minimize poverty increasing economic capacity, bring equality through social justice and make efforts in improving social status. Hence, early community development initiatives in India, emerged as rural development experiments in 1920s, 1930s and 1940s, emphasized more on beneficiary oriented development. For instance, Sriniketan experiment, Martandam experiment, Gurgaon experiment, Sevagram experiment and Etawah experiment more or less focussed on improving quality of life, capacity building, self-help and self-reliance, self-sufficiency, equality, removal of illiteracy and orthodox beliefs, casteism etc. Again, the CDP of Government of India started in 1952 insisted on agriculture, co-operatives, education, health, social welfare and establishment of *panchayats* to upgrade socio-economic standards of life. Thus, by and large, most of the community development efforts initiated before 1960s focused more on beneficiary oriented development.

Basic infrastructures such as roads, electricity supply, telecommunications, housing facility, irrigation opportunity and so on influence community development. Poor infrastructures are the obstacles to socio-economic progress. Having realized the need to have infrastructures which have bearing on poverty reduction, Government of India started many programmes since 1960s. A few programmes are Minimum Needs Programme (1974-78), Twenty Point Programme (1975), Pradhan Mantri Gram Sadak Yojana (2000), National Common Minimum Programme (2004) etc. In order to improve a particular region, there are also several programmes, such as, Drought Prone Area Programme (1973-74), Desert Development Programme (1977-78), Tribal Area Development Programme started in the Fifth Five Year Plan (1974-1978) etc. Of course, there is no specific year or clear cut demarcation to understand beneficiary oriented development *versus* infrastructure or region oriented development. Moreover, since 1960s, all types of programmes together (i.e. beneficiary oriented or infrastructure or region oriented) are in operation.

The issue of *environmental concern in community development* domain emerged after the Brundtland Commission published its report entitled "Our Common Future" in 1987. Thereafter, people talk about sustainable community development (Hope, 1996), natural resource management for local area development (Reddy, 2008), locally appropriate technology for rural development (Pathare and Varghese, 2015) etc. In this discourse, off and on, it is argued that nature should provide the norms for our techno-economic system (Jacob, 1994).There is also study (Agnimitra, 2014) recommends that development in neo-liberal context should foster protection and promotion of environment and State as well as voluntary organizations must participate in it. Dr. Agnimitra's this recommendation is based on a study conducted in the Garhwal Himalayan region.

In India, at present, environmental concern in community development programmes is a grave issue. Twelfth Five Year Plan (2012-17) wanted environmental sustainability of economic growth. Hence, Ministry of Rural Development insisted on greening rural development that includes improving natural resource conservation, minimizing negative impact on environment, strengthening climate resilience of the communities and contributing to climate change mitigation (UNDP, 2012). A couple of programmes, those are already cited in the previous section (I), are being implemented today with environmental concern. For instance, Mahatma Gandhi National Rural Employment Guarantee Scheme (as most of the activities under it are linked with water, soil and land), Integrated Wasteland Development Programme (aims to restore ecological balance and help to provide sustainable livelihood), Mahila Kisan Sashaktikaran Pariyojana (MKSP) under National Rural Livelihood Mission (NRLM) (as it identifies regeneration and sustainable harvesting of non-timber forest produce species), Indira Aawas Yojana (green results include efficient use of resources like water, energy and construction material), and Swachh Bharat Abhiyan (as it wants to stop open defecation and insists on solid and liquid wastes management) are remarkable.

Beginning of globalization is another facet. Craig (1998) has corroborated with example and theoretical interpretation that community development is very often understood as local approach to mitigate problems, but it requires having global perspective as globalization has taken place. Globalization is a process of structural adjustments within an economy of a country. Some of the opponents say, it is modified version of imperialism (Ramanjaneyulu, 2005). Some equates it with capitalism (Reddy, 2005). In India, globalization started in 1991 and brought several positive changes in the economic system. Simultaneously, it has presented numerous challenges increasing vulnerability among the peasants, agricultural laborers, artisans, dalits, tribals, women and people under BPL. The community development workers engaged in rallies, demonstrations and legal advocacy to restore peace, harmony and integration in the communities. They became more alert with the unpleasant incidents when farmers' suicide increased (Deshpande, 2002) and unskilled as well as illiterate workforce was more exposed to occupational hazards (Pathare and Varghese, 2015). Hence, social safety nets have been suggested by countless scholars in the social science literatures. Moffatt *et al.* (2011) show, in India, community workers who fight for social justice and rights of the marginalized communities, face challenges in organizing their efforts due to adverse results posed by globalization process and therefore, there is a need to rethink on the guiding principles on community practice.

III. Emerging Issues

Using the historical perspective, much has been expressed in the above deliberations. It is true that community development is a continuous process and a purposeful initiative at the local level to improve situation. Change is inevitable in its approach. Therefore, let us throw some light on the changes or issues that are being observed in the contemporary days.

Recent trend in the areas of intervention: Community work in India, from the beginning of last century as cited above (in Section I), intended to transfer lives of the poor, exploited and marginalized. The then emphasis on intervention included income generation activity, co-operative movement, adult and continuing education, formal school for educational up-gradation, health awareness and health care, training for agriculture and animal husbandry etc. In the second half of the last century, responding to local level situation, countless people's organizations emerged. Community workers became instrumental to form and to strengthen those organizations. Many of those organizations are still active and continue to exist today. For instance, various social movements (tribal movement, dalit movement, ecology movement etc.), mass-based struggles to resist acquisition of land for industrialization (e.g. struggle in Andhra Pradesh, Maharashtra, West Bengal etc.), Self-Help Groups (SHGs) for micro-finance etc. can be cited.

During the 1980s and 1990s, the issue of social justice and equality minimizing the discrimination against dalits, tribals, marginalized and women were very prominent focus of community workers. After the emergence of globalization, areas of social exclusion, marginalization, farmers' suicide, environmental concern, and like became important. Now, considering the issue of fundamental rights, rights-based approach is very much on the agenda. Community workers' activities revolve around right to education, right to access to health care, right to housing, right to food, right to safe drinking water, rights of the disabilities, and so on. Research-based innovative approach with regard to any local concern, evidence-based practice, resilience perspective and corporate involvement to fulfill social responsibility are also emerging concerns in community work.

Professional mingling: Community work, now-a-days, occupies a major place and makes its roots firmed within the larger development domain. It is a concern or an area of interest of many subjects/disciplines studied in the contemporary academia, for instance, engineering, environmental studies, social work, sociology, development studies, public health, political science, regional development/planning etc. An NGO or an international development organization committed or engaged in community work takes the help of a couple of professionals like engineer, sociologist, environmentalist, social worker, public health professional, regional planner etc. simultaneously. Therefore, the notion that community work is only concern or a dominating area of social work discipline is gradually becoming irrelevant. Community work has been appearing as a trans-disciplinary subject (Andharia, 2009). Professional mingling thus is an emerging issue in community work today.

Authentication of theories: Community work has been taking place in India under the government sector, voluntary sector (now-a-days called NGO) and corporate. In the history of its last 100 years, areas of intervention and strategies of work have evolved and undergone various changes. These changes were not willful or forced creation of the human society. It was the outcome of social order or social processes. Change was felt necessary according to the social condition, political situation and economic structure of the then society. A critical look on the historical evolution of community work in India shows that old approaches (that means approach followed in the early days, i.e. during 1920s and 1930s) of work (such as focussing on self-reliance, self-determination, participation etc.) and the influence of international trend of working focus in development sector (e.g. issue of human rights) are emerging now-a-days as theories of community work. The contemporary authors of the books/articles on community work/community development/social development (Schuler, 1996; Kenny, 2007; Pawar, 2014) are authenticating these theories. For instance, rural development experiments started in India in 1920s & 1930s, as cited above in Section-I, already established several concepts such as self-reliance, self-determination, participation etc. as essential aspects of community work. Mozumdar (1971) confirmed those again during 1970s. Those concepts have been reconfirmed/authenticated as strong pillars or essential principles of community work by Pawar (2014) today.

Financing to initiate work: Finance or resource base is very crucial issue in community development, whether initiated by GOs or NGOs or corporate bodies. Now-a-days, it is a trend that most of the activities at community are undertaken in project mode for a particular duration. A community development project whether economically viable or sustainable depends on sources of funding or resource support mechanism. In India, funds for community work come from Central and State Governments, Reserve Bank of India (RBI), National Bank for Agricultural and Rural Development (NABARD), Co-operative Credit Agencies (CCAs), Commercial Banks (CBs), Regional Rural Banks (RRBs), and Foreign Funding Agencies like bilateral partners and multilateral partners (Singh, 2009). Of course, there is shifting in funding landscape. Other potential sources are corporate houses. Corporate Social Responsibility (CSR) partnership in community is increasing (Bingham and Walters, 2013). Many-a-time, these funding agencies work through grassroots level NGOs. In other words, a large number of grassroots-level NGOs generates funds from the above cited funding agencies. It is a hard reality that raising funds is a challenging task. Financial services innovation in community development, hence, is on the agenda for last two decades

(Leibsohn, 1999). The emerging trend today in this regard is that countless development professionals serve as consultants to mobilize funds for grassroots level NGOs.

Emergence of research on community work as a welfare business: Community development is a purposive intervention in a particular context and therefore evaluative research has got a special importance to it. Despite of the fact, research had very little scope during 1970s (Voth and Martin, 1974) throughout the world. Although community development programmes in India flourished that time, issue of research was negligible. Thomas (1980) rationalized and insisted "community work research" in 1980s as community-level workers were less interested in research than in action. In fact research has been understood as a tool in community work (Smith, 1981). In the contemporary scenario, research is taken very seriously and there are many new approaches to "community work research" (Holland *et al.*, 2011). Qualitative techniques are used more than the quantitative techniques. Mixed method design, focus group discussion and case study get more preference to evaluate a community-level project (Shaw, 2003). In addition to the more importance on "community work research" today, the same area is well-liked for making money. It would be better to say that this area has become popular as *welfare business*. For instance, most of the funding agencies now want evaluation research after the project termination and hence seek applications like tenders. This sort of research is done within very limited time, sometimes as a formality, to rationalize money spent for the project. There are many consultancy firms or individuals who carry out this task to earn money and therefore this area is emerging as a *welfare business*.

In brief, the chapter has given an overview of community development initiatives in modern India particularly since the beginning of twentieth century. It has epitomized how various landmarks became instrumental and various government sponsored programmes have come into effect. In the course of deliberation, few facets of community work such as approaches, beneficiary oriented development *versus* infrastructure or region oriented development, environmental concern, and impact of globalization have been analyzed logically. The last section of the chapter has brought out some emerging trends which the contemporary academia are observing, i.e. recent trend in the areas of intervention, how professional mingling is taking place, how theories are being authenticated, trend in financing to initiate work, and how "community work research" has appeared as a "welfare business". It can be concluded by saying that community development programmes in India are very diverse in nature and it has been flowing spontaneously with the passage of time or social order or social change.

Notes

1. In order to establish more democratic system and empower middle and working classes people in Britain and North America, social reforms were taking place gradually. To know more, visit: http://www.ohcc-ccso.ca/en/courses/community-development-for-health-promoters/module-one-concepts-values-and-principles/defini-0
2. Robert Owen was born in Wales in 1771. He was a social reformer and founders of Utopian socialism and cooperative movement. His community experiments in Scotland and Indiana are well-known. For details, visit: https://en.wikipedia.org/wiki/Robert_Owen
3. Antigonish movement emerged to improve the condition of small resource base communities in Canada. It is also a liberal Catholic movement. For details, visit: http://www.thecanadianencyclopedia.ca/en/article/antigonish-movement/
4. The definition is very popular and has been cited in different places. For instance, a few websites are: https://canadianglobalresponse.ca/portfolio/community-development/https://www.kansascityfed.org/en/publications/community/connections/articles/4-30-2015/2015-april-traditional http://www.ohcc-ccso.ca/en/courses/community-development-for-health-promoters/module-one-concepts-values-and-principles/defini-0
5. Cited in Mozumdar (1971), p. 10.
6. This experiment was started by YMCA at Martandam in South Travancore, presently under the Kanyakumari district of Tamil Nadu. It adopted self-help approach and utilization of local resources. For details, see Sreedhar and Rajasekhar (2014), p. 17.
7. Rabindranath Tagore undertook the Sriniketan experiment for socio-economic changes of the rural masses in and around the villages of Sriniketan and Santiniketan, West Bengal. He wanted to

reorganize the fragmented rural society. For details, see Sreedhar and Rajasekhar (2014), p. 16.

8. F.L. Brayne, who was the Deputy Commissioner of Gurgaon district, Punjab, initiated it based on four principles such as village organizations, mass education, leadership, and spirit of service. For details, see Sreedhar and Rajasekhar (2014), p. 18.
9. It is known as Boroda experiment that started with 10 villages and later on extended activities in 35 villages. For details, see Sreedhar and Rajasekhar (2014), p. 19.
10. For details, see Singh (2009), pp. 69-72.
11. Etawah project was basically an extension programme focusing on self-reliance and local level needs. It wanted to improve agricultural production, technologies, public health, adult literacy and village leadership. For details, see Sreedhar and Rajasekhar (2014), p. 21.
12. Grow More Food Campaign (GMFC) was started after the Bengal Famine in 1943. GMFC was reviewed in 1948 and was reoriented with few recommendations. In 1952, Grow More Food Enquiry Committee evaluated the GMFC further and made several other recommendations. Those recommendations were the basis for Community Development Programme (CDP) of Government of India started in 1952.
13. *Op. cit.*
14. http://www.muintir.ie
15. http://www.combatpoverty.ie/publications/TheRoleOfCommunityDevelopment-LiteratureReview_2006.pdf

References

Andharia, J., 2009. "Critical Explorations of Community Organization in India (Editorial)", *Community Development Journal*, 44(3): 276-290.

Agnimitra, N., 2014. *Going Green : Women and Grassroots Environmentalism*. New Delhi: Shipra Publications.

Bingham, T. and Walters, G., 2013. "Financial Sustainability within UK Charities: Community Sports Trusts and Corporate Social Responsibility Partnerships", *Voluntas: International Journal of Voluntary and Non-Profit Organizations,* 24(3): 606-629.

Campfens, H., 1997. *Community Development around the World: Practice, Theory, Research and Training.* London and Toronto: University of Toronto Press.

Cearbhaill, C.O. and Varley, T., 1996. "An Irish Community

Development Movement's Experience of Crisis Conditions: Muintirna Tire's Struggle for Survival", *Journal of the Community Development Society,* 27(1): 1-16.

Craig, G., 1998. "Community Development in a Global Context", *Community Development Journal,* 33(1): 2-17.

Deshpande, R.S., 2002. "Suicide by Farmers in Karnataka: Agrarian Distress and Possible Alleviatory Steps", *Economic and Political Weekly*, June 29.

Hope, K.R., 1996. "Promoting Sustainable Community Development in Developing Countries: The Role of Technology Transfer", *Community Development Journal,* 31(3): 193-200.

Holland *et al*., 2011. "Understanding Neighbourhoods, Communities and Environments: New Approaches for Social Work Research", *The British Journal of Social Work*, 41(4): 689-707.

Jacob, M., 1994. "Toward a Methodological Critique of Sustainable Development", *Journal of Developing Areas,* 28(1): 237-252.

Kenny, S., 2007. *Developing Communities for the Future.* Melbourne: Thomson.

Koerin, B., 2003. "The Settlement House Tradition: Current Trends and Future Concerns", *Journal of Sociology and Social Welfare,* 30(2): 53-68.

Leibsohn, D.M., 1999. "Financial Services Innovation in Community Development", *Journal of Affordable Housing and Community Development Law*, 8(2): 122-131.

MacAuley, S., 2001. "The Community Economic Development Tradition in Eastern Nova Scotia Canada: Ideological Continuities and Discontinuities between the Antigonish Movement and the Family of Community Development Corporation", *Community Development Journal,* 36(2): 111-121.

Moffatt *et al*., 2011. "Community Practice at a Crossroads: The Impact of the Global on the Local in India", *Community Development Journal,* 46(1): 104-121.

Mozumdar, S.N., 1971. *Community Development in India*. Santiniketan: Visva-Bharati.

Nayar, B.R., 1960. "Community Development Programme: Its Political Impact", *The Economic Weekly,* September 17, 1401-1410.

Neale,W.C., 1983. "Community Development in India: Progress or Rip-Off?", *Asian Survey,* 23(11): 1209-1219.

Pathare, S. and Varghese, J., 2015. "Rural Community Development in India: Emerging Issues, Challenges and Strategies", In S. Roy and B.M. Dash, *New Perspectives in Community Development,* New Delhi: Atlantic.

Pawar, M., 2010. *Community Development in Asia and the Pacific*. New York and London: Routledge Publications.

Pawar, M., 2014. *Social and Community Development Practice*. New Delhi: Sage Publications.

Ramanjaneyulu, M., 2005. "Impact of Globalization on Rural Development in India", In Narashimha Rao, C. (Ed), *Rural Development in India— A Multi-Disciplinary Analysis,* New Delhi: Serials Publications.

Reddy, S., 2008. "Natural Resource Management through Rural Cooperatives', In V. Reddy and Yadagira, C.M., *Rural Development in India: Policies and Initiatives,* New Delhi: New Century Publications.

Reddy, V.V., 2005. "Globalization and Rural Development", In Narashimha Rao, C. (Ed.), *Rural Development in India—A Multi-Disciplinary Analysis,* New Delhi: Serials Publications.

Schuler, D., 1996. *New Community Networks: Wired for Change*. New York: CAN Press.

Shaw, I.F., 2003. "Cutting Edge Issues in Social Work Research", *The British Journal of Social Work,* 33 (1): 107-116.

Singh, K., 2009. *Rural Development: Principles, Policies and Management*. New Delhi: Sage Publications.

Smith, T., 1981. "Reviewed Work", *The British Journal of Social Work,* 11(1): 101-102.

Sreedhar, G. and Rajasekhar, D., 2014. *Rural Development in India: Strategies and Processes.* New Delhi: Concept Publishing Company (P) Ltd.

Synzka, P., 2002. *Community Organizing and the Alinksy Tradition in Germany*, for details, please visit: https://comm-org.wisc.edu/papers2002/szynkag.htm

Thomas, D.N., 1980. "Research and Community Work", *Community Development Journal,* 15 (1).

UNDP. 2012. *Greening Rural Development in India*. New Delhi: UNDP.

Voth, D.E. and Martin, M.J., 1974. "Evaluative Research on Community Development in Non-metropolitan Communities", *Social Service Review,* 48 (3): 438-441.

Westoby, P. and Dowling, G., 2013. *Theory and Practice of Dialogical Community Development—International Perspectives.* London: Routledge Publications.

Westoby, P. and Hope-Simpson, G., 2011. "Re-thinking Tradition and Community Development Practice", *European Journal of Social Work,* 1-15.

2

Tagore's Experiment in Rural Reconstruction

A Model for Community Development in India

Prasanta Kumar Ghosh

In 1883, when Tagore was 22 years old, he wrote "We may get many things from the British by begging, but never self-reliance; what is obtained by begging can never last; what is achieved by our own efforts has permanence" (Sen, 1943). His vision on society and culture, the way it was moving, leaving aside its own social and cultural heritage and self-reliance moved him to work for the suffering humanity and decaying earth. The dependence was found to be damaging our potentialities to achieve self-sufficiency as we had in the past. The seeds of rural reconstruction was sown in by Gurudev at the end of 19th century while he was entrusted with the responsibilities of administration of his ancestral estates at *Silaidaha* and *Patisar,* the then undivided Bengal of India but now in Bangladesh. While visiting the communities as a landlord he observed how the social and economic conditions of the people and society were decaying. To Tagore, service to suffering human being, to the down trodden, should be the bench mark of selfless service to mankind. To quote from *Gitanjali* (song offerings) No. 10:

> "Here is thy footstool and there rest thy feet
> Where live the poorest, the lowliest, and lost"
>
> —*[Gitanjali, (English) No. 10]*.

Founding the model school named '*Brahmacharya Ashram',*

now called *'Patha Bhavana'* combining the old education system in consonance with cultural heritage of this country he went further with higher education naming the organization as Visva-Bharati, where the world unites in a single nest. He wished to have cultural assimilation and exchange of thoughts ideas freely and fairly. His dream was to make everyone complete person. Tagore in his immortal poem wrote,

> "Where the mind is without fear and the head is held high
> Where knowledge is free
> Where the world has not been broken up into fragments
> By narrow domestic walls
> Where words come out from the depth of truth
> Where tireless striving stretches its arms towards perfection
> Where the clear stream of reason has not lost its way
> Into the dreary desert sand of dead habit
> Where the mind is led forward by thee
> Into ever-widening thought and action
> Into that heaven of freedom, my Father, let my country awake".

Tagore was trying to upheld humanity with truth. Education is the preconditions for any change in attitude and behaviour of a person. With true concern and a greater cause of the farmers he also tried to address the problems of the rural mass on his own. e.g. he experimented with cultivation of new varieties of crops at *Silaidaha* adjacent to his *Kuthibari* (Bangladesh) between 1899 and 1906 (Sinha, 2010). During this period he had sent his son Rathindranath and his friend's son Sontosh Chandra Majumdar to University of Illinois (Urbana-Champaign Campus), USA, to study agriculture and animal husbandry. Later, he deputed his son in law Nagendranath Gangopadhaya to the same institute to learn agriculture in the larger interest of farmers and the farming systems of India. The objective was to bring in change with the pattern of cultivation for higher yield that benefits the farmers. His second drive for rural reconstruction could be observed between 1908 and 1909 when made an attempt at *'Birahimpur'* to solve the all sorts of social, cultural, and economic problems, the people faced by using their own strength on a holistic approach. In *Pabna* conference (1908) Kalimohan Ghosh was influenced by the philosophy and approaches to rural reconstruction of Tagore and joined as worker of the team and continued to work all along his life at Sriniketan. Relying on his observations as landlord in three districts (now in Bangladesh) he planned for Sriniketan Experiments in Rural Reconstruction, in 1922 formally, though the work of Sriniketan was initiated at Surul Village Extension Centre in 1917 at Sriniketan *Kuthibari* bought in 1912 from Sinha Family of *Raipur*.

Tagore first met Leonard Knight Elmhirst, a British citizen in New York while he was studying agriculture at the Cornell University of USA. Knowing his interest in agriculture in India, Tagore invited him to come and work at Sriniketan. He joined Sriniketan Experiment in Rural Reconstruction as the first Director of the Institute of Rural Reconstruction from 6th February, 1922. During the initial days of L.K. Elmhirst at Sriniketan, he encountered a number of hurdles beginning from languages to health and suspicion from the adopted communities as they were not very clear about the programme objectives and its outcome. Being concerned about, naming the project, Elmhirst wrote quoting Tagore "A fuller description of how our programme for village rehabilitation grew and developed must be given later. It was later too that the Poet came to give 'Sriniketan' as the name for the whole project instead of more clumsy title 'Institute for Rural Reconstruction' (Elmhirst, 1975). He was very much affirmative about the potential contribution from Elmhirst once he conceptualize and plan for implementation. However, Elmhirst could not continue at Sriniketan owing to his ill health but he and his wife Dorothy Straight Elmhirst continued to support Sriniketan experiments even after the demise of Tagore in 1941. He was deeply and emotionally involved with the philosophy and approaches of Tagore on rural reconstruction. Elmhirst had to leave for his motherland by 1925 and established Dartington Hall at Devon as replica of Sriniketan experiment of Tagore. Later he became the Chief Consultant to the Ministry of Agriculture of the government in the country.

Tagore emphasized and focused on the self-development through knowledge, skills and attitude as good citizen first. He believed that the capacities of our people is to be mobilized at the right direction for an awaken self. '*Atma Shakti*' i.e. potentialities inherent in individuals but not used by '*Atmiya Samaj*', i.e. relative society, the platform we all belong to; the society where we all are in relations to each other. Hence, need for collaboration and cooperation as the traditional Indian society was bestowed upon. The mission under rural reconstruction programme was to bring back those social and ethical values to live in peace with happiness. '*Ananda*' (the bliss), is the ultimate aim to achieve by human being. He believed in holistic education to make a complete human by nurturing them in nature following the natural law. As a humanist, he has not only described the pains of the poor and vulnerable people but tried to find out the way to sustainable system, inbuilt in Indian society and its culture through promotion of self-help, building civil society organizations, and cooperative societies in his experiments in rural reconstruction.

Serving the poorest of the poor and other vulnerable sections of the society was the philosophy of two other contemporary great sons of India, Mahatma Gandhi and Swami Vivekananda who were socio-political and spiritual leaders respectively. Here, the thoughts of Gurudeva are in consonance with them, i.e. God lives among the people, especially, the poor and the backward classes. At the inaugural address of *'Silpa-Bhandar'* (store for the products from the faculties and students of Handicrafts) at Sriniketan in 1345 BS he said, "Those who worship physical quantity often say that the field of our operation is very circumscribed and, therefore, as against the need of the entire country, the result will be insignificant. But we should remember that truth establishes itself on its own dignity and not on its quantitative measurements in terms of length and breadth. In whatever part of the country we establish ourselves through discovery of truth, we establish ourselves over the whole India" (Banerjee, 1966).

The third phase of his work seems to be gaining maturity between 1915 and 1940 when he finally established the experimental project at Sriniketan with the following objectives: "to bring back life in its completeness into the villages, making the rural folk, self-reliant and self-respectful, acquainted with the cultural tradition of their own country and competent to make an efficient use of the modern resources for the improvement of their physical, intellectual and economic conditions" (Tagore, 1922). His basic philosophy and approaches to reconstruction was based on self-help and mutual help, upon which the communities lived with happiness during the older times in India. He wanted to bring back and reconstruct those values and principles of the society. This is why he did not use the word 'development' but 'reconstruction' in his experiment in rural India. He said, "do not insult the villagers with your help … it will harm more than your help. We shall not uplift the villages as such but see that upliftment takes place naturally and internally with the efforts of the people of the community. He motivated and organized the villagers to establish health cooperatives, credit cooperatives, consumers cooperative, weaver's cooperative, farmers' cooperatives, and cooperative banks at the village level combining a cluster of communities on self-help basis. As these organizations are made and maintained by the people it will be sustainable to continue to benefit the poor farmers, weavers, carpenters and other vulnerable populations. His interventions started with education at the communities, skill up-gradation of the rural artisans, and formation of nucleus organizations with youth and women of the villages. He was convinced that if life is equipped with necessary knowledge, skills, attitude and belief, their livelihood is made forever. In fact, Tagore wanted to channelize the inherent capacities of the people and the planet to legitimize a good quality of life within the existing social order of the rural inhabitants in India which is indigenous, hence sustainable. The system will eliminate all kinds of dependency of the people on the state and other charitable organization. He wished to make one such model village for replication across the country and that will represent true India.

Rationale of Sriniketan Experiment to be the Model of Rural Reconstruction

In the late 1930s Sudhir Sen took over the charges of Sriniketan Economics as it had to face multiple problems and mainly on financial crisis to maintain the establishment and run the programme. On his arrival to Sriniketan he studied and went around the communities, speaking to the poverty stricken people. He then found two main obstacles:

(a) "rural poverty could be reduced only if much more wealth were produced within the village; and
(b) to produce more wealth one must rely overwhelmingly on agriculture, including wide range of agri-related activities and rural industries" (Sen, 1943).

Since then, the focus of Sriniketan activities was redesigned to explore the means to produce more wealth within the communities by applying the high yielding variety of crops and allied income generation programme like, animal husbandry, etc. On the other hand training in cottage industries was also intensified bringing in diversity in product design, inclusion of new crafts trades. Rathindranath Tagore and his wife Pratima Devi were instrumental in taking the crafts with new product like artistic leather crafts, *Batik* on clothes, etc.

Tagore was pained to see the sufferings of the people with poverty, illiteracy and ill health, that is why in his address to Sriniketan workers in 1939, he said "It seemed to me a shameful thing that I should spend my days as *Zamindar* (Landlord) concerned only with money-making and engrossed in my own profit and loss account" (Sen, 1943). A deep sense of solidarity for the vulnerable rural communities, and therefore, giving back to such people for whom he survived and prospered.

Having experimented successfully in farm and non-farm products, education for rural youth and organizing the communities with organizations of varies nature according to the needs of the people in these communities, later it became a pioneer project on models of community development of the Government of India launched since 2 October, 1952. He shared philosophy and approaches to rural reconstruction with Mahatma Gandhi during his visit to Santiniketan. They agreed on the development of eternal strength among the people though Gandhiji differed in being dependant on funding projects from outside and modernization and mechanization of the whole production.

Tagore's Unique Strength Based Interventions for Community Development in India

- To his understanding the people in general suffer due to illiteracy and education to deal with the problems they encounter in life. Therefore, development of knowledge keeping in mind the traditions of the country-using indigenous methods and updating it from time to time in tune with the emerging changes in society. Convergence of knowledge with current practise was another important factor for reconstruction with self-reliance and achieving a good quality of life. He said, do not insult the villagers with your help from outside, it will harm more than the benefits to the communities.
- Organising the communities and setting their attitude for a positive change in the larger interest of the people and the planet. He observed that rural habitants are not organised as they were in the past. There was time when each one was concerned about others—a sense of fellow feeling inculcated from belief in spirituality learned from generations. Industrial revolutions brought in a self-centred lifestyle and individual differences on issues of citizenship and governance affecting the normal life as were in the past. It continued to damage our unity which furthered the sufferings of the masses as the days passed by. The salvation from poverty, illiteracy and ill health was lying with the affected people themselves believed Tagore. He also firmly believed that they possess all those strengths required to tackle the issues but not channelized appropriately. Therefore, tried with an experiment in Sriniketan planning a strategic intervention over the years to make model village.
- For the purpose of organising the communities he thought that formation of self-supported rural organisations could be the vehicle for rural development alongside the cultural

tradition of the country. He planned to form *'Mahila Samities'* (Women's Group/Cooperatives), Weavers' Cooperatives, Health Cooperatives, Credit Cooperatives, Consumers' Cooperatives, and Farmers' Cooperatives, etc. to promote mutual help and assistance. These organisations were planned by the people and implemented with their own strength of organising for a better living. He was convinced that these organisations will play a pivotal role in their life. Any systematic activity like building an organisation for achieving a goal to serve the essential needs of the targeted population for poverty alleviation needed a great amount of lessons, honesty, and integrity, felt Tagore, hence he stressed on the education and health first before intervening with other problems.

- Learning before serving. "There is nothing so dangerous as in expert service, ... if we want to serve we must learn". He was of the opinion that if one wants to serve the people and the communities he/she must learn to serve through training and develop the required skills in observing, analyzing, and mobilizing the people for a positive and desired change. The principles and participation and involvement of the people in programme planning, executing, and evaluating the impact are essential skills one has to apply in organising and uplifting the communities. Social work as a profession emerged in the third decade of the 20th century but Tagore planned and applied its principles and methods in the second decade of the same century without coining it as social work. He also observed that people in the villages did not understand the value of self-respect and potentialities they possess. His interventions with the communities focussed on the inculcation of self-respect and self-confidence, which in turn helps people to achieve the desired goal in life. He coined the designations of workers of rural reconstruction as the *'gram karmis'* (village workers) who are solely responsible for all types of activities carried on in the communities adopted for social, cultural, and intellectual improvement. Interestingly, he used all the indigenous resources and methods available in the social and economic systems available in the ancient and medieval India.

- Capacity-building of the individuals, groups and communities at the grassroots level mobilizing the people and available resources. Since, illiteracy and ill-health coupled with poverty were identified as the vicious circle to all the rural problems, he stressed upon building the capacities of the ... by bringing out the inherent potentialities as believed today by the social work professionals. Since, the farmers and other inhabitants of the communities were busy during the day, he opened night schools for the farmers, women and youths to learn. Beginning with literacy to skill development in different trade and crafts were the objectives. Education on farming systems for the farmers was incorporated in the subjects of learning curricula, although there were no formal syllabi as we have today. While describing the role of universities, he said, 'the university should play the role of a brain in human body, which spreads its nerves for free flow of blood to keep us alive, similarly, the university should spread over its branches in the communities for education and dissemination of knowledge to the people to give life to the country.' Establishing learning centres at each community was an essential parts of the programme of interventions in rural reconstruction.
- Organizing village scouts with young boys and girls. Trusting on the power of the youth in any community, he advised his workers to organize the boys and girls scouts in each adopted community and teach them disciplined physical exercises, health and hygiene, and above all citizenship which will go a long way in building the rural communities to make model village. He wanted to channelize the power latent in youth to awaken the people in their communities—the finesse thought the great social thinker and modern philosopher had and we find its appropriateness even after a century. The Government of

India including the state governments have initiated a number of programmes for the development of the youth in the country. Of late, the Rural Extension Centre of the Institute of Rural Reconstruction continue to train the boys and girls scouts in about 50 villages around Sriniketan which is named as *'bratachari'*.

- Health cooperatives on self-help basis for disease prevention and cure was the second agenda after the studies were carried on in the pilot communities. There was no health service for the Indian villages during the British regime. He then organised a cluster of villages to come together to form a health cooperative and succeeded in doing it in 1932 which was followed in about 180 communities making a total of a dozen of health organisations. Each family had to subscribe a meagre amount annually to fund for a Doctor, a Pharmacist, and a Cleaner for the dispensary. Pharmacist normally used to keep the accounts of the health cooperative. Almost all such cooperatives became obsolete when the government introduced health services by 1980s but the second one located in *Surul* village still survives and provides services to the poor and needy with a minimum subscription per annum.
- Producers' in agriculture, dairy keepers, weavers, carpenters, blacksmiths, and other rural artisans suffered from a number of setbacks, owing to low yield, intensive labour with low return, paucity of raw materials and over all the inadequate capital made them fall on the moneylenders lending on high and exorbitant rate of interest. He thought if they could be put together with funds contributed by members forming cooperatives for higher return and to stop exploitation of the moneylenders, they could be saved from further decay. Following the successful cooperative movement in Europe, he Indianized the policies' of cooperatives in his writings on 'Cooperative Principles' suiting to the requirements of this country. Initially, this movement had received a very positive

response and successfully implemented for the benefit of the communities.

- His effort in building model village under Visva-Bharati University at the beginning of 20th century is finesse and proactive interventions in strength based practice. Unfortunately, we are talking and trying to implement the same in the form of university community partnership at the turn of the 21st century. Never late than ever, time has come to produce evidences of successful implementations of the welfare and development programmes at the community to maintain good citizenship and governance with our knowledge and skills. Strength based practice facilitate the evidence based practice in social work. Tagore felt it a century ago and tried out with limited resources and got success at the time of interventions. Anything cannot remain static in a changing society with the advent of fast ever changes, we have to change with speed to catch up, using the methods to which Gurudev said, " if you try to swim against the flow, you will find yourself in grave". Alongside changing society and its culture we have to adopt some keeping in view the traditions of the country. Use of information and technology is inevitable in our life and make a rationale use of these developments.

Conclusion

There is no explicit mention of the term social work in the works of Tagore that is understood and defined professionally. A close approximation used by Tagore to explain social worker is '*Viswakarma*' and social work is *'Viswakarm'* (Banerjee, 1975). The other reference we come across the term social worker in Tagore's work is the organisation and administration the rural extension services at Sriniketan. The workers who were posted at the village were called *'Samaj Karmis'* or social workers and those at the senior level called *'Kendra Karmis'*, i.e. Centre Workers. The '*Gram Karmis*' were responsible for implementation of the plan at the village level and the *'Kendra Karmis'* were responsible for a cluster of communities. The social workers were placed at the lowest level of hierarchy of the organisation but they were given due importance as primary functionary at the community level and the success of each programme depended on the performance of social workers.

Tagore also applied professional approaches to organise the communities and asked his workers to win the friendship of the villagers taking a real in their concern, their welfare and making lively effort and assist them in solving the most pressing problems.

Tagore also reflected on the professional and personal self of the social workers. He envisaged the true social worker having a balanced personality, instinctive humanity, definite amount of tact, patience and adequate insight into the human nature. In his essays of spiritual union he explained some qualities of a social worker (Joseph and Ghosh, 2002). To quote him "In order to be united with Him we have to divest to our work of selfishness and become '*Viswakarma*', the 'World Worker', who works for all. I do not mean for a countless number of individual. All work that is good, however small in extent, is universal in character. Such work makes for the realization of '*Viswakarma*'. The world workers who works for all. In order to be one with Mahatma, 'The Great Soul', one must cultivate the greatness of Soul, which identifies itself with soul of all people and merely not with that of one's own" (Tagore, 2000). '*Viswakarmas*' are now named International Social Work Practitioner if we relate to modern social work practice.

According to Tagore, social worker should work that serves the interest of the community both at micro and macro levels and these services should be altruistic in nature. He used to say that even if one village could carry out the programme he visualized, it would be like a lamp from which light could radiate in all direction (Kabir, 1961). The main thought of Tagore was strictly confined to holistic community welfare. He used to appreciate and recognize the voluntary workers who work without any expectations in return. But he never negated the concept of paid and professional workers as he maintained many such workers at Sriniketan.

The framework of values to Tagore was mainly intrinsic in nature of the people upon which the traditional Indian society followed from generations. He believed in Truth, Beauty, Goodness, Freedom and Bliss which plays pivotal role in shaping the life of people in India. These are also identified as the strength of the people and the community as a whole. The wholeness of a person's life is more important and decline in it amounts to decline in the social order in which we live. Therefore, he tried to intervene to preserve and promote these values in his efforts in strength based practice in rural reconstruction.

The decaying social and physical environment pained him to that extent he tried regenerating the social and cultural traditions of the country to make it sustainable on the basis of self-help and self-reliance. He began teaching about the environment at the turn of 20th century when we have taken it at the undergraduate level at the end of 20th century. His vision on rural community development is as relevant as it was a century ago. Considering the above discussions on Tagore's rural reconstruction effort we can say that all his interventions were based on strength of the individual and the community emerging from the village level which has been done by government under 73rd Constitutional Amendment Act almost eighty years later. What Tagore thought about a century ago is still relevant even today and that is why it is a sustainable human development in true sense and can be replicated anywhere in the universe.

References

Banerjee, H., 1966, *Experiments in Rural Reconstruction*, Kolkata: Visva-Bharati Publishing Department.

Banerjee, G.R., 1975, *Papers on Social Work—An Indian Perspective, Series No. 23.* Bombay: Tata Institute of Social Sciences.

Elmhirst, L.K., 1975, *Poet and Ploughman*, Kolkata: Visva-Bharati Publishing Department.

Joseph, S. and Ghosh, P.K., 2002, Sriniketan: From Experiment to Experience. Research Document, Department of Social Work, Sriniketan in Association with PRIA, New Delhi & IDS, Sussex, UK (Unpublished).

Kabir, H., 1961, *Rabindranath Tagore: Towards Universal Man*. Mumbai: Asia Publishing House.

Sen, S., 1943, *Rabindranath Tagore on Rural Reconstruction,* Kolkata: Visva-Bharati Publishing Department.

Sinha, D., 2010, *Rabindranather Gram Unnyan Prayas (Bengali),* Kolkata: Bangiya Sathiya Parisadh.

Tagore, R., 1922, *Sriniketan*, Santiniketan: Visva-Bharati.

Tagore, R., 2000 (Reprint), *The Religion of Man*, Kolkata: Visva-Bharati Publishing Department.

3

Analysing Social Work Intervention for Community Development

A Process Towards Mainstreaming

Sudeshna Lahiri, Suvashree Roy Chowdhury and *Rupa Ghosh*

Introduction

The concept of charity goes back to ancient times, and the practice of providing for the poor has roots in many major ancient civilizations and world religions. However, it is required to distinguish between 'charity' and 'social work' which most of the people fails to fathom and often mistakenly use interchangeably. The term 'charity' is the *practice of benevolent giving and caring* (Reference: http://en.wikipedia.org/wiki/Charity*),* where Social work has its roots in the social and economic upheaval wrought by the Industrial Revolution, in particular the struggle of society to deal with poverty and its resultant problems. Because dealing with poverty was the main focus of early social work, it is intricately linked with the idea of charity work, but it must now be understood in much broader terms. For instance, it is not uncommon for modern social workers to find themselves dealing with the consequences arising from many other 'social problems' such as racism, sexism, homophobia, and discrimination based on age or on physical or mental ability. Modern social workers can be found helping to deal with the consequences of these and many other social maladies in all areas of the human services and in many other fields besides.

Whereas social work started on a more scientific footing aimed at controlling and reforming individuals (at one stage supporting the notion that poverty was a disease), it has in more recent times adopted a more critical and holistic approach to understanding and intervening in social problems. This has led, for example, to the reconceptualisation of poverty as more a problem of the haves versus the have-nots rather than its former status as a disease, illness, or moral defect in need of treatment. This also points to another historical development in the evolution of social work: once a profession engaged more in social control, it has become one more directed at social empowerment. That is not to say that modern social workers do not engage in social control (consider for example statutory child protection workers), and many if not most social workers would likely agree that this is an ongoing tension and debate. There are also different views on how 'social work' is and should be defined. Observing that the Scottish social work legislation dates back to the 60s, the Minister commented: 'Expectations are very different in the 21st Century'. In June 2004, the Scottish Minister for Education and Young People announced a fundamental review of social work in the 21st Century. The Deputy Minister subsequently defined three key issues for the Review. 'What is the core purpose of social work in modern Scotland? .... How can we best deliver services? .... Essential services must have clear lines of accountability'. As part of the Review, the Scottish Executive commissioned a discussion paper on 'the need for social work intervention'. Subsequently, it is not just social work but 'social work intervention'. In practice and at present, this refers largely to local authority social work services which have powers and responsibilities to intervene in the lives of individuals and families, generally with their consent but compulsorily in specified circumstances. It is in these areas of social work that many of the tensions and conflicts arise, not only for social workers but for people using their services and for the public. In this regard, Social Work Intervention (SWI) is intended to aid clients in alleviating problems impeding their well-being. The interventions used by social workers are those that are identified as potentially helpful on the basis of the social worker's ongoing assessment of these seekers. Effectiveness of SWI depends on depth of knowledge, skill, gender and awareness of exact needs of the marginalized. A strategic planning is of utmost importance here not only for community's sustainable development but also to intellectually prepare the underprivileged to seize the opportunities and turn them to their advantage. As Vickery (1974) examines that the contribution that general systems theory can make to social work with individuals and families. Using the perspectives of a systems approach it identifies interaction between people and organizations as being the appropriate focus for social work. It includes the examination of problems of choice in relation to social work goals, targets of intervention and client systems; and emphasizes the need for the social worker with individuals and families to be knowledgeable about and related to community structures and resources. Within a defined social system it examines crucial points for intervention in the transactions between client and environment systems. To further probing the effectiveness of SWI, Cohen (1999) explore that the pursuit of an integrative strengths-based intervention/supervision paradigm can contribute to the development of a positive, innovative vision of direct practice, a vision congruent with historic social work values, relevant to working with social work's clientele, and distinct from the other helping professions. Social Works Intervention Towards Community Development (CD) may be a crucial area of research as Community Development (CD) is both an occupation and (such as a community development worker in a local authority) and a way of working with communities. Its key purpose is to build communities based on justice, equality and mutual respect. Thus, how education as a vehicle of social reform and transform, could be the tool for SWI towards Community Development may require an analysis.

Objectives

The present chapter focuses on two main objectives in relation to 'education' as a tool and 'teachers' as social workers as follows:

- To discuss the importance of Social Work Intervention (SWI) for Community Development towards community and individual who are socially marginalized by virtue of its gender; physical disability and social exclusion.

- To analyse the required professional approach from the interventionists in the form of therapy through education and health improvement to make the weaker sections self-reliant and decision-maker in their life.

SWI for Community Development to Determine Teachers as Social Workers

> In the 21st century when few of us stay in the same job all our lives, I would like to think there was flexibility so teachers could become social workers, or foster careers become teachers.
>
> —*Estelle Morris*

The above quotation is so much true in its every sense. A teacher is that one person who needs to play the role of a social worker in our school and the community. Social work is a discipline within human services which needs the assistance of education. No society can function without education and no social work can be carried out without the partnership of education.

Social work has been there since time immemorial. In this present era Social work is usually a part of the Human Services Department of a Government. It serves as a link between the government's clients and other government resources, such as: manpower training leading to employment, welfare payments towards financial assistance, legal consultation in dealing with legal problems, food and water relief at times of drought, famine and war, etc. As a social worker, one works closely with medical professionals in order to provide medical care for clients; with school personnel to identify children who are in need of help and with counsellors and psychologists in order to provide psychological counselling. Today the problems faced by individuals and families are often complicated, and assistance from many agencies is needed.

Today, social workers are not only the bridge linking clients to other helpers, they also provide their clients with hope, and encourage their first steps towards a new life. Social workers usually stand in the front line, and reach out to the clients soon after problems occur. They provide an initial assessment of the situation and mobilize other needed services. Social work uses a team approach and is multi-disciplined. Its goal is to provide a service to those who need help especially the old, young, poor, abused, mistreated, handicapped, and jobless, the sick and the homeless. Its approach is to use available resources to solve problems in order to empower clients to help themselves in the long term.

To speak from the view point of education, it is the most powerful instrument that can create huge difference in alleviating social evils and contribute to social service. Schools are most important places to carry our social work because it is in the schools where the inaccessible population is to be found. Social work in schools should be the application of social work principles and methods to the purpose of the school. Goals should centre upon helping pupils attain a sense of competence, a readiness to continue learning, and an ability to adapt to change. Increasingly, the focus of school social work should centre on cognitive areas such as learning, thinking and problem-solving, as well as traditional areas of concern, like relationships, emotions, motivation and personality. It is important for the school social worker to be concerned with the relationship of the school to other social institutions in the community.

Ethics of a Teacher as a Social Worker

Respecting the dignity of the individual student under any critical situation is the most essential as the basis for all social relationships. The teacher is to believe and imbue confidence and have faith in the capacity of the student to advance towards his/her goals of solving the crisis. Base the relations with others on their qualities as individuals, without distinction as to race, creed, colour, or economic or social status. Recognize that the greatest gift to another person may be to give an opportunity for him/her to develop and exercise his/her own capacities. Too much of intervention in the personal affairs of an individual without his/her consent, except in an emergency, where they must act to prevent injury to him/her or to others. Believe and accept the differences and individuality of others, and endeavour to build a useful relationship on them.

Base one's opinion of another person on a genuine attempt to understand the whole person, his/her situation, and what it means. Constantly try to seek understanding and control one's self, attitudes, and the prejudices which may affect relationships.

Should Teachers be Social Workers?

The English press has echoed concerns expresses by some teachers and teaching unions about the demands placed upon teachers that go beyond the purely academic. In research conducted by Furedi (2003), observed that an academic dealing with social policy has articulated this argument by stating that teachers should not be social workers. He asked why English education and social policy appeared to give parents the role of educators whilst teachers are encouraged to be carers and that professionalizing the management of children's relationships, parenting and community attitudes weakens the ability of people to conduct their own affairs. However, school teachers, parents and school could collaborate for Social Work intervention for addressing the need and problems of children with disabilities. In this regard, the Responsiveness to Intervention (RTI) process, used in USA, is a multi-tiered approach to providing services and interventions to struggling learners at increasing levels of intensity. RTI can be used for making decisions about general, compensatory, and special education, creating a well-integrated and seamless system of instruction and intervention guided by child outcome data. RTI calls for early identification of learning and behavioural needs, close collaboration among teachers and special education personnel and parents, and a systemic commitment to locating and employing the necessary resources to ensure that students make progress in the general education curriculum. School personnel can play a number of important roles in using RTI to identify children with disabilities and provide needed instruction to struggling students. The time has come that we should identify the role of teachers as Social Workers towards Community Development on the eve of RTE (2009), in India, as Right to Free and Compulsory Education for children requires primary education to reach every strata of society. The teacher training courses, i.e., B.Ed and M.Ed, may cater to recognize the need and role of social worker to its trainee teachers. The course curriculum has 'Community Outreach' in their one year programme. However, it becomes the privilege of Teacher Training Institutes how they will translate this part of the curriculum and not many institutes take up 'Community Teaching' as 'Community Outreach'. This may be the cause that teachers fail to recognize themselves as Social Worker.

Guidelines for Teachers as Renderers of Community Help towards Students

In a conference held in Swaziland, 2000, UNESCO provided few guidelines on how teachers can become social workers. The gist says that establishment of a counselling relationship with the students are must in order to see the relationship as a process of giving the student an opportunity to grow, develop, and ultimately to understand and discover himself, and make appropriate choices. Acceptance is the next important virtue that the teacher must imbibe in her or herself. She has to recognize the worth of the individual regardless of his/her circumstances, status, religion, race, politics, behaviour, and wish to foster human dignity and self-respect. Self-determination simply means to encourage self-help as a means of growing in self-confidence, and the ability to take on more responsibility for one's own affairs. Freedom to Choose the students must be able to make appropriate choices, and consider how his/her choice may affect others. The teachers has to respect and care for clients as individuals without ridicule. Confidentiality is to be maintained to the hilt as the relation of a teacher and a student is based on trust. You must recognize that what passes. Being empathetic simply denotes being sensitive to the client's feelings putting oneself in the position of the student. The teacher must be genuine and not defensive, be open, real and honest.

Professional Approach from Interventionist Helping Society

Though Indian economy is enjoying a change of status from underdeveloped to developing country it still suffers from problems like unlimited growth of unskilled population, absolute poverty, illiteracy, unemployment and corruption. All these have their spill over effects on the economy with the rise of criminal activities, flesh trading, substance use, low paid jobs, exploitation, juvenile crime, domestic violence and environmental degradation. Removal of economic inequality and establishment of social justice have always been one of the major objectives of economic planning in India. While moving in the path of economic development, Indian planners have realized that economic development of our nation is deeply associated with the improvement in the standard of living of the country's citizens and that is the area where we lack. An economy cannot be called developed when a section of the population are enjoying all the luxuries of life whereas 37 per cent of the population are struggling to enjoy two square meals a day. Social activists in India are neither economists nor policy-makers but their love for humanity motivates them to work for the marginalized and underprivileged to relieve their sufferings working individually or in groups. Social activists therefore, are the social reformers and they are the true change agents in an economy.

Around the world, social workers face various expressions of the social question, like violence, poverty, unemployment, no health care, no education, unemployment, homelessness etc. These Social Workers as professionals intervene in situations where the elderly have their constitutional rights violated, children and teenagers are involved in drug trafficking, women are victims of physical abuse, in short, those are a few of the social question expressions they come across in the work processes in which the social workers are inserted. As a vehicle of social reform, 'Education' may be used as tool for Community Development as a holistic approach. It may be used as awareness campaign and for rehabilitation of women who are ostracised and children with disability who are marginalised. Although, teachers have expanded role as social worker but social workers are relatively independent, for they lack the resources required to set their workforce in motion. Hence, the institution that hires and offers some of the means of work also organize the work process in which social workers take part by assigning them roles (Iamamoto, 2005). It may be difficult for a teacher with a full time profession , especially when social work is not its job profile, to pursue as Social Worker. Ferriera (2010) mentions that several professionals who work as teachers are not familiar with the dimension of the dialectical-critical method; they believe that the social question is unable to explain the phenomena found in society and that many needs social workers come across cannot be analyzed based on capitalism's founding contradiction. A few topics in (family violence, drug use etc.) are dealt with from an individualizing perspective, as though separate from the production relationships, which leads students to look for references in other fields of knowledge because they are not aware that their own field provides the theoretical and methodological inputs for them to intervene on certain needs. Sometimes, differences in academic requirement to be a professional social worker become a little short of for a teacher to become social worker. However, area which may be genuine requires teachers to involve as Social Worker.

Apprehending such situations as expressions of the conflict between capital and labour marks off the specific features of Social Work in the socio-occupational arena. That is why people from other fields working in the institution not always have the same understanding of the institutional needs. Social Workers seek to understand how the processes deriving from society's economic framework. The Professional approach of Social Workers could be substantiated with the research conducted. A study by Weisner (1977) on Southern Gujarat regarding utilization behaviour in the health sector reveals that geographic and socio-economic conditions play an important role in determining community health work policy. A study made by Sarkar (2005) on social work in India reveals that the targets for social work in India includes human rights violation, gender discrimination, persons living with HIV/AIDS, environmental destruction, crisis of governance, effects of globalization, etc. Also in spite of governments endeavour in protecting human rights through the Protection of Human Rights Act (1993), the condition of the pavement and slum dwellers, dalits, minorities, tribal children and common people and in case HIV infected people and providing services to them social workers faces toughest challenge in our country. Though the NGO's emerged in India soon after Independence but according to Chatterjee (2006), it became popular only in the 1980's as the Government did not realize at all the impact that these voluntary organizations can make to the society. At present India has a strong and vibrant NGO sector but unlike western countries it suffers from lack of funds. It is well understood now that social work intervention requires not only the state but also the market and civil society to have an impact. India Government's initiative through National Rural Employment Guarantee Act (NREGA), 2009 in providing 100 days employment to one member of rural household though definitely made an impact by increasing wage rate but still it has lot more to do for the poor. The diversity of the area of Social Work could be understood in the research by Peters, Yezbeck & Sharma (2002) reveals that the use of tobacco is higher among illiterate men and unskilled workers in urban and rural areas of India and these people are more vulnerable to suffer from coronary heart diseases and hypertension. These people also suffer from serious mental disorders and psychosis.

We are well aware with the saying that the hand that rocks the cradle rules the world and in our country the women suffers the most from the burden of poverty. They not only suffer from gender discrimination but also physical and mental abuses, domestic violence, human trafficking and not given access to basic education. Some of the NGOs who are working towards Community Development (CD) with professional approach are enlisted as:

(i) The Akshaya trust in Madurai works for the helpless, forsaken, mentally ill, old, sick and the road side destitute with love and affection, healthy food and rehabilitation opportunities.

(ii) Gudiya another NGO targets women as an asset, works for women empowerment and spreads awareness regarding Government policies.

(iii) Goonj takes care of the clothing problems of the underprivileged, establishes partnerships between rural poor and rich urban schools and also assists natural disaster stricken people.

(iv) Sammaan Foundation strives for empowering poor by linking them with the main-stream through education, training and financial support. Sammaan works for women empowerment, health services, employment generation, micro credit and children's education.

(v) Pratham is one of the largest NGO which works towards educating the underprivileged children in the slums of Mumbai. It takes the initiative to increase the number of enrollments in schools and also tries to increase the learning levels of those.

(vi) LEPRA promotes quality health care through various health programmes in the prevention and control of diseases like AIDS, Leprosy, and Tuberculosis, etc. Their focus is mainly on the communities which are poor comprising women and children.

(vii) Deepalaya works for the slums of Delhi and initiated rural development in Haryana and Uttarakhand. Working with both governmental and non-governmental agencies it makes interventions in the state's policy-making. Their area of work includes education, health-care, gender equality, vocational training, empowering other NGOs which have the same vision and upliftment of the differently-abled.

(viii) Uday Foundation provides support to the families of children suffering from critical disorders, congenital defects and other diseases and syndromes which affect their health, growth and education.

(ix) Help Age India strives to raise resources to protect the rights of the senior citizens of the country.

The intervention is all about must strive for the change of attitude in the first step. The change of attitude has to come from each able bodied citizens to work for their poor brothers and sisters. The patriarchal society of India has to realize that women are the kingpins; they play a crucial role not only in the economies but for the local economy also. Women when educated are likely to have fewer and healthier children, would be able to educate their children and lessen the burden of poverty to be experienced by future population.

Discussion

According to Planning Commission of India (1950), Development is a process which calls for effort and sacrifice on the part of the entire body of citizens. In India, we have representative democracy rather than participatory democracy and elected politicians are well aware that they are not answerable to those who have elected them about each of their decisions and this makes the situation tougher for the poor's and downtrodden.

Educating the girl child is the key to fight poverty. Actually, they are the change agents and this has to be identified first. India is a multi-cultural country and each and every religion has its own hindrances, the social work intervention therefore, has to be objective specific. The interventions should be first and foremost of providing financial services and medical help. While medical help along with psychological should have continuous therapy financial help should also not be of one time show. It is necessary to build their entrepreneurial skill but first of all their outlook must have to be changed so that they can believe in themselves.

As market will never take care of the deprived as it takes care of those who are able to pay and nor our politicians it becomes the responsibility of us who can aspire to change at least the life of one person of this marginalized group. Although, micro-finance has gained tremendous popularity in recent years but still it is unable to reach the poorest of the poor because of their critical needs, lack of skills and confidence. Hence, Social Work intervention needs young minds, newer thoughts and more female workers as they only can penetrate easily to bring a change. It must be made mandatory that each student in high school and college has to be given the responsibility of educating one poor with the premise 'Each one teach one' and it should come under internal assessment while providing character certificate to the student while leaving school or college. In colleges also the National Service Scheme (NSS), Ministry of Youth Affairs and Sports and Leadership Training Services (LTS) should be given more autonomy and made as separate cells. Teachers should by rotation work in this cell to work with the students as their influence makes a lot of difference. Teachers can also form groups and help the underprivileged to form self-help groups so that they can work independently and become self-reliant.

References

Chatterjee, P., 2006, *The History of NGOs in India*, For details, please access: www.amaidi.org/pdf/HistoryofNGOs.pdf

Cohen, B., 1999, "Intervention and Supervision in Strengths-based Social Work Practice", *Families in Society: The Journal of Contemporary Human Services*. For details, access: www.uta.edu/ssw/faculty/helton/documents/Supervision%20in%20 Strength%20Based%20Social%20Work%20Practice.pdf

Ferreira, J.W., 2010, "Social Question and Professional Intervention by Social Workers", *Textos and Contextos (Porto Alegre)*, 9(2): 200-208.

Furedi, F., 2003, *Therapy Culture: Cultivating Vulnerability in an Uncertain Age*, London: Routledge Publications, For details, www.frankfuredi. com/index.php/about/article/188/

Iamamoto, M.V., 2005., *O Serviço Social Na Contemporaneidade: Trabalho E Formação Profissional*. São Paulo: Cortez.

Peters, D.H.; Yazbeck, A.S. and Sharma, R.R., 2002, *Better Health Systems for India's Poor: Findings, Analysis, and Options*, Washington, DC: World Bank.

Sarkar, A.K., 2005, "Social Work—A Commentary from India", *Present and Future of Social Work in Asia Pacific Countries*, Seoul: Korean Association of Social Workers. For details: www.apple.welfare.net/board/download.asp?filePath=%5C...fileName.

Vickery, A., 1974, "A Systems Approach to Social Work Intervention: Its Uses for Work with Individuals and Families", *The British Journal of Social Work*, 4 (4): 389-404.

Weisner, S., 1977, "The Impact of Community Intervention", *Social Service Review*, 51 (4): 659-673.

Websites

http://www.anand.to/india/ngo.html

http://www.cesj.org/thirdway/economicjustice-defined.htm

http://agropedia.iitk.ac.in/?q=content/community-development-programme

http://www.employmentnews.gov.in/Current_Prospects_Social_Work_India.asp

http://www.interventions.org/fraising.html
www.naswpressonline.org
http://www.telegraph.co.uk
http://cec.vcn.bc.ca/cmp/modules/adv-sw.htm
http://www.unesco.org/education/mebam/module_3.pdf`
http://www.socialworkscotland.org.uk/resources/pub/NeedforSocialWorkIntervention.pdf
http://www.sswaa.org/userfiles/file/NewRolesinRTI.pdf

4
Social Work and Community Development

Rakesh Dwivedi

Introduction

The poor and impoverished have been always part of society and effort has been made to improve their condition. These are the peoples those are not able to survive their own lives themselves. They mostly depend on charity. In ancient and medieval era, there was a widespread tradition of giving alms and donation to the needy (deprived) person in a courtesy manner. The charitable work taken-up by individuals and some voluntary organisations came to be termed as social work in the due course of time. The most frequent misconception seen about social work is that people use to give charity, alms and voluntary activities as social work, but in reality this is not social work, as it does not provide any permanent solution to the person's problems and does not empower a person to face their problems by themselves.

The Social work is a profession which works on psycho-social problems of individuals, groups and community and help to maintain relationship between the individual and his social environment. It deals with various problems and issues systematically and scientifically with scientific methods and empowers individuals, groups and communities, increases utilization of resources and enhances their social functioning.

Social work originated as a philanthropic activity by few well-to- do individuals as groups, but gradually grew as a profession in between these temporal and conflictual processes of change in values, facts and means.

Definitions of Social Work

"Social Work includes all voluntary attempts to extend benefits in response to needs which are concerned with social relationships and which avail themselves of scientific knowledge and methods" [Cheyney Alice (1926) cited in Singh, 2016].

The International Association of Schools of Social Work and International Federation of Social Workers (2001) defined social work as "*A profession that promotes social change, problem solving in human relationships and the empowerment and liberation of people to enhance well-being vitalizing theories of human behaviour and social systems. Social work intervenes at the point where people interact with their environments. Principles of human rights and social justice are "fundamental to social work*" (cited in Dhawan, 2011).

Indian Perspective of Social Work

Social work in India is as old as the Indian society itself. Every aspect of Indian culture is predominated by humanitarian philosophy. In Indian context the social work profession is influenced by the socio-economic as well as political cultural changes across the nation. Political dependency and economic backwardness have been the main obstacles in the development of social work in India. Some of the definitions of Indian writers have been given below:

> "Social Work is a welfare activity based on humanitarian, philosophy, scientific knowledge and technical skills for helping individuals or groups or community, to live a rich and full life."
>
> — Indian Conference of Social Work (1957)

> "Social Work, helps an individual in his social functioning, It is based on certain knowledge foundation, calls for skill in human relationships on the part of its practitioner, and has a set of values furnishing its philosophical base."
>
> — Khinduka (1962)

Social Work in its various forms focuses on the multiple, complex transactions between people and their environment. Its mission is to enable all people to develop their full potential, enrich their lives, and prevent dysfunction.

There are three primary methods of Social Work:

- **Social Case Work**: This method deals with an individual to solve the psycho-social problem. It applies the scientific methods and techniques to modify the behaviour of person. This method helps a person in improving his social functioning and self-decision making.
- **Social Group Work**: The objective of this method is development of person through the group. This method guides interaction in programme activities that they may relate themselves to each other and experienced growth opportunities in accordance with their needs and capacities to the desired needs of individual and development.
- **Community Organisation**: Community Development is the term used to describe efforts to bring about adjustment, development or change among groups and organization in regard to social needs or problems. It is a process of people coming together to address issues that matter to them. It also helps to increase interaction among people.

And three auxiliary methods are:

- **Social Work Research**: This method aims to find out answers of problems with the help of scientific tools and testing of social work functions and methods.
- **Social Action**: This method aims to effect social institutions, laws, customs etc. This method works in bringing desired changes through education, propaganda, persuasion etc.
- **Social Welfare Administration**: This method plays a major role in transforming social policies in to social action. Social welfare administration and social work research keep social work as a profession well-aware of the emerging problems and issues, and the modifications required to cope with such challenges by updating knowledge, skills and techniques.

Community

As a whole, it is a unit of action. In community we can see "WE" feeling. When we think of community, we think in geographic terms. Our community is the city, town or village where we live. When community is defined through physical location, it has precise boundaries that are understood and accepted by others. Community can also define by common cultural heritage, language, and beliefs or shared interests.

Community Development

Human resource is an asset to any society and their appropriate utilization decides the development of any nation. The primary aim of development should be welfare of the people or community. A conquer development means development of the people of that community and which can be brought by the people of community themselves. It can be understand as the development of the people, by the people and for the people.

The community development programme has been the biggest rural reconstruction scheme undertaken by the government of India. In 1952, Fifty five community development projects were launched under Community development programmes on the birth anniversary of Mahatma Gandhi. The programme was extended to wider areas even after the duration of the First Five Year Plan including all villages of India.

Community development seeks to improve the quality of life by improving through adjustment with the environment. Effective community development results in mutual benefit and shared responsibilities among community members. Community development helps in building capacity among communities in order to address and take advantages of opportunities, find common grounds and interests. It is a skill based process. It is one of the main sources of initiating change in community. The nature of various development programmes depends on the situation from country to country, state to state and from community to community. Effective community development should be a long term endeavour, well planned, holistic and integrated in to a wide picture.

The planning commission defined the community development programme in these words: "Community development is an attempt to bring about a social and economic transformation of village life through the efforts of the people themselves."

"Community is a process designed to create a condition of economic and social progress for the whole community with its active participation and the fullest possible reliance upon the community initiative". The UN Bureau of Social Affairs, 1955 (cited in Patil, 2013).

"Community development is a movement designed to promote better living for the whole community, with the active participation and if possible on the initiative of the community, but if this initiative is not forthcoming spontaneously, then by the use of techniques for arousing and stimulating it in order to secure its active and enthusiastic response to the movement" [Mukherji (1961) cited in Patil, 2013].

It provides an opportunity to individual as well as community to grow and change according to their needs and priorities. It also pays attention to the fact that this development does not take place at the cost of oppressing other groups or communities. Community development programmes exhibits several characteristics. These are as following: (a) It promotes self-confidence among the community members. (b) It develops self-reliance among individuals and develops ability to take initiative. (c) The community development programme effects change at the psychological-level of the community persons. (d) It seeks to create new administrative machinery suited to the manifold needs of the village. (e) Community thinking and collective action are encouraged through people's institutions like the *panchayats* , co-operative societies, vikas mandal etc. and (f) It promotes problem solving approach.

The role of community development programme in context of the rural community cannot be gainsaid. The programme is instrumental in raising the standards of living of the rural persons and reconstructing the rural India. People involves in their community problems, they co-operate each other to formulating and executing their plans and programmes to solve the problem. They show interest in solving the problem actively.

Therefore, community development is successful only with the total participation of the people. In order to achieve community development, people must be enabled to develop their capacity to identify their problems and plan way to solve things. The community development process involves following cycles:

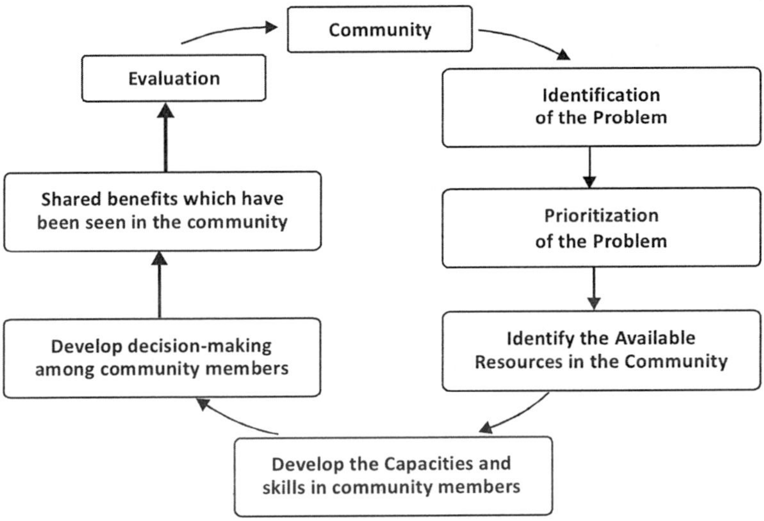

Fig. 4.1: Cycles of Community Development Process.

Source: Patil, A.R. (2013).

Community Development through Social Work Practice

In the field of community development social work practice is applied in variety of settings at individual as well as community-level. The community social work practice attempts to identify various issues that are responsible for social problems in a specific community.

Community Organization is a process of bringing people together to address issues that matter to the with the belief that acting together have a great capacity to improve their own circumstances, as they have first-hand knowledge of the situation and needs of the community to bring desired changes for betterment. It increases interaction among people and tries to integrate and coordinate with existing groups for helping people to identify their needs and fulfil them and helps to bring out voices to add collective power and strength on the issues.

The difference between community development and community organisation can be understood by following points: (a) Community Organisation is a method and Community Development is a programme to bring social change in the community. (b) People are engaged in executing and planning of programmes to their issues in Community Organization. Whereas people participation is optional and external agencies plan the programmes in Community Development. (c) Community Organisation emphasise on the process whereas Community Development emphasise on goal/aim. (d) Community Organisation is a continuous process, where is no time bound to achieve the goal and it is up to people participation, but in Community Development there is time limit to take action and achieve the goal. (e) People participation is very important in Community Organisation, whereas development of people is more important in Community development.

Community organisation is the one of the major method of Social Work which plays a very significant role in development of any society. Community social worker uses the steps of community organisation to bring development in the society. Firstly, it is very important for a worker that she/he must know the community very well and collect the all required information on all aspect and dimensions of the community in which community worker has to do work. Community worker should collect the information regarding demographical, political, social, geographical situation of the community. Through these information worker becomes closer to the community and build the rapport between the community members. It provides the information of community's capacity and that will help in to solve the problems of community very easily.

Community worker enhance the leadership quality of community member who can shoulder all the responsibilities of the community. This community member will represent the whole community. Leader of the community will identify the problems which are facing by the community members and discuss on the priority of the problems. Leadership plays a significant role in the overall development process of community. Community worker empowers the people with the skills needed for improving their living conditions. In this work people's participation must be important to improve the situation and taking necessary action to fulfil needs of the society. In this process, people learn by doing and gain experiences.

Community Worker plays an important role in identification of resources and tells require utilization of local as well as outside resources at the optimum level. For example, community social worker works with various section of society like women, children and elderly by using specific methods with each group. Community Worker can also work for comprehensive development of community by mobilizing internal and external recourses appropriately.

Conclusion

Community social worker can be instrumental in various ways such as creating awareness among community members regarding available resources so that community members solve their problems themselves. All the available resources within the community should be proper utilized by the community members. Community organization as a method of professional social work by which the worker makes intervention regarding the needs and skills when once community members have knows about their capacity they must be involved to make development in community. Social worker must take opportunity to review their role with community work and ensure that old prejudice is not rekindled. In this way, Community will be empowered to use their considerable knowledge, skills and methods in a meaningful constructive way. Social Work has important role to play in addressing community issues—poverty, inequality and social exclusion, but it requires long term planning and commitment part all of those community people involved.

References

Dhawan, N., 2011, *Social Work Perspectives (Philosophy and Methods)*, Lucknow: Bharat Book Centre.

Guha, R., 2013, *Community Organization and Social Action*, New Delhi: Centrum Press.

Mandal, N.K., 2011, *Community Work and Social Action*, New Delhi: Centrum Press.

Palmer, S. D., 2011, *Social Work and Community Practice*, Canada: Apple Academic Press.

Patil, A.R., 2013, *Community Organization and Development*, New Delhi: PHI Learning Private Limited.

Roy, S. and Dash, B.M., 2015, *New Perspectives in Community Development*, New Delhi: Atlantic Publishers.

Singh, S.K., 2016, *Social Work: Principle and Practice*, Lucknow: Navjyoti Simrranjeet Publications.

http://www.peernetbc.com

http://www.youarticleliberary.com

5

Gandhian Philosophy of Sustainable Development and Success Stories of Ralegan Siddhi and Hiware Bazar, Maharashtra

Jaimon Varghese

Introduction

Mahatma Gandhi was an outstanding personality who synthesised spirituality with politics in his personal life. He was a socio-political philosopher with a spiritual bent. He was deeply spiritual and deeply religious. Religion, morality and spirituality are synchronised in his saintly life. He advocated and nourished inclusive spirituality—a spirituality that is wide enough to include all the religions and even the atheists. He was a *Sannyasin* with a great political vision. His *ashrams* were open to people of all religions, castes, nationalities, languages and races. Everyone lead a deeply religious life dedicated to service. He described his religion as religion of truth. Truth is God. He hesitated to describe God as truth. God is more abstract than truth. Truth is close to everyone and being truthful is everybody's responsibility. Even atheists are expected to pursue truth. Therefore, a religion of truth is inclusive of theists and atheists. Non-violence (*ahimsa*) and selfless service (*seva*) are the means to realise truth or God. His political commitments were just his religious duties. Everyone finds meaningful life while losing oneself in continuous and continuing service of others. Gandhi remains in history as an embodiment of spirituality and service.

According to Gandhi, human nature is essentially good, spiritual and divine (IGNOU, 2011). Therefore, being truthful is natural to human being. Humans have a natural aptitude towards truth. Since truth is God, pursuit of truth is a spiritual pursuit. Taking personal suffering in pursuit of truth would influence the oppressors even. Gandhi's spiritualistic philosophy has been translated into *Satyagraha* (passive resistance), *Sarvodaya* (development of all), *Gram Swaraj* (village republic), *Swadeshi* (indigenisation) and *Sarvadharma Samabhavana* (religious harmony). All these enterprises essentially promote global peace, harmony and sustainable development. *Satyagraha* is the proven means for peace building at local, national and even at international levels. It is a globally tested strategy for building sustainable peace. *Sarvodaya* and *Gram Swaraj* are means for sustainable community building. With the 73rd and 74th Constitutional Amendments of 1992 and 1993 respectively, the Government of India expressed its will to establish participatory democracy at the local levels in all the villages and towns in India. Several villages in India have attempted to realise the Gandhian ideal of *Gram Swaraj*. Ralegan Siddhi and Hiware Bazar in Ahmednagar district of Maharashtra present two such success stories across the country.

Padmashri Anna Hazare and Shri Popatrao Pawar have developed their villages, Ralegan Siddhi and Hiware Bazar respectively, as self-reliant communities through a systematic process of social change through people's participation. They set role models of dynamic leadership and demonstrated how we could realise Gandhian models of *Gram Swaraj* in the contemporary era. The key strategy of rural reconstruction being practised in these villages is called '*Panchasutri*' (5-point programme) that includes ban of drug abuse, ban of tree felling, control on free grazing of cattle, family planning and *Shramdan*. By sustained cooperation and participation of the people, both these villages accomplished successful water harvesting enterprises in their villages. Natural resource management is the primary concern of sustainable development. Through effective implementation of water harvesting and soil conservation projects, the villages set the sustainable base for progress. Prosperity and community development were only the by-products of these endeavours. With this achievement, people's capacity for self-determination and self-governance improved. Finally, these model villages attained self-reliance in every sense. Their success stories contribute to the body of knowledge as well as the skill base of professional social workers who are committed to rural community development.

Sustainable development is the buzzword today among the social workers and the development professionals. We can pinpoint the key aspects of sustainable development in Gandhian ideals of *Gram Swaraj* and *Sarvodaya*. In this chapter, Gandhian thought on sustainable development explored with the help of two successful Gandhian model villages of Ralegan Siddhi and Hiware Bazar in Ahmednagar District, Maharashtra.

Gandhi's Inclusive Spirituality

Gandhi accomplished a dynamic unity between morality and religion. There is no distinction between ends and means. The core of good life has to be reflected in the whole life of human beings. Religion is culture specific articulation of a community's moral vision. The fundamentals of morality are same across all the religions (IGNOU, 2011). Gandhi professed the holistic nature of human life. According to Gandhi, one's religious, moral and political life can not be segregated. There is unity and integrity in the lived experience of human beings. His political commitments were religious and moral obligations. All responsibilities are means for spiritual progress.

Gandhi has initiated a revolutionary spiritual philosophy. According to Gandhi, truth or *Satya* is God. *Satyagraha* is quest for truth. *Satya* comes from *Sat* which means existence. *Sat* or existence is metaphysically the only undeniable fact. Truth is clearer and closer to man than the mere abstract concept of God. The ambiguous concept of God can be doubted or even denied. However, denying truth is self-contradictory. Truth is completely universal, comprehensive and provides a common platform for both the theists and atheists to work together for common goal. Gandhi was aware of the fact that blind religious notions about God have done immense damage to mankind. Therefore, he shifted the emphasis from God to truth (IGNOU, 2011). His spirituality is so inclusive that he took inspiration from Jainism, Buddhism, Islam, Christianity, *Gita* and *Upanishads* and welcomed both the theists and atheists in his ashrams. Gandhi was a *sage* in true sense and he preferred to live in community of *sages*.

Gandhi started four *ashrams* during his life time. Two of them are still attracting the attention of people across the world. Phoenix Settlement established in 1904 in South Africa spread over 100 acres of land and gave training to *Satyagrahis* who hailed from all religions and nationalities. Tolstoy Farm established in 1911 in South Africa spread over 1100 acres accommodated aspirants from Hindu, Christian, Muslim and Parsi religions and practiced the Tolstoy's tenets of peace and harmony. *Satyagraha Ashram* started by Gandhi in 1915 at Sabarmati in India, apart from promoting inclusive spirituality, strived for eradication of untouchability, emancipation of women and encouragement of self-reliance by imparting training to the inmates on weaving, carpentry, cooking and sanitation. *Sevagram* established at Wardha in Maharashtra in 1936 spread over 300 acres of land has a common kitchen for all castes. *Nai talim*, the innovative education enterprise for life skill training, is the distinction of *Sevagram*. The *Ashram* rules set by Gandhi reflect inclusive spirituality. Major *ashram* rules were truth (*satya*), non-violence (*ahimsa*), self-control (*brahmacharya*), non-stealing (*asteya*), detachment (*aparigraha*), control of palate, fearlessness, removal of untouchability, bread labour, equality of religions and *swadeshi* (*khadi*) (IGNOU, 2011). Practice of inclusive spirituality is essential of community development. No village can achieve self-reliance and prosperity without promoting inclusion of all ideologies, religions and castes. Inclusion is the basis for sustainable development. Gandhi was very much aware of this fact and had been keen to promote the same since the start of his political career in South Africa. We have contemporary models of Gandhian inclusive thought demonstrated at Ralegan Siddhi and Hiware Bazar in Ahmednagar District of Maharashtra.

It is relevant to distinguish inclusive spirituality from exclusive spirituality. Exclusive spirituality believes in exclusivity of truth. From this perspective, there is only one truth or only one true religion. All other religions are mistaken paths or ignorant ways who need correction or in the evolutionary path who need to grow and mature. According to exclusive spirituality, bringing everyone to the single truth is the mission of true religious person. Else the unfaithful would perish in vain. Life lived or sacrificed for the promotion of religion is the supreme goal of life on this earth. It can be seen that the fanatic, dogmatic and superstitious trends are visible in exclusive spirituality.

Inclusive spirituality, advocated by Gandhi, believes in inclusive reality or religious pluralism. Every religion has truth or every religious truth has relevance in its own cultural and historical context. Being true to one's own religion is good enough for salvation. Every religion has the scope for enlightenment and salvation. Life on this earth is as important as life after death. Being compassionate, loving and serving all people is the true expression of religion and they are the real means for salvation or meaningful life. Loving and serving mankind and other living beings on earth is the visible service to the invisible God. One should not die for the sake of religion or God. Religion is for the good of man. Serving others is the real religious service. Life is more important than religion. Religion is just one of many social institutions for promoting the interests of man, like state or cultural institutions. A life exclusively lived for religion is not worth living. Inclusive spirituality is human centred or nature centred. It is not centred on the supernatural or the life after death. All the religions are cultural expressions of people at different historical and geographical contexts. No religion is superior to the other.

It is both interesting and surprising to see that every religion has people who follow exclusive as well as inclusive spirituality. There are religious missionaries who spend their entire life in promotion of their own religion. There are also compassionate people in the same religion, who spend their life in the service of all people without caring for promotion of own religion. Religion had always been inspiration for many to set apart their life for humanitarian service. There are several great visionaries and missionaries who have set-up noble humanitarian enterprises in the world. There are also many world leaders who are deeply religious with inclusive spirituality. Gandhi is one such world leader who was deeply religious with a vision for inclusive spirituality.

From historical point of view exclusive spirituality was more popular than inclusive spirituality during the ancient and medieval period. During those years there lived a large number of religious martyrs. Gradually, there has been a shift from exclusivity to religious toleration and inclusiveness during the modern and contemporary era. Today, from the sustainable development perspective, we talk about religious harmony, ideological tolerance, pluralism, unity in cultural diversity and preservation of all cultural resources. When we are more engaged with inclusive growth and development, the exclusive approach becomes outdated.

We can not however, ignore the fact that the exclusive spirituality is still prevalent in certain corners of the world and has posed the greatest challenge for the sustainable development of world today. Being adamant to exclusive spirituality is taking the world several centuries backward. Such attempts are termed as radicalisation and countries worldwide condemn it. What is required today is clear shift from exclusiveness to inclusiveness. True and sustainable spirituality for us is inclusive spirituality. Gandhi firmly believed in inclusive spirituality and strongly advocated the same through his *ashram* life. Communalism is an expression of exclusive spirituality. Gandhi himself had been a victim of dangerous expression of exclusive spirituality.

Ahimsa and Satyagraha— A Means for Sustainable Development

According to Gandhi, politics cannot be alienated from moral enterprise. Politics is the spiritual exercise for moral growth. Politics offers a great opportunity for people to serve others and facilitates one's spiritual growth. *Ahimsa* (non-violence) and *Satyagraha* are the only means to achieve any moral, economic, political and social end. Non-violence is the greatest force available at the disposal of mankind. It is the soul-force or love-force used by *Satyagrahi*. Non-violence is humble, brave and free from hatred. Positive meaning of non-violence is love and compassion. It is the foundation of human civilisation and the fundamental principle of existence and survival. Non-violence is the law of the strong, not the weak and the coward. Violence, on the other hand, is the law of the brute who are generally weak (morally) and coward (IGNOU, 2011).

Non-violence condemns the evil, but loves the evil doer. *Satyagraha* fights the tyranny, aggression and evil systems. While taking loss and suffering upon themselves, *Satyagrahis* bring about a transformation of mind and attitudinal change in the enemies. *Satyagraha* may be regarded as the collective name of all the methods and techniques of Gandhian Social Work, namely persuasion, auto-suffering, fasting, non-cooperation, boycott, civil disobedience, picketing, strikes, etc. All these methods are based on Gandhian values and principles of truth and non-violence (Billore, 2010[1]:325). A *Satyagrahi* is always ready for an honourable settlement with the opponent but he has not to arrive at a compromise with issues which are not moral. As a *Satyagrahi* has to be ready even to fight injustice, he is to welcome peace in an honourable manner. He cannot surrender his moral principles. Gandhi believed that in the path of *Satyagraha*, negotiations and compromise are essential at some stage or the other because if they are attempted in the very beginning the conflict may be avoided (Gaur, 1977:63). They engage in constructive work during the peaceful time, such as eradication of poverty, building cooperatives, establishing village industries and improving educational facilities.

While analyzing Gandhian thought, one can understand that he has staunch belief in the goodness of human nature. According to him goodness and honesty are essential to human nature. Ignorance and greed often block our perception of our own basic good nature. The effectiveness of *Satyagraha* lies in his unflinching faith in good human nature. "The exploitative attitude is not human but one conditioned and fostered by bourgeois materialism and greed, while the quiescent attitude is of the rebel who tries to escape the bourgeois world and voices his idealist protest against bourgeois greed" (Raj Kumar and Vijendra Kumar, 1999:104). A *Satyagrahi* can change the mind of the oppressor by removing his ignorance at the cost of own suffering.

Success of *Satyagraha* has been demonstrated in South Africa, Czechoslovakia, Chile, Iran, Rumania and Philippines. October 2 is celebrated as the United Nations International Non-violence Day. *Satyagraha* is considered as the only way to escape hatred, violence and war. Violence breeds violence. Non-violence breaks the cycle of violence and brings sustainable peace. *Ahimsa* and *Satyagraha* are not only the means for political gains, but also the means for sustainable development. For, peace is essential for development. By establishing sustainable peace, non-violence prepares the ground for sustainable development and prosperity.

Sustainable Development Goals

On 25th September, 2015, the United Nations' General Assembly passed the resolution A/70/1 with the title, "Transforming Our World: The 2030 Agenda for Sustainable Development". It was endorsed by 196 countries. It consists of 17 goals with 169 targets. When the first round of ranking was completed, India stood at 110th position (*The Indian Express*, 23.07.2016). The sustainable development goals (Table 5.1) are close to the objectives of *Sarvodaya* and *Gramswaraj*.

Table 5.1: Sustainable Development Goals

Goal 1	End poverty in all its forms everywhere.
Goal 2	End hunger, achieve food security and improved nutrition and promote sustainable agriculture.
Goal 3	Ensure healthy lives and promote well-being for all at all ages.
Goal 4	Ensure inclusive and equitable quality education and promote life-long learning opportunities for all.
Goal 5	Achieve gender equality and empower all women and girls.
Goal 6	Ensure availability and sustainable management of water and sanitation for all.
Goal 7	Ensure access to affordable, reliable, sustainable and modern energy for all.
Goal 8	Promote sustained, inclusive and sustainable economic growth, full and productive employment and decent work for all.
Goal 9	Build resilient infrastructure, promote inclusive and sustainable industrialization and foster innovation.
Goal 10	Reduce inequality within and among countries.
Goal 11	Make cities and human settlements inclusive, safe, resilient and sustainable.
Goal 12	Ensure sustainable consumption and production patterns.
Goal 13	Take urgent action to combat climate change and its impacts.

(*Contd.*)

(*Contd.*)

Goal 14	Conserve and sustainably use the oceans, seas and marine resources for sustainable development.
Goal 15	Protect, restore and promote sustainable use of terrestrial ecosystems, sustainably manage forests, combat desertification, and halt and reverse land degradation and halt biodiversity loss.
Goal 16	Promote peaceful and inclusive societies for sustainable development, provide access to justice for all and build effective, accountable and inclusive institutions at all levels.
Goal 17	Strengthen the means of implementation and revitalize the Global Partnership for Sustainable Development.

Source: sustainabledevelopment.un.org

Gandhian Philosophy of Sustainable Development

Gandhi was aware of the hypocrisy of modern civilisation which is unsustainable and brings only cruelty, oppression, exploitation and indignity. Industrialised and capitalist economy breeds hunger for wealth and greed for worldly pleasures. Industrial mode of production reduces man in to a mere cog in the machine. By maddening conveniences, man transgresses natural limits. Large scale production and transportation cause famine. Big machines displace man from his natural habitat and work. Machines and mechanical devices are introduced at the cost of spiritual progress and happiness. Education is pre-occupied with occupation where character formation is neglected. Gandhi called for a return to simple village life which is more sustainable, humane, spiritual, nature-friendly and healthy.

Gandhi is not an academic philosopher, but a practical philosopher. Whatever, he preached were practiced by him and all his thoughts and words were meant for practice in the field. Gandhian trinity of *Sarvodaya*, *Swaraj* and *Swadeshi* were the three-fold strategy to establish a sustainable social, economic and political order by getting rid of the centralised, exploitative, unsustainable and violent system of governance and economics of greed. *Sarvodaya* is an all comprehensive vision assuring the total good of every individual which includes religious, moral, social, political and economic well-being. *Sarvodaya* is based on three principles. Good of individual is contained in the good of all. From livelihood perspective, lawyer's work has the same value as that of barber's. A life of labour such as tilling the soil or handicraft work is worth living. *Sarvodaya* has several goals. Primary goal of *Sarvodaya* is greatest good of all living beings to which everyone contributes according to his ability. It aims at a liberated society where rights and dignity of every human person is respected. It is a new social, political, economic and moral order which is just, non-violent, non-exploitative, non-material, non-imperialist, non-racist, non-consumerist, egalitarian, liberated, human and decentralised. It assures self-realisation of every individual. Main features of *Sarvodaya* are trusteeship with regard to wealth, economic equality and networking. It is against intimidation, coercion, persecution and organised violence of the state machinery. It stresses on party-less democracy and decentralised governance (*Gram Swaraj*) (IGNOU, 2011).

Gandhi strongly believed that the villagers are wise enough to form *Gram Swaraj*, a self-reliant village republic, if given the opportunity and encouragement. Gandhi is regarded as the first social thinker in India who presented a complete picture of an ideal Indian society based on rural realities, giving thought to every aspect, such as nature of the State and its administration, defence, health, sanitation, housing, education, employment, development of weaker sections and eradication of various social problems such as untouchability, alcoholism, poverty etc. (Billore, 2010[2]:338-339). While the world around is running after an urban oriented development model, Gandhi advocated for a rural model of national development. Gandhi had great faith in the villagers' ability for *Gram Swaraj* and he had the vision of ideal development model for the nation based on rural reconstruction. He had a dream of village based republic of India, where each village in the country is politically free and economically prosperous and self-reliant.

It is interesting to note that Gandhi used the word *Gram Swaraj* with a double meaning in the context of Indian National Movement. Gandhi promoted in the concept of *Swaraj*, or 'self-rule', advocating Indian Independence from foreign domination. Simultaneously, he also discussed his belief in *Gram Swaraj* ('village self-rule'), asserting that the Indian village should be self-sufficient and autonomous. Considering that over two third of Indians are still living in villages today, Gandhi's philosophy is still relevant. Gandhi termed his ideal society as '*Ramrajya*', i.e. the kingdom of God on earth. In Gandhi's '*Gram Swaraj*' all people will proudly, joyously and voluntarily be bread labourers. Gandhi's ideal society is predominately a rural society. The real India lies in the villages. If Indian civilization is to make its full contribution to the building up of a stable world order, it is this vast mass of humanity that has to be made to live again. Gandhi had full faith in the wisdom of the rural people (Billore, 2010:270-271).

Gandhi had worked out the minute details of a *Gram Swaraj*. Hard work, cattle rearing, recreation, prohibition, education, irrigation, cooperation, *Satyagraha* and compulsory *Shramdan* had their own place in *Gram Swaraj*. Gandhi's idea on village republic is bold and comprehensive. According to Gandhi, village panchayats should have full powers and little interference from the State. Emphasizing on autonomous village republic is the way to promote participatory model of rural development. Rural prosperity begins with the formation of all powerful village panchayat that would self-impose the rules and regulations for self-reliance and sustainable development. Such self-rule of the village panchayat has been demonstrated at Ralegan Siddhi and Hiware Bazar.

Gandhi has outlined the framework of a strong village self-government. As a political thinker, he has worked out the powers and functions of the village *panchayat*. Gandhi believed that villages have moral functions. Village *panchayats* need to promote honest and industrious living. Justice and speedy resolution of disputes are essential functions of village *panchayats*. There should be total ban on intoxicating drinks and drugs. Untouchability and casteism are to be eliminated from village scenario. Religious harmony should be the face of model village.

Gandhian thought on model village can be summarized by the 19-point Constructive Programme. The 19-point Constructive Programme is a unique contribution of Gandhi's ingenuity and imagination to the theory of social reconstruction and peaceful revolution (Parmeshwari Dayal, 2006:269). Gandhi called his 19-

point Constructive Programme a programme for construction of total or complete independence *(Poorna Swaraj)* consisting of not only political, but social and economic independence as well through truthful and non-violent means. The reconstruction programme aims at eradication of social problems like untouchability, alcoholism and unemployment and backwardness of weaker sections through programmes on communal unity and economic equality (Billore, 2010[3]:304). The 19-point on the Constructive Programme can be classified into three categories, *viz.* (a) *Economic Regeneration—Khadi*, Village Industries, Economic Equality, Improvement of Cattle, Kisan and Labour; (b) *Social Reform*—Removal of Untouchability, Prohibition, Uplift of Women and Adivasis, Education in Health and Hygiene, and Lepers; and (c) *National Character Building*—Communal Unity, Village Sanitation, Basic Education, Adult Education, Provincial Language, National Language and Students (Parmeshwari Dayal, 2006:270-271).

Peace and social harmony are by-products of an ideal *Gram Swaraj*. The economic structure of Gandhian Thought is based on the absence of exploitation, decentralization of producing units, cheaper defense organization, less inequality of income and self-sufficiency among the communities (Palsapure, 1972:66). Gandhi was stern against corruption of the public offices. When someone wanted to honour Gandhi, he exhorted, 'I, therefore, beseech you that if you want really to do me a honour, do not give me a shower-bath of addresses and honours. The best way to honour me is to do my behest and carry my principles into practice'(Tendulkar, 1951:223-224).

"Rural Development is concerned with economic growth and social justice, improvement in the living standard of the rural people by providing adequate and quality social services and minimum basic needs becomes essential. The process of sustainable development envisages that people should not merely participate, but be in charge of their own development. Village economy is based on its natural resource management. Natural resource management has to be the key pin for an effective strategy for rural development. Most of the rural development models have therefore, considered natural resource management as the means for rural transformation" (Shahaji and Arya, 2004:208-209). In this regard sustainable rural development is essentially economic development in tone with the ecological and environmental conservation.

Gandhian model of *Gram Swaraj* is the ideal model for sustainable development. *Gram Swaraj* promotes bread labour (universal productive work), consumption based production (to replace commercial production), local distribution (replacing interstate or international transportation) and local self-reliance. Mass production, huge scale collection in cold storages and warehouses, mass movement and large scale transportation lead to greed, competition and unsustainable development. Such development leads to wastage of economic resources, unwarranted exploitation of natural resources, huge cost of recycling and replenishing of exhausted resources. *Gram Swaraj* advocates total decentralisation of political and economic powers as well as activities. Every village would become self-reliant economic and political unit with minimum need for inter- dependence. Poverty, illiteracy, unemployment, poor sanitation, poor drainage, poor water supply, poor connectivity and poor health have to be dealt with locally (at village level). Eradication of all these social evils at state or national level is a myth. We need strategies to deal with all these problems at village-level. No uniform solution can be provided for all the villages. Every village has unique problem demanding unique solution. From Gandhian perspective, the key for sustainable development is to plan for localised model for self-reliant villages and towns. Ralegan Siddhi and Hiware Bazar have provided such unique solutions in Maharashtra.

Success Stories of Ralegan Siddhi and Hiware Bazar

Ralegan Siddhi and Hiware Bazar are two medium sized villages in Parner block of Ahmednagar district. Ahmednagar District is geographically the largest District in the State of Maharashtra having 5.66 per cent of the area of the State (www.ahmednagar.nic.in). Due to scarce rainfall, Ahmednagar often suffers from drought. Ahmednagar is named after its founder, Ahmed Shah Nizam Shah (1494 A.D.). Ahmednagar Fort, being considered as the strongest fort in India, was used as the state prison by the British to house Jawaharlal Nehru and other Indian nationalists during the Indian Independence Movement. During his confinement by the British at Ahmednagar Fort, Nehru wrote the famous book *'The Discovery of India'*. Ahmednagar city was the Indian base of the British Army's Royal Tank Corps and Indian Armoured Corps. Today, Ahmednagar Tank Museum has the second-largest display of military tanks in the world.

Ahmednagar district has an area of 17,412 sq. km. and has approximately fifty lakhs population today with 12 per cent Scheduled Castes and 7.5 per cent Scheduled Tribes people. The district has 1581 villages and 18 towns. It has 14 *Panchayat Samitis* (tehsils), 1310 *Gram Panchayats*, 1 Municipal Corporation, 8 Nagar Parishads and 1 Cantonment Board. Ahmednagar has the maximum number of sugar factories (19 sugar factories) and is the birth place of the sugar cooperative movement in India. The first cooperative sugar factory in Asia was established at Pravara Nagar (www.ahmednagar.nic.in).

Ahmednagar has made significant contribution in the field of rural development in the past. Ahmednagar is the birth place of National Service Scheme (NSS), a Government of India Programme for the student community of the higher education. Based on his experience of implementing the Rural Life Development Project with the support of the students of Ahmednagar College and the Centre for Studies in Rural Development (CSRD) in about 100 villages in the district of Ahmednagar, Prof. Hulbe, the founder director of CSRD prepared the basic guidelines of the National Service Scheme which was implemented by the Government of India in 1969 as a nation-wide programme. Today, hundreds and thousands of students of colleges and universities render their voluntary services towards rural reconstruction activities through NSS.

Upon the successful implementation of Employment Guarantee Scheme (EGS) of the Government of Maharashtra in various villages in Ahmednagar district, such as Hiware Bazar, the scheme has been adopted as a nationwide programme in 2005. Employment Guarantee Scheme (EGS) was started in the year 1972. The projects to which EGS employment contributed included moisture conservation and water conservation works (e.g. percolation and storage tanks), soil conservation and land development works, afforestation, roads, and flood protection schemes. Successful demonstration of EGS is visible in several villages in Ahmednagar. EGS had a significant role in the path of transformation of Hiware Bazar the model village in Ahmednagar. In December 2004, a bill was tabled in the Parliament of India, the National Rural Employment Guarantee Bill, which proposed to extend the EGS to the poorest 150 districts of the country. It became National Rural Employment Guarantee Act in 2005 and today it has become a highly popular and successful scheme under the name of Mahatma Gandhi National Rural Employment Guarantee Act (MGNREGA).

Adarsh Gram Yojana is yet another Government of Maharashtra Scheme under implementation since 1994 based on the lessons learnt from Ralegan Siddhi, a model village in Ahmednagar transformed by *Padmashri* Anna Hazare. The transformation of his village Ralegan Siddhi began in the year 1975 based on Gandhian ideals. Since 1989, Hiware Bazar village in Ahmednagar district followed the Ralegan model of rural transformation and in a shorter span time, they demonstrated its success. Adarsh Gram Yojana is being implemented in phase by the Government of Maharashtra in various parts of the State. Training centres established at Ralegan Siddhi and Hiware Bazar for imparting training for local body functionaries are the nerve centres for the implementation of this scheme. Adarsh Gram Yojana of the Government of Maharashtra is the predecessor of Sansad Adarsh Gram Yojana of the Government of India.

Ralegan Siddhi has an area of 982 ha. It has approximately 2000 people living in 325 households. Marathas of Khatri caste out-number other castes and constitute nearly two-third of the families. Backward classes (Scheduled Castes and Scheduled Tribes) constitute 14.23 per cent of the total population. When Shri Annasaheb Hazare, a retired army man, first returned to his village in 1975 it was an extremely degraded village. There was a large scale outward migration, ill health, low productivity and a flourishing business in the illegal distilling of alcohol, resulting into violence especially against women. Having been elected to the leadership of the village, he stressed on his five-point programme of ban on open grazing, ban on tree felling, ban on consumption of liquor, family planning and donation of labour (*Shramdan*).

Annasaheb started the work of rural reconstruction with the watershed development and widespread afforestation by cheap, local, and maximized use of local resources especially labour. The villagers worked patiently and continuously over 20 years to demonstrate the lasting impact. Most of the water-harvesting structures were acquired by the villagers through 100 per cent *Shramdan*. The water harvesting structures include 48 nulla bunds, 5 cement check dams and 16 Gabion structures, continuous contour trenches and loose boulder structures on 500 acres of land. The watershed development work helped in conserving each drop of rainwater in the village itself and in recharging the groundwater aquifers. This ultimately raised the water table and expanded the area under cultivation. Along with agriculture, the dairy business has also flourished as a subsidiary to agriculture. The per capita income of the villagers increased from Rs. 225 to Rs. 2500.

Since last 25 years, thousands of visitors have visited Ralegan Siddhi to study the impact of watershed development. A training institute to impart training in watershed development has been established at Ralegan Siddhi. *Padmashri* Anna Hazare has set the role model for Gandhian social workers. His greatest investment was his own honest, hardworking, genuine and positive personality. His involvement in various social issues and mass movements in the nation is nothing but his natural reaction as a responsible citizen of the country.

The Gandhian ideal of *Gram Swaraj* has also been achieved at Hiware Bazar 20 years after the success of Ralegan Siddhi. Hiware Bazar has the total geographical area of 976.84 hectares. The population of Hiware Bazar is approximately 1200 where the Marathas constitute the dominant caste (185 out of the 205 households). In 1989, Shri Popat Rao Pawar completed the Master of Commerce Degree from New Arts College, Ahmednagar. In the same year, he was elected and became the *Sarpanch*. He had been the force behind all the changes that transformed Hiware Bazar since 1989. Hiware Bazar, the "Adarsh Gaon", is a unique model based on the twin principles of self-governance and self-reliance. The *Gram Sabha* has the power to decide on a range of issues, including identifying sites for water and types of crops to be cultivated (Neha Skhuja, 2008:30-31).

On 15th August, 1994, the Hiware Bazar village *Gram Sabha* established the "Yashwant Krishi Gram and Watershed Development Trust" for implementing watershed development programmes in the village. Funds were drawn from Employment Guarantee Scheme and Joint Forest Management to manage the water harvesting programmes. The Total cost of Watershed programme sanctioned by Government of Maharashtra State was Rs. 6.60 million and the villagers of Hiware Bazar contributed Rs. 2.10 million through *Shramdan* (voluntary labour). Activities undertaken included the construction of contour bunds, continuous contour trenching on hill slopes and planting of local hardy trees, bushes and grasses over the watershed. Under these schemes, about 52 earthen bunds, two percolation tanks, 33 loose stone bunds were constructed. About nine check dams have also been constructed in a series on the downstream *nallah*. New constructions and repairs of loose boulder bunds, cement bunds, farm bunds, farm tanks and percolation tanks have also been undertaken from time to time.

Along with the implementation of water harvesting project, in 1995, the Adarsh Gaon Yojana was launched. Hiware Bazar was selected as the village that could be developed as the model village in the district. The village adopted the five-point Adarsh Gram Yojana Programme of *Shramdan* (voluntary labour), ban on tree cutting, ban on grazing of cattle in forest or in pasture land, ban on liquor and implementation of family planning. The *Gram Sabha* added five more principles by consensus. The additional five rules for village development were ban on using a borewell for irrigation, ban on cultivating water intensive crops such as banana and sugarcane, ban on selling of land to outsiders, ban on any feeling of full and private ownership of groundwater occurring in individual farms and use of borewells only for drawing drinking water. In fact, these self-imposed additional rules made Hiware Bazar distinct and on the fast track to become Adarsh Gram in a very short period. During the Adarsh Gram Yojana decade (1995-2004) the village witnessed significant progress in various sectors. Water table rose from 70-80 ft to 20-25 ft. Area under irrigation increased 3.18 times (250 to 795.23 hectares). During summer it increased 10.28 times (7 to 72 hectares). Annual Per Capita Income increased from Rs. 832 to Rs. 30,000. Today people from far and wide have paid visit to the village. Delegates from 122 nations have so far visited Hiware Bazar.

Conclusion

There is connection between spirituality and sustainable development. Gandhi's vision of spiritualist philosophy has applicability towards the goal of sustainable development. Gandhi achieved in his life and advocated for others the principle of inclusive spirituality which is essential for establishing global peace, communal harmony and sustainable development. *Sarvodaya*, *Gram Swaraj* and *Swadeshi* have similar goals with that of sustainable development goals endorsed by United Nations in 2015. *Ahimsa* and *Satyagraha* are means for establishing egalitarian societies, global peace and sustainable development. Gandhian ideal of *Gram Swaraj* has already been successfully demonstrated in various parts of the country. Ralegan Siddhi and Hiware Bazar are two such model villages in Ahmednagar District of Maharashtra which exhibit development of sustainable villages based on Gandhian principles of *Gram Swaraj*.

Notes

1. Billore, S.R., 2010, "Gandhian Social Work: Methods and Techniques", in Gracious Thomas (Ed.): *Origin and Development of Social Work in India,* New Delhi: IGNOU, School of Social Work.
2. Billore, S.R., 2010, "Gandhian Social Work: The Historical Perspective", in Gracious Thomas (Ed.): *Origin and Development*

of Social Work in India, New Delhi: IGNOU, School of Social Work.

3. Billore, S.R., 2010. "Gandhi's Charter of Social Reconstruction", in Gracious Thomas (Ed.): *Origin and Development of Social Work in India,* New Delhi: IGNOU, School of Social Work.

References

Billore, S.R., 2010, "Gandhi's Perception of an Ideal Society", in Gracious Thomas (Ed.): *Origin and Development of Social Work in India,* New Delhi: IGNOU, School of Social Work.

Gaur, V.P., 1977, *Mahatma Gandhi—A Study of His Message of Non-violence.* New Delhi: Sterling Publishers Private Ltd.

IGNOU, 2011, *Gandhian Philosophy (MPYE 15),* New Delhi: Indira Gandhi National Open University, School of Interdisciplinary and Trans-Disciplinary Studies.

Kumar, R. and Kumar, V., 1999, *Mahatma Gandhi— Life, Ideology and Thoughts: A Vision for 21st Century,* Jaipur: Mangal Deep Publication.

Palsapure, P.Z., 1972, "Gandhiji's Ideas on Social and Economic Life and its Progress", *Proceedings of the Seminar on Gandhian Thought*, Pune: Pune University Press.

Parmeshwari, D., 2006, *Gandhian Theory of Social Reconstruction,* New Delhi: Atlantic Publishers and Distributors.

Phand, S. and Arya, H.P.S., 2004, "Adarsh Gaon Yojana—Way Towards Gandhi's Dream Village: Self-Sufficient, Prosperous and Peaceful," *Journal of Rural Development*, 26(2).

Skhuja, N., 2008, *Hiware Bazar Calling—Down to Earth*, New Delhi: Centre for Science and Environment.

Tendulkar, D.G., 1951, *Mahatma Life of Mohandas Karamchand Gandhi,* Vol. I, New Delhi: Ministry of Information and Broadcasting, Government of India.

www.sustainabledevelopment.un.org

www.ahmednagar.nic.in

www.hiware-bazar.epanchayat.in retrieved on 14th November, 2011.

www.nrsl.wordpress.com/2005/04/04/hiware-bazaar retrieved on 14th November, 2011.

www.annahazare.org/Ralegan-siddhi.html retrieved on 14th November, 2011.

www.breds.org.in/gandhi.html retrieved on 14th November, 2011.

www.rainwaterharvesting.org/rural/Hirve.htm retrieved on 14th November, 2011.

www.rainwaterharvesting.org/rural/Ralegan.htm retrieved on 14th November, 2011.

www.telegraph.co.uk/earth/earthcomment/geoffrey-lean/8081883/Hiware-Bazar-putting-a-price-on-nature.html retrieved on 14th November, 2011.

www.thebetterindia.com/2264/hiware-bazar-model-village-india retrieved on 14th November, 2011.

www.yehhailife.com/2010/10/26/hiware-bazar-an-indian-villages-journey-from-poverty-to-riches retrieved on 14th November, 2011.

6

Grassroots Level Planning

A Tool for Community Development

Ram Prasad Das

Planning is a process of preparing a blueprint of actions to attain stated objectives within a timeframe. The determination of objectives, the specification of targets, the strategy for mobilisation of resources, the allocation of resources of different development sectors, the blueprint of actions and service delivery system etc., are the main issues for any planning exercise. It involves prioritizing needs and setting up of clearly defined goals. It also includes critical analysis of the existing and to be acquired resources in terms of men, money materials, organisations and technologies so as to obtain maximum results with minimum costs. Social planning is done with the inherent goal of obtaining economic growth with social justice, maximizing work opportunities, self-reliance, enhancing income, removing regional and caste-class disparities, alleviating poverty leading to improve the quality of life of the nation as a whole. This approach as a tool is applicable to grassroots level planning for the development of villages also.

As long as the rural masses remain deprived of adequate developmental opportunities, any thought of making the country one among the developed nations would be futile. The "trickle down approach" could not bring about fruitful result till first four decade after Independence rather non-involvement of target group in rural area remained a problem in the planning process. The institutions for planning, the officials and administrators of higher level would decide upon the plans and programmes to be implemented for the rural areas. Therefore, with the passage of time, a marked shift in the planning process, that is, from plan from above to plan from below. Various measures of democratic decentralisation have been taken up, so that, the target population participates in the planning process. At this grassroots level planning, the people themselves prioritise their needs and problems and make plans for the development of the village. In order to institutionalise people's participation, democratic decentralisation came into effect in the form of 73rd Constitutional Amendment Act in 1992.

This Act provides constitutional status to the Panchayati Raj, plugging in many of the loopholes observed in the earlier system. The new system ensures involvement of all sections of the society, including the disadvantaged, women, SCs, STs, OBCs, in the process of economic, social and political development through appropriate reservation of seats.

In recent time, a number of steps have been taken for agricultural development, housing, health and education sector to improve the quality of life for the rural masses. People's participation through certain grassroots level institutions, village *panchayats*, *Gram Sabhas*, *Mahila Mandali*, youth clubs, *Krishak Charcha Mondali* has been tried but, these grassroots- level institutions were largely voluntary, without statutory back-up. A vast sum of money was spent on rural development through different sectorial departments trying to reach the rural people directly without appropriate field level functionaries. Several new programmes and schemes were launched every now and then without paying any attention to the ground realities and priorities of the rural masses. Weak planning at the block level and absence of effective village based institutions of the people's participation compounded the problems of grassroots level planning which led the target group to remain as mare passive receiver of the programmes and services.

Hence, there was a need for involvement of rural people in the planning process for the development of their own community. With the view of amending the lacunae in the planning and implementing of policy and programme for rural masses, there was a paradigm shift in social planning. Instead of "planning from top" focus was on "planning from below" which is the inherent theme of grassroots-level planning. Grassroots-level planning ensures participation of those who are the final targets of developmental planning.

Grassroots-level planning means a form of planning lower institutional-levels of the block and village, where people from all sections of the society get together and enlist and prioritise the areas of intervention, take view of their resources and formulate, execute and supervise the plans for the development of their own community, but also power to use resources for effective implementation and to supervise the whole process. It also involves for the socio-economic development of their own community as well as that of the nation.

Under the Panchayati Raj System of the rural people elect the village *panchayat* members who are responsible for executing the plans and programmes for rural development. The village members participate in the planning of rural development programmes and its monitoring, supervision and evaluation through *Gram Sabhas.* One of the unique features of this democratic decentralisation is the involvement of all sections of the society in the planning and execution process. The weaker sections of the society are involved in decision-making process for community development and given legal right to be part of the grassroots-level planning. The scheduled castes, scheduled tribes, the other backward classes and women have been given due reservation of seats in various constituencies. The inherent theme behind the involvement of representatives of weaker sections has been to secure the well-being of their respective fellowmen. In the same manner, women are expected to raise issues related to the welfare and well-being of females during planning process in *panchayat*.

In the grassroots planning, the *panchayat* deals with many issues pertaining to rural development like regulating building construction, protection of public land against encroachment, maintenance of traditional drinking water sources, collection and disposal of solid wastes and regulation of liquid waste disposal, maintenance of environmental hygiene, management of public markets, vector control, protection of roads and other public properties, street lighting and its maintenance, adoption of immunisations programmes, agriculture-related activities like cultivating waste lands and marginal lands, soil protection, encouraging horticulture and vegetable cultivation etc.

The scope of grassroots-level planning is too vast. It also includes other crucial areas like animal husbandry and dairy farming, minor irrigation, fishing, social forestry, small scale industries, rural housing, water supply, electricity and energy, education, public works, public health and sanitation, social welfare, poverty alleviation, development and welfare and of scheduled castes and scheduled tribes, promotion of sports and cultural affairs, public distribution system, relief work during natural calamities etc. Apart from all these areas of intervention, it is the duty of the *panchayat* to ensure people's participation in all the activities for the development of the village and to maintain transparency in their work. Therefore, decentralisation has been seen as necessary and desirable for the participation of the people in the process of planned development which is being operationalized on the basis of 73rd Constitutional Amendment Act of 1992.

A *Gram Panchayat* functions as a unit of self-government and, in order to achieve economic development and secure social justice for all through preparing a development plan for five-year term of the office of the member and also to prepare an annual plan for each year for development of human resources, infrastructure and civic amenities and to implement schemes for economic development and social justice in the area.

According to the 73rd Constitutional Amendment Act there are several items covering different aspects of socio-economic life of the villages such as regulatory functions to maintain civic amenities, social service and infrastructure, development and enhancement of economic resources of the village and welfare and development of weaker sections, particularly the families below the poverty line. The major sectors under the Panchayati Raj Institutions (PRIs) are:

(A) Agriculture and Allied Activities

(1) Agriculture and extension

(2) Land improvement, land reform, consolidation, soil and water conservation
(3) Minor irrigation
(4) Animal husbandry, dairying, poultry etc.
(5) Fisheries

(B) Forestry and Environment
(6) Social and farm forestry
(7) Fuel and fodder
(8) Minor forest products
(9) Non-conventional energy resources

(C) Industries
(10) Small industries including food processing
(11) *Khadi*, village and cottage industries

(D) Infrastructure, Minimum Needs, Social Services
(12) Roads, culverts, bridges, ferries etc.
(13) Rural electrification
(14) Drinking water
(15) Rural housing
(16) Education
(17) Technical and vocational education
(18) Adult and non-formal education
(19) Libraries
(20) Cultural activities, festivals etc.
(21) Health, sanitation etc.
(22) Family welfare
(23) Public distribution system
(24) Markets and fairs

(E) Social Welfare
(25) Women and child welfare
(26) Social welfare including welfare of handicapped and mentally retarded.
(27) Social welfare of scheduled castes and scheduled tribes

(F) Poverty Alleviation

A number of poverty alleviation programmes have been initiated at the grassroots level for the last couple of years. The village *panchayats* play a vital role in terms of identifying and selecting the beneficiary list and implementing various schemes at the village-level.

(G) Maintenance of Community Assets

There are many items/activities under a district which are handled by Panchayati Raj Institutions (PRIs). It is estimated that there are as many as 290 activities of which 108 are district components, 87 block components and 95 village components. Therefore, village panchayat, block panchayat and district panchayat have to play their respective role for implementing various components/ activities. Village panchayats may have very important assets in its locality and to be maintained accordingly.

The proper execution of village development plans depends on the financial resources available with the village *panchayat*. There are three types of activities for which finances are required by the village panchayat. First, for maintaining panchayat office, which includes salary of the office bearers, maintaining office building, electricity, water, furniture and other office materials. Second, activities are related to maintenance of civic services, physical infrastructure and panchayat assets. The third investment is required for the construction of new infrastructure and developmental activities including poverty alleviation and social welfare programmes. According to the 73rd Constitutional Amendment, a Finance Commission has been constituted in each State to determine the principles on the basis of which adequate financial resources is ensured for *panchayat*.

A large portion of finances comes in the form of state grants through many programmes like Jawahar Rojgar Yojana etc., the village *panchayats* have the right to develop self-reliance by collecting taxes, for example, house tax, property tax, cattle tax etc. and the cost of civic services provided to the community to meet the maintenance expenditure. However, as a number of families are poor and not in a position to pay the actual cost of the services, they could be asked to pay a lower rate for a certain period and till that time, the state is to compensate to the *gram panchayats*.

The village *panchayats* shoulder the overall responsibility to supervise the developmental works in their respective communities.

Nevertheless, the Panchayat Samiti and Zilla Parisad also depute official and non-official functionaries to monitor the developmental activities of the village *panchayats* and advise them where corrective measures are required. However, the prime role of social auditing and supervision and evaluation lies with the *Gram Sabha*.

The *Gram Sabha* has been assigned a key role for effective role for the effective functioning of *panchayats*. Based on the need-assessment of the community, the *Gram Sabha*, decides what developmental work is to be undertaken by *panchayats* on priority basis. Gram Sabhas can also question and scrutinize the decisions of panchayats in their meetings and discuss the annual financial statements of *Gram Panchayats*. Under the Act, the *Gram Sabha* itself has been vested with a wide range of powers including ownership of minor forest produce, approval of developmental plans, selection of beneficiaries under various programmes, management of minor water bodies, control of mineral leases, management of village markets and regulation/prohibition of sale of intoxicants.

Gram Sabha has been given the task to perform one of the most important roles of social audit at a time when the corruption at all levels of administration is often thought to be rampant. This social auditing is expected to be done by the gram sabhs members. This makes the members of the village panchayat directly answerable the voters. In order to introduce public accountability, the *Gram Sabha*'s role of social auditing should be given due importance. The completion of the works is approved by the *Gram Sabha* and only after it, the utilisation certificate is granted by the authorities concerned. Without *Gram Sabha* approval, the completion certificate issued by the government departments is not treated valid.

At the initial stage of village level planning process, the village panchayat members hold their meetings regularly in according to the Panchayati Raj Acts. In a village panchayat meeting, which is held either in *panchayat* bhavan or at any common place in the village, the quorum of two-thirds of the members is required. The members of the village panchayat share responsibilities for planning and executing various developmental works among themselves in the form of various sub-committees as per the rules and regulations specified in the Panchayati Raj Acts. *Panchayat* meetings have a formal structure where, usually, the president or *Sarpanch* chairs the sessions and decisions on any issue related to the working of panchayats are by majority. Further, *Gram Sabha* meetings are held at least once in three months. The quorum of the *Gram Sabha* is 10 per cent of the number of voters of its area. In case, the quorum for *Gram Sabha* is not complete, the meeting is called again. In the meeting of the *Gram Sabha*, resolutions are passed on majority basis. Role of *Gram Sabha* is very important. It assists in preparing developmental schemes for the village and supervises the implementation of such schemes.

Gram Sabha has the power to supervise activities of village *Panchayat*. It evaluates the progress of the developmental programmes in the village. The village panchayat is to place a report of the existing and the proposal projects in front of *Gram Sabha*. This village assembly of voters scrutinizes the expenditure undertaken during the current year and the proposed one. It checks the annual statement of accounts and the administration report of the preceeding year. If, in any circumtances, any decision of the *Gram Sabha* could not be implemented, the president or *Sarpanch* shall report the reason of it before the *Gram Sabha*. The village panchayats, the block panchayats and the district panchayat shall give due consideration to the suggestions of *Gram Sabha* in accordance with the provision of the 73rd Constitutional Amendment Act.

It can be said without hesitation that no single approach is good enough to deal with rural poverty; rather it requires multi-dimensional approach for bringing about effective change in this field. Till date, the Government of India has given a lot of emphasis on economic opportunity for the rural masses but very little attention has been given to social opportunity, namely, education and health. The policy-makers are yet to find out effective method for how panchayats machineries can be properly used for intervening in the field of social opportunity. It would not be wrong to express the views that whatever good result could have been brought about in the name of poverty alleviation through *panchayats*, it had not happened so owing to political nature of PRI system neglecting the field of social opportunity. Policy-makers have perhaps assumed that village planning is the highest level of micro-approach, giving meaning to homogenous character of village people—there can not be any kind of exploitation/ deprivation within the village community. It can not be denied that every village is a political power centre. Political power in a village community operates both at micro-level and at macro-level backed by agro-caste relationship. While implementing poverty alleviation programmes, the ruling class or the powerful group within the village community find the programmes very important and imperative for their political survival, rather, what actual development would take place among the poorest of the poor. The poor are politically powerless and there is a relationship between Government sponsored economic benefits and, political liberty and democratic rights. If the poor are given a choice between economic benefits/needs and democratic rights, obviously, they will choose the first one. Since, Government sponsored economic benefits are being implemented through *panchayats*, i.e., political agency, therefore, legitimate demands can not be achieved without political bargaining process, unfortunately, they couldn't achieve that power. Thus, in spite of having good constitutional provisions for economic upliftment and social justice for rural poor, the desired result can not be achieved without safety nets for the under-privileged. The idea of *Gram Sabha*, theoretically, seems to be encouraging, but, what happens in reality, when conducting *panchayat* election becomes very difficult and candidates are afraid of filing nomination, particularly, in the politically polarised state like West Bengal? How do the members of *Gram Sabha* opine freely for the development of their own village?

References

Jain, S.P., 1997, "The *Gram Sabha*: Gateway to Grassroots Democracy", *Journal of Rural Development*, 16(4).

Jha, S.N. and Mathur, P.C., 1999, *Decentralisation and Local Politics,* New Delhi: Sage Publications.

Mathew, G. (ed.), 2000, *Status of Panchayati Raj in the States in India*, New Delhi: Concept Publishing Company.

Sen, A., 2000, *Development as Freedom,* New Delhi: Oxford University Press.

SECTION-II
Disadvantaged and Community Development

7
Community Health Insurance Schemes (CHIs) in India
Can Those be Partners in Providing Financial Health Risk Protection to the Poor?

Paramita Roy

Introduction

There is an increasing acknowledgement of the fact that risks play a great importance in the lives of the poor. Risks from sudden and lump sum expenditures on health are a major cause of a fall in household savings and an increase in informal borrowings by the poor people. There is a strong positive link between health and poverty reduction at low income levels (Holzmann and Jorgensen, 2000). The state in most developing countries has not been able to grant health security to its poor. A low budgetary support for health care services, inefficiency in public health provision, unacceptably low quality of public health services, and the increasing out-of-pocket expenses are reflective of the state's inability to meet health care needs of the poor. In the last decade, the "health care crisis" led to the emergence of many community- based health insurance schemes (CHIs) in different regions of developing countries, particularly in sub-Saharan Africa (Wiesmann and Jütting 2001, Preker *et al.*, 2001). The decentralisation process unleashed in these countries to empower the lower layers of government and the local community further fuelled their emergence. The success of community-based micro-credit schemes may have also contributed to the emergence of community-based health initiatives designed to improve the access through risk and resource sharing (Dror and Jacquier 2000, Brown and Churchill, 2000). Elsewhere, particularly in regions of Asia and Latin America, community-based health initiatives have come about independently and as part of income protection measures or to fill the void created by missing institutions.

Of all the risks facing poor households, health risks probably pose the greatest threat to their lives and livelihoods. A health shock thrusts health expenditure on a poor household precisely at a time when they can ill-afford it due to income shortfall resulting from the shock. Moreover, the uncertainty of the timings of illness and unpredictability of its costs make financial provisions for illness difficult for households receiving low and irregular income (Tenkorang, 2001). Furthermore, given the strong link between health and income at low income levels, a health shock affects the poor the most.

Many health risks such as those relating to illness, injury, disability, maternity and the like are considered to be eminently insurable as these risks are mostly independent or idiosyncratic, that is, not correlated among community members. Two, insurance separates time of payment from time of use of health services for each member, and thereby makes possible demand for such services by its members who would not have otherwise been able to afford the cost. Insurance is particularly beneficial to the poor who often bear high indirect costs of treatment due to their limited ability to mitigate risk on account of imperfect labour and credit markets. Also, community-based insurance is considered to be pro-poor as it strengthens the demand side and thereby helps the poor to articulate their own needs (Develtere and Fonteneau, 2001).

In 2003, the Government of India constituted a Consultative Group on Micro-Insurance to examine existing insurance schemes for rural and urban poor concentrating on outreach, pricing, products, servicing and promotion and to examine existing regulations with a view to promoting micro-insurance organisations with specific reference to capital requirements, licensing, monitoring and review, etc. The report of the consultative group has brought out the following key issues: (i) Micro-insurance is not viable as a standalone insurance product; (ii) Micro-insurance has not penetrated rural markets. Traditional insurers have not made much headway in bringing micro-insurance products to the rural poor. (In addition, the Committee feels that micro-insurance has not penetrated even among the urban poor); (iii) Partnership between an insurer and a social organisation like NGO would be desirable to promote micro-insurance by drawing on their mutual strengths; and (iv) Design of micro-insurance products must have the features of simplicity, availability, affordability, accessibility and flexibility.

The draft chapter prepared by the Consultative Group to Assist the Poor (CGAP)[1], a working group on micro-insurance defines micro-insurance as "the protection of low income households against specific perils in exchange for premium payments proportionate to the likelihood and cost of the risk involved." The chapter deliberates on the key roles to be played by all stakeholders—insurers, regulator and the Government. The working group also agrees that the cost of such cover should be affordable.

A study commissioned by the United Nations Development Programme (UNDP) titled "Building Security for the Poor—Potential and Prospects for Micro-insurance in India"[2] states that 90 per cent of the Indian population—some 950 million people—are not covered by insurance and signify an untapped market of nearly US$2 billion. This enormous "missing market" is ready for customized life and non-life insurance, but first, serious mismatches between the needs of the insured and the insurers must be overcome, pitting priorities against profits.

The UNDP report has analysed six key issues pertinent to the growth of the micro-insurance industry in India, capturing the concerns of different stakeholders as indicated below: (i) There are specific reasons for low demand for insurance in spite of intense need. Suppliers have their own concerns which help to explain why there have been so little efforts at market development. Consequently, the rural market is characterized by limited and inappropriate services, inadequate information and capacity gaps; (ii) There are challenges in product design, which has resulted in a mismatch between needs and standard products on offer. Efforts at product development/diversification have been limited; (iii) Pricing, including willingness to pay and the availability of subsidies, influence the market. In the absence of a historical data based on claims, premium calculations are based on remote macro aggregates and overcautious margins. Building and sharing claims histories can help in aligning pricing decisions with actuarial calculations, thereby reducing prices; (iv) Difficulty in distribution is one of the most cited reasons for absence of rural insurance. The high costs of penetrating rural markets, combined with under-utilization of available distribution channels, hinder the growth of rural insurance services. This adds to costs, both, managerial and financial. Like inclusive credit, inclusive insurance is expected to be a "low ticket" business, requiring volumes for viability; (v) Cumbersome and inappropriate procedures inhibit the development of this sector; and (vi) Contrasting perspectives of the insured and the insurers, lead to low customization of products and low demand for what is available.

The UNDP report further states that micro-insurance solutions should, therefore, attempt at addressing key issues that will improve customer satisfaction (demand-supply gaps, appropriate products and pricing), provide distribution efficiencies for better outreach and remove procedural hassles facilitating easier renewals and claim settlements. With a view to reduce costs, the report has also suggested that the premia payable on micro-insurance be exempted from payment of service tax, which will also enable greater penetration in rural markets.

Community Health Insurance Models

Community Health Insurance (CHI) is a recent innovation that has taken roots in Africa and is now being introduced into Asia. CHI uses the strategy of health insurance wherein people pay a small contribution at the beginning itself. These contributions are pooled to provide benefits (medical costs) for those who need it. In CHI it is that the community that usually initiates the scheme and manages it. This characteristic is very important, as it implies that the CHI is developed to meet local needs. The main strengths of a CHI are that it is owned by the community and so there is a strong will to make it succeed. The design suits the local needs and requirements. And finally the scheme is usually co-managed by the people, so the administrative overheads are low. Its main weakness is that it is small and so the risk sharing is low. This makes such schemes vulnerable to bankruptcy in the event of any catastrophe. Also there is limited technical expertise and this may be a major handicap in developing the scheme and making it work effectively and efficiently. And finally CHI, like all insurance programmes, does not protect the poorest sections of the population.

There are three broad models of CHIs in India—the provider model; the insurer model and the linked model (see Fig. 7.1). In the provider model, the initiating NGO is both the insurer and the provider of care. In the insurer model, the NGO is the insurer and assumes the financial risk of managing the fund. Independent institutions provide the care. And finally in the linked model, the NGO collects the premium but passes this onto an insurance company. Similarly, independent institutions provide health care. It is true that community health insurance is not for the poorest of the poor but such schemes has a lot of scope for the informal sector workers and certain target groups like the students in formal institutions. To prescribe a uniform design of CHIs is not a feasible alternative as it will be decided by the facilitating institutions, the target beneficiaries, etc.

Community Health Insurance (CHI) is not a new phenomenon in India. The oldest scheme is more than 50 years old. Currently, there are more than 100 such schemes in India, most of them initiated by Non-Governmental Organizations (NGOs). The main objectives of these schemes are to improve access to health care and to protect households from high medical expenditures (Devadasan, 2005). They typically cover between 20 and 40 per cent of their target population; the number of members ranges from 1000 to 100,000. Most of the CHI schemes cover hospitalization services in private or NGO hospitals. Administration responsibilities are shared between the community and the NGO (Devadasan, *et al.*, 2006). Many CHI schemes have linked up with formal insurance companies to expand the risk pool and make the scheme more sustainable (Devadasan, *et al.*, 2004). Given the political will of the government it should be possible to expand the CHI movement and cover more people.

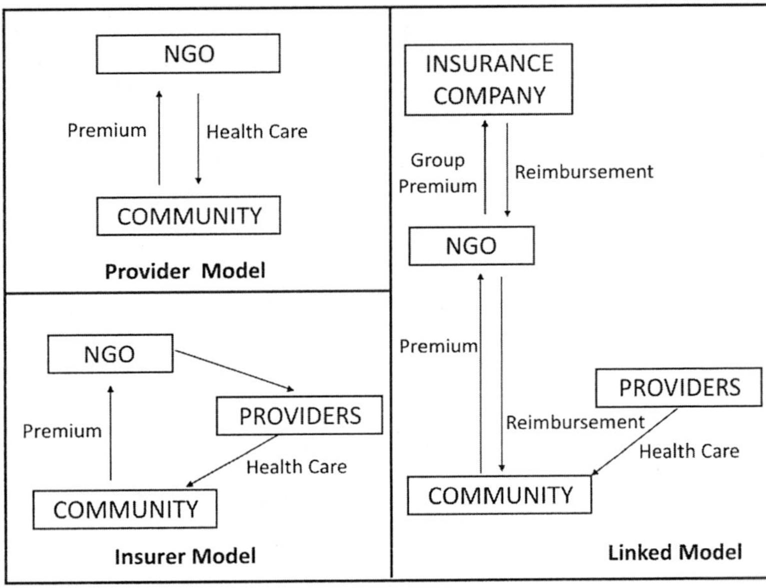

Fig. 7.1: Models of Health Insurance.

Source: Devadasan *et al.*, 2006.

Thematic Analysis of Two Selected Cases

(I) ACCORD-AMS-ASHWINI (AAA)

ACCORD is an NGO; AMS is a tribal union and ASHWINI is the health provider. It was initiated in 1992 and provides health insurance coverage to all the tribal members of the AMS living in Gudalur Taluk. ACCORD is based in the Niligiris and was founded in 1986 with a mission to "fight against the unjust alienation of the adivasi lands and other human rights violations by organising them as a strong group." The area of operation is largely inhabited by tribal groups such as Paniyas, Kurumbas, Irulas, Kattu Naickens and Kothas, who have been working as landless labourers with little or no rights. ACCORD promoted '*sangams*' or village groups to organise these adivasis to protect their rights and demonstrate against the occupation of their traditional lands by outsiders. Some 200 sangams were federated and called as "Adivasi Munetra Sangam" or AMS and it severely protested against the injustice. Finally, when it achieved its goal, it subsequently became the representative body of the tribals to defend their cultural rights. The federation works closely with ACCORD and ASHWINI on various socio-economic development activities of the tribal groups. ASHWINI is the sister NGO of ACCORD and it is mostly managed and staffed by tribal youth. During the implementation of the community health programme by ACCORD, there was an increasing demand from the *adivasis* for a hospital. Finally, an adivasi hospital was set-up in December 1990. Following this, ACCORD decided to insure the tribals, accessing health services in the hospital. It started negotiating with various national insurance companies and finally, made a deal with the New India Assurance Company (NIAC). In 1992, ACCORD launched the "Composite Tribal Health Insurance Package" (Fig. 7.2).

Objectives

Its main objectives were: (i) To access health care with dignity by not depending on charity or handouts; (ii) To encourage health seeking behaviour by offering comprehensive health care with minimal payment at the time of use of the services; (iii) To enhance the feeling of solidarity among the members of the AMS; (iv) To protect the AMS members from catastrophic health expenditure; (v) To enhance the feeling of ownership of the health programme among the members of the AMS by contributing towards their own health care; and (vi) To provide a stable income for the ASHWINI hospital.

The Community

All the members of the AMS (~12,000), between the age of six months and sixty years and residing in Gudalur Taluk, are eligible to join this scheme. These members are distributed all over the Taluk over a radius of 50 km. Most of the Taluk is heavily forested and the terrain is hilly. The tribals are traditionally hunter-gatherers and also daily wage earners—earning an average of about Rs. 1000 per month (~ US$ 22 – November, 2003). The local economy is a plantation economy, mostly tea and some coffee and pepper. Most of the tribals work as casual labourers in these estates, some have small land holdings and grow paddy, tea or coffee and pepper.

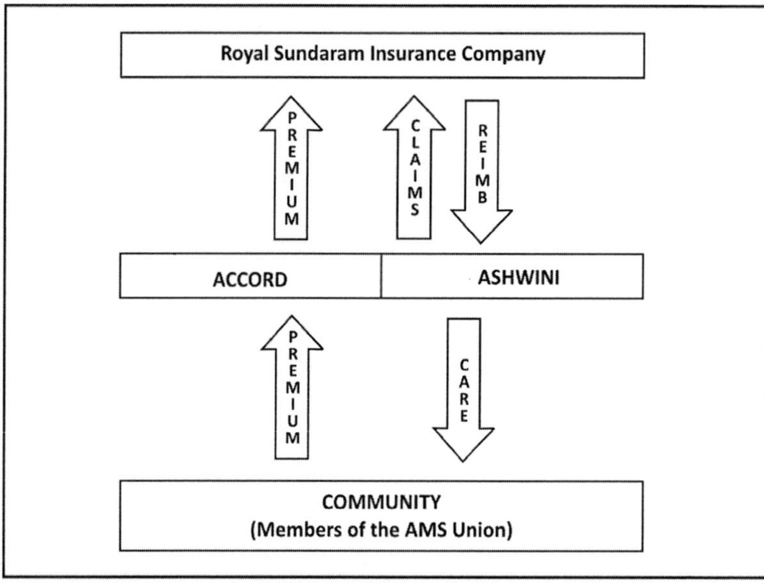

Fig. 7.2: The Design of the AAA Community Health Insurance Programme

Source: Devadasan *et al.*, 2006.

The Insurer

The formal insurance company is the prime insurer of this scheme. From 1992 to 2002 it was the New India Assurance Company (NIAC) and then from 2003, it is the Royal Sundaram Alliance Private Limited.

Provider

ASHWINI is the main provider of health care. ASHWINI has a network of village health workers, Health Centres (manned by nurses and distributed all over the Taluk) and a 20-bedded hospital with all basic facilities. The health centres provide a mixture of curative and preventive care. The hospital provides medical, paediatric, surgical and obstetric care and has a well-equipped laboratory.

Premium

As stated above, the premium has to be seen at two distinct levels. In 1992, ACCORD/ASHWINI/AMS negotiated with NIAC to insure. All the AMS members for a period of five years. This enabled AAA to avail of the long-term discount as well as the group discount. This plus the fact that AAA has a limited the coverage to Rs. 1,500 reduced the annual premium from Rs. 48 to Rs. 13 per person per year. ACCORD thus paid the premium of Rs. 65 per tribal (Rs. 13 per year for five years) and covered 6000 tribals in the first round. The lump sum amount of Rs. 3,86,318 was provided by CEBEMO, a Dutch agency. New members who joined subsequently were enrolled on a *pro rata* basis. The scheme was renewed in 1997 for another five-year period; the premium remained the same and once again CEBEMO/BILANCE helped meet the lump sum payment of Rs. 4,83,000 to insure 9000 tribals for five years.

In 2002, NIAC hiked the premium by a substantial amount, so ACCORD/ASHWINI/AMS approached Royal Sundaram Alliance Pvt. Ltd. They agreed to provide hospitalisation coverage upto a limit of Rs. 1000 for a premium of Rs. 20 per tribal per year. The AMS members have been insured for a year from 2003-2004. This amount was paid by the Sir Ratan Tata Trust, Mumbai. The tribals were not able to pay the lump sum amount of Rs. 65 towards the premium. So, it was collected in annual instalments. In the initial years, as insurance was a new concept, the premium was heavily subsidised. In 1992, no premium was collected, but in 1993, the AMS members were asked to pay Rs. 4 per person per year. In the next year, this was raised to Rs. 6 per person and in 1995, Rs. 8 was being collected. Thus, by the year 1997, the entire annual premium amount was being paid by the tribals. In the subsequent years, the premium amount was raised and currently they pay Rs. 22 per tribal per year. Thus, while the ACCORD/ASHWINI insured tribals *en masse* with the formal insurance company and paid their premiums, upfront; the tribals repaid this premium on an annual basis.

Benefit Package

The benefit package also has to be viewed at two levels. A package provided by the insurance company to ASHWINI and another (more comprehensive) provided by ASHWINI to the tribals. NIAC assures only hospital care with an upper limit of Rs. 1500 per patient per year. It also has important exclusions—pre-existing illnesses, diseases due to substance abuse and self-inflicted illnesses. Deliveries and family planning operations were initially excluded, however, while renewing the policy in 1997, ACCORD managed to include the first two deliveries and family planning operations into the benefit package. The current policy with RSAIC covers hospitalisation to Rs. 1000 and the first 2 deliveries to Rs. 500. There are no exclusions.

As per the initial policy there was additional coverage for damage to hut and personal accident coverage for the head of the household. However, this was removed in 1997 as AMS felt that this coverage was not very beneficial. While removing this coverage, the company agreed to replace it with the pregnancy cover.

While the above was the benefit package provided by the NIAC to ACCORD, ASHWINI provides a more comprehensive package to the tribal patients. For the insured patient, both OP and hospitalisation is provided for a small co-payment of Rs. 10 per visit. There Compilation of community health insurance schemes in India are no exclusions and no upper limits. If required they may be referred to a tertiary centre like the Government Medical College at Calicut for further treatment. The patient has to pay only for the food and ambulance expenses.

ASHWINI also provides promotive, preventive and basic curative care through its network of Village Health Workers (VHWs) and Health Centres. This benefit is provided to all the AMS members, irrespective of their insurance status. While theoretically the patient has to be referred by the Health Centre for admission, in reality this is not adhered to very strictly. Thus, while the formal insurance company provides a hospitalisation package, ASHWINI uses its resources to provide a more holistic cover. External resources as well as from the profits generated from non-tribal patients meet the difference in the benefit package. As ASHWINI provides comprehensive care it encourages people to live a healthy life and to seek care at the earliest when ill so that problems are addressed close to home at the area centre or at the hospital. This cuts down morbidity and expenses—a truly win-win situation. This positive feedback loop is the greatest strength of the programme.

Claims and Reimbursements

At the end of the hospitalisation, three copies of the hospital bill are made. One copy is handed over to the patient (but the patient does not pay any amount). One copy is kept for records and the third copy is forwarded by ASHWINI to the insurance company (on a monthly basis). Claims are made to a maximum of Rs. 1000 only. Any excess of Rs. 1000 is met from ASHWINI's general funds. The average hospital bill is about Rs. 750 per patient per episode of illness. This is a slightly subsidised cost as the doctors and the nurses draw relatively low salaries. The insurance company in turn reimburses ASHWINI on a regular basis. The lag time with NIAC was around 3-6 months, but with RSA it is less than a month. The reimbursement rates have been in the range of 95-100 per cent.

The ASHWINI and ACCORD field staffs as well as the AMS leaders collect the premium. The field staff has other work and collecting premium is an additional responsibility that they have undertaken. The AMS leaders do it on a voluntary basis. A system of receipts and strict accounting measures prevents fraud.

Measures to Control Adverse Selection

While the individual is the unit of enrolment, AAA encourages family enrolment. Also for the insurance company; there is very little adverse selection as the entire tribal community is enrolled.

There is an initial waiting period of 30 days and a definite collection period. All these help in limiting adverse selection.

Measures to Control Moral Hazard

Provider induced moral hazard is negligible as the medical officers are paid a fixed salary. So, there is no incentive for cost escalation. Most of the disease conditions are treated using a standard treatment protocol. Patient moral hazard is minimised by the fact that patients have to incur all indirect costs e.g. transportation, food costs, loss of wages and cost of accompanying relatives. These are an effective deterrent to unnecessary hospitalisation.

Measures to Control Cost Escalation

Cost escalation is minimal as there is no incentive for the providers. Also generic drugs, an essential drug list and standard treatment guidelines help in keeping costs low as well as standard. This plus the fact that most of the staff draw very low salaries help in containing costs well below the market rates.

Achievements

The coverage of the AMS members is shown in Fig. 7.2. The average coverage was initially in the fifties, but has now declined to around 35 per cent. Various reasons have been attributed to this fall in coverage. One important reason is the fall in income of the households due to the fall in tea prices. Further analysis needs to be done to understand this fall in coverage.

The utilisation of the hospital has been high-ranging from 105 to 150 per 1000 insured member. While this is much higher than the national average, it is in keeping with the Kerala figures (Gudalur Taluk is adjacent to Kerala). One of the objectives of the AAA CHI was to mobilise resources from within the community. But it was never intended that the insurance programme meet the entire costs as the founders felt that it was not equitable for the poorest to bear the total burden of their health care. Thus, throughout the 11 years, efforts were made to supplement the community efforts by raising funds from other sources.

(II) Vimo SEWA

Vimo SEWA is one of the oldest member-based organisations (along with ACCORD) to link up with formal insurance companies to provide insurance cover for its population. It started in 1992. The main objectives were to protect women from indebtedness resulting from: (i) sickness requiring hospitalisation; (ii) the death of a spouse; or (iii) loss of working assets.

Vimo SEWA is an integrated micro-insurance scheme protecting the health, life and assets of its members and their families. Vimo SEWA is a part of the SEWA family, which is a labour union of self-employed women workers in Gujarat and other parts of India. The combined strength of the SEWA movement is 700,000 (530,000 in Gujarat itself). Other than insurance, SEWA provides the following services: (i) SEWA Bank—a women-led micro-finance institution with about 200,000 depositors and about Rs. 1 billion working capital; (ii) Child care—for the children of members; (iii) Health care—for the members and their families; and (iv) Housing—for the members and their families. For a large part, SEWA has linked up with existing insurance companies to develop the products. However, for a few years between 1994 and 2000, SEWA de-linked from the insurance companies for health and asset insurance.

Design

Vimo SEWA is one of the first linked models of CBHI. Vimo SEWA collects the premium and hands it over to the formal insurance company. When patients fall sick, they seek care from any provider. After discharge, the patient submits the necessary documents to the Vimo SEWA staff that checks the document and verifies its authenticity. Once this is cleared, the patient receives the cheque, from the insurance fund. In the meantime, the claim documents are sent to the insurance company for reimbursement and they reimburse Vimo SEWA. This insurance fund is created by a floater fund from ICICI-Lombard (Fig. 7.3).

Community

The target community is mainly the SEWA union members, though the scheme is not limited to them only. These are mainly self-employed women, their spouses and children from three months to 18 years of age. While initially women between 18 and 58 were the only ones who were eligible to enroll in the insurance programmes, other members of the family were included in stages. When compare the general rural Gujarati households with Vimo SEWA members appear slightly "poorer" than the general population—and significantly so for indicators of food security.

Premium

There are two schemes. Currently, the premium for Scheme 1 is Rs. 100 for a woman, Rs. 170 for woman and her husband and Rs. 250 for the entire family. This premium covers life, health and asset insurance.

The breakdown of the premium for the woman under Scheme 1 is as follows:

Rs. 20 for natural death cover;
Rs. 7 for accidental death cover;
Rs. 33 for health insurance;
Rs. 10 for asset insurance; and,
Rs. 30 for administrative expenses.

The premium is usually collected annually (October-December) by community-based leaders called *Aagewans*. These *Aagewans* are responsible for collecting premiums, processing claims and helping with any other related matter. They are paid for each day of work put in. They collect the premium and hand it over to the district insurance coordinator, who in turn hands it over to the Vimo SEWA office in Ahmedabad. Each insured family receives a receipt to acknowledge its insurance status and payment

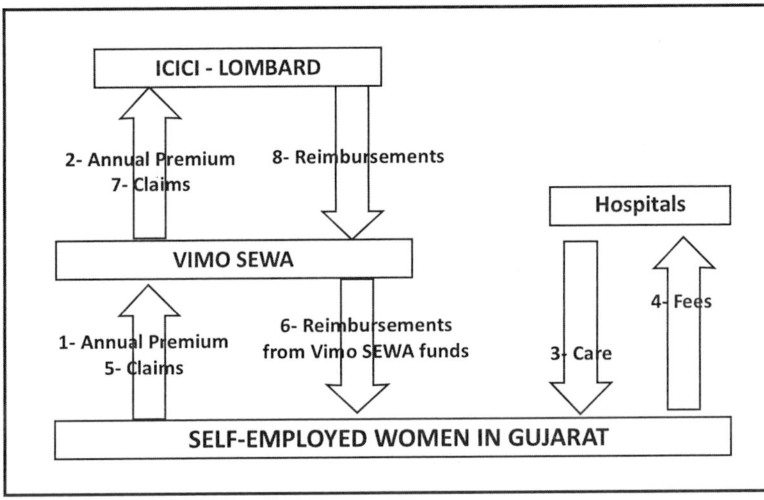

Fig. 7.3: The Design of the SEWA Community Health Insurance Programme

Source: Devadasan *et al.*, 2006.

of premium.

Yet another mechanism for paying the premium is through the fixed deposit. A deposit in the SEWA Bank of Rs. 2100 will ensure that her premium is paid on an annual basis from the interest on the deposit. This saves tremendously on administrative expenses.

Much effort goes into the community before the collection period. Meetings are held at the village level, IEC material is distributed and even door to door campaigns are conducted.

Benefit Package

The insured family receives a comprehensive cover. The benefits under Scheme 1 are as follows:

- Natural death of insured member—the nominee receives Rs. 5,000.
- Accidental death of insured member—the nominee receives Rs. 40,000.
- Accidental death of husband of insured woman—the wife receives Rs. 15,000.

- Illness of insured member—hospital expenses upto Rs. 2,000 per year.
- Damage to house and its belongings—Upto a maximum of Rs. 10,000.

Vimo SEWA is experimenting with a system of prospective reimbursement to hospitalized members, wherein Vimo SEWA pays the patients in the hospital itself within 24-48 hours of hospitalisation.

Provider

Currently Vimo SEWA allows the patient to go to any hospital for care. While they do encourage public hospitals, the ultimate choice is with the patient. After discharge, the patient is supposed to collect the relevant documents and hand it over to the Aagewan or to the insurance coordinator at the district SEWA office. Vimo SEWA has not negotiated with the providers for either cost control measures or quality of care. In fact, most of the providers are not aware of the insurance status of the patients, until discharge when the patient requests for the documents. One of the drawbacks of a "free choice" is that at times the patient receives poor quality of care or the documentation is inappropriate. So, Vimo SEWA is experimenting with 'preferred providers'. Using specific criteria, they are trying to identify hospitals with good track record. As a first step, they identify hospitals that have been used fairly regularly by our members for a period of years. From among these, they then try to select facilities that fulfil certain requirements pertaining to quality of facilities, availability of doctors and nurses, cost etc. Members are visited individually in their homes and given information about these preferred providers. Also the prospective reimbursement is operational in these preferred provider's hospitals only.

Claims and Reimbursements

The process of claims and reimbursements is clearly well-organized and run professionally. The patient is expected to provide the following documents for filing a health claim: (i) insurance receipt, (ii) a discharge summary, (iii) bills from the hospital, pharmacy and laboratory, (iv) prescriptions, and (v) laboratory results.

This is handed over to the insurance coordinator at the district-level, who then visits the patient at his/her house and confirms the details of the admission. If necessary, the coordinator also visits the admitting hospital to get further information. The documents are then handed over to an empanelled doctor who checks whether the treatment received was appropriate or not. Finally, all this is presented to the insurance committee (at the district level in some districts, but at Ahmedabad in others) that meets every week. The insurance committee, comprising of representatives from the member community and one to three staff members of SEWA (including somebody from Vimo SEWA's central office in Ahmedabad), is the final decision-maker. It decides on whether the patient should be reimbursed or not, and if yes, how much should the reimbursement be.

Insurer

Currently Vimo SEWA is linked-up only with private insurers. They are Aviva Life Insurance for life insurance and ICICI-Lombard for health, asset and accidental death insurance. The reason why they shifted to private health insurers is that they received better offers in terms of benefit package as well as better service in terms of faster claims processing and providing a floater fund. While there were periods when Vimo SEWA took the financial risk of managing the insurance funds, they found it too risky. Some events, like the 2000 floods and 2001 earthquake, made them realise that without reinsurance and spreading the risk in a larger pool, they would be exposing themselves to high risks. Hence, they decided to link up with insurance companies, though they had problems with the insurance companies like inflexible products, long lead times between claims and reimbursements and partial reimbursements.

Administration

A large part of the administration is through paid staff of Vimo

SEWA. This is possibly one of the contributing factors to the relatively high administrative costs in Vimo SEWA as compared to other Community Health Insurances, where most of the administrative burden is shared by community volunteers. However, given the size of the ISSS of Vimo SEWA, it may not be possible to rely on volunteers to cover the target population. The various administrative tasks are:

Creating Awareness

Awareness in the community about Vimo is created primarily through community meetings and *Gram Sabha*s (village level meetings). House-to-house visits to educate members about Vimo are being carried out in a few talukas on a pilot basis.

Collection of Premium

The *Aagewans* have been given specific zones and they market the insurance product with great zeal. They are paid on a daily wage basis. They are provided with all the necessary support in terms of information material; receipt books and stationary. They are also trusted by Vimo SEWA to handle the money.

Monitoring the Scheme

Vimo SEWA probably has one of the most detailed MIS systems among the CHIs in India. It is fully computerised and up to date. Middle management also uses this data regularly to monitor trends in utilisation and enrollment.

Measures to Control Adverse Selection

Vimo SEWA has used a collection period and a waiting period to minimise adverse selection. While earlier, the individual was the enrolling unit, today they are encouraging family as the unit of enrolment. This also has a positive control on adverse selection. Yet another measure is the exclusion, during the initial six months of membership, of coverage of chronic and pre-existing illnesses.

Measures to Control Moral Hazard

Co-payments in terms of fees paid over the upper limit are the only measure used to control either supply side or demand side moral hazard. Also a medical doctor checks all claims to ensure that admissions are appropriate. Other mechanisms like cost control or a referral system could have been used.

Measures to Control Cost Escalation in Claim Amounts

No specific measures or incentives have been instituted yet. But given the low ceiling of Rs. 2,000 the members have a strong, personal interest in keeping the costs down.

Achievements

Vimo SEWA started as a small CHI, but has been growing by leaps and bounds over the past few years. This is clearly reflected in their enrolment rate.

Vimo SEWA is one of the most famous CHIs in India. It is a very professionally managed as compared to other CHIs that are dependent on volunteers. Due to the large size of its membership, direct participation of the members in the management of the scheme is not possible. However, Vimo SEWA is committed to ensuring that the needs and interests of members guide the scheme design and implementation. Community participation in Vimo SEWA governance occurs in two ways. First, the governing body is made up of representatives of the member community (including insurance members). Major decisions such as premium and coverage amounts, and expansion of the scheme to new geographic areas are taken in consultation with, and after approval by, the elected representatives. Second, members of the insurance programme actively express their feedback and their needs *vis-à-vis* the scheme to the workers who market and service the scheme. These inputs are incorporated into the design of the scheme to the extent possible. Yet another mechanism for community participation in the scheme is the Claims Committee which scrutinizes and approves claims that are submitted. The mediclaim committee, which scrutinizes and decides on each health insurance claim submitted, is made up of SEWA *aagewans* representing different trades practiced by SEWA members. This mechanism ensures community participation and transparency in the claims decisions.

Vimo SEWA has been offering an integrated insurance package to its members since 1992. The primary aim of the insurance, *viz.*, to protect SEWA's members from risky events and associated financial losses, has stayed the same over the years. The operational aspects of the scheme have changed with time, always in response to the needs of the members. For instance, Vimo SEWA de-linked from the insurance companies for a few years because members were not being satisfactorily served by the insurance companies. However, once it was able to negotiate better servicing, it linked up again with the insurance companies, thus shifting the risk from the member based union to the insurance company.

In terms of risks covered, the package has enlarged its coverage to the husbands and children of members because, that is, what the member demanded. Coverage amounts have also been increased to offer better protection to SEWA's members; this has been possible in part due to the improvement of SEWA's negotiating power *vis-à-vis* the insurance companies. Vimo SEWA current efforts are focused on improving its services to its members by improving its internal efficiency. Vimo SEWA is also strengthening its links with health. Another benefit of a having community members on the claims committee is that it reduces the information asymmetry that occurs when insurers and insured belong to different socio-economic backgrounds. care providers, with the twin objective of ensuring better quality services to its members and cost-containment of health claims.

The Scope of CHIs as Health Insurance Providers

The two Community Health Insurance (CHI) scheme described in this chapter are well replicable in other parts of India and the globe. The figure below depicts the concepts and the linkages very important for an CHI to be affordable, cost-effective and sustainable.

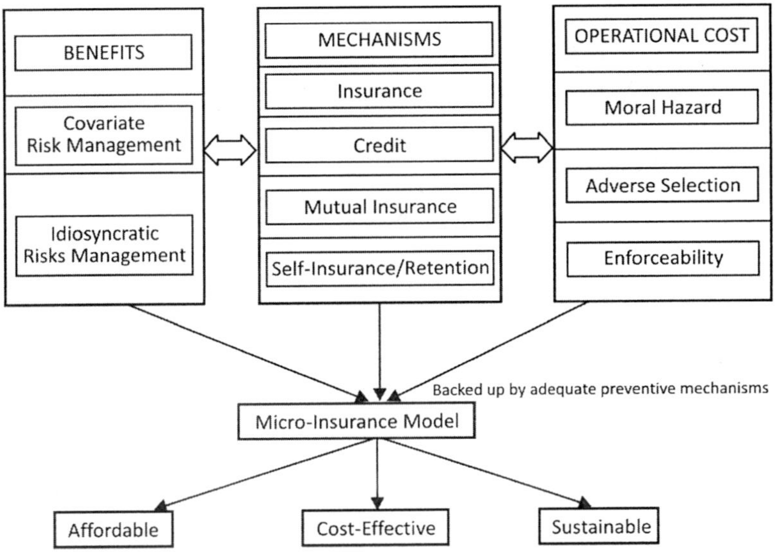

Fig. 7.4: Conceptual Linkages of a Community Health Insurance Programme*

* The flowchart can be generalised to represent all micro-insurance schemes including the CHIs.

Source: https://www.nabard.org/pdf/Chap_XI.pdf

The following are some of the issues that all CHIs should deeply consider in order to make them viable partners in providing health insurance to the vulnerable sections of the society and who otherwise would be unable to afford a formal health insurance.

(i) Leveraging Existing Network for CHIs

For a CHI, it would be difficult to establish a vast network for distribution of any micro-insurance products. They need to utilize existing Government organizations, banks, MFIs, NGOs and SHGs to increase the outreach of micro-insurance to the poor. The advantages of these entities are that they find greater acceptability among the financially excluded, and with a better understanding of their needs are well equipped to advise them on the choice of products. In India with a vast rural population characterized by challenges and complexities, it makes sense to latch on to an existing mechanism operating in these segments to lower costs and to help the insurer to leverage on the faith already generated by the entity. Hence, it would be prudent to choose a partner-agent model for delivery where the insurer underwrites the risk and the distribution is handled by an existing intermediary.

(ii) Linking Micro-credit with CHI

It is becoming increasingly clear that any CHI needs a push and guidance from the Government. There is, therefore, a need to emphasise linking of micro-credit with micro-insurance. Linking micro-insurance with micro-finance makes good business sense. Further, as it helps in bringing down the inherent risk cost of lending, NABARD[3] should be regularly involved in issues relating to rural and micro-insurance to leverage on its experience of being a catalyst in the field of micro-credit. The various SHGs (Self-Help Groups), cooperatives, etc. could form useful collaborators of health security *vis-à-vis* income security as well.

(iii) Human Resources Requirement and Training

As indicated earlier, the UNDP[4] report states that there is a huge untapped market—of around 950 million people and nearly US$2 billion—for insurance in India. IRDA[5] may consider putting in place an appropriate institutional structure for deciding on service packages including premia and formulating strategies for effective promotion of micro-insurance. There is also a felt need for development, of both full-time and part-time staff from the community, through effective training in insurance marketing and servicing concepts.

(iv) Operations and Systems

To address the requirements of the huge market potential available, appropriate systems should be evolved for tracking client information, either manually or using technology. While a technology platform may take time for setting-up, in the long-run, the same will be cost-effective and reliable. Similarly, the procedures for premium payments, claims and other services should be formalized along with increased customization of products to stimulate demand. Since, most CHIs are linked to a collaborating institution, such use of technology should not be difficult.

(v) Development of Adequate Feedback Mechanism

Keeping in view the diverse nature of market requirements, suitable mechanisms to collect market intelligence, collating and interpretation of the same, in a formally structured manner, is important for product development and process refinement. Insurance companies should go beyond devising new products to improving their processes for building awareness, marketing enrolment, premium collection, claim settlement and renewal. For this they need use innovative channels such as business correspondents, SHGs, NGOs and MFIs as also cooperatives and mutual associations. Further, the use of technology such as mobile phones and ATMs for premium collection should be encouraged to keep transaction costs low.

(vi) Consumer Education, Marketing and Grievance Handling

The CHI sector is unique in the sense that there is an ongoing challenge to explain the concept and benefits to the insured. Creating awareness through the use of pictorial posters, local folk arts and street theatres might be useful to explain the mechanisms of insurance. Local community-based organisations could organize premium collections, as they have better access to the local people. To make it more acceptable to the people, micro-insurance products, apart from covering only risks, should also provide an opportunity for providing long-term savings.

Notes

1. www.cgap.org
2. UNDP, Sept. 2007, (https://unp.un.org/details.aspx?entry=E07150)
3. NABARD is National Bank for Agriculture and Rural Development.

4. UNDP is United Nations Development Programme.
5. IRDA is Insurance Regulatory and Development Authority.

References

Brown, W. and Churchill, C., 1999, "Providing Insurance to Low-Income Households, Part I: Primer on Insurance Principles and Products", *USAID Micro-enterprise Best Practices Project*, November.

Devadasan, R. Damme, W. and Criel, B., 2004, "Community Health Insurance in India: An Overview", *Economic and Political Weekly*, 39: 3179-83.

Devadasan, N. Manoharan, S. Menon, N., 2004, "Accord Community Health Insurance—Increasing Access to Hospital Care", *Economic and Political Weekly*, 39: 3189-94.

Devadasan, N., 2005, *Community Health Insurance in India: A Compilation of Case Studies*, Ahmedabad: Friends of Women's World Banking (FWWB).

Devadasan, N. Ranson, M.K. Van Damme, W. Acharya, A. Criel, B., 2000, "The Landscape of Community Health Insurance in India: An Overview-based on Ten Case Studies", *Health Policy*, 78:224-34.

Devadasan, N., *et al.,* 2010, "Community Health Insurance in Gudalur, India, Increases Access to Hospital Care", *Health Policy and Planning,* 25:145-154.

Develtere, P. and Fonteneau, B., 2001, "Member-based Organizations for Social Protection in Health in Developing Countries", Paper Prepared for ILO/STEP (Strategies and Tools against Social Exclusion and Poverty).

Dror, D. and Jacquier, C., 2000, "Micro-Insurance: Extending Health Insurance to the Excluded", *International Social Security Review*, 52 (1): 71-98.

Holzmann, R. and Jorgensen, S., 2000, "Social Risk Management: A New Conceptual Framework for Social Protection, and Beyond", *Social Protection*, Discussion Paper No. 0006, Washington, D.C.: The World Bank.

Preker, A., *et al.,* 2001, "A Synthesis Report on the Role of Communities in Resource Mobilization and Risk Sharing", *CMH Working Paper Series*, Paper No. WG3: 4.

Tenkorang, D.A., 2001, "Health Insurance for the Informal Sector in Africa: Design Features, Risk Protection, and Resource Mobilisation", *CMH Working Paper Series*, Paper No. WG3: 1.

Wiesmann, D. and Jütting, J., 2000, "The Emerging Movement of Community Based Health Insurance in Sub-Saharan Africa: Experiences and Lessons Learned", *Afrika Spectrum,* 2: 193-210.

8

Panchayati Raj Institutions and Social Inclusion in India

Moumita Laha

Introduction

Panchayati Raj Institutions (PRIs) form grassroots of Indian democracy. They have provided new dimensions to rural development and are means of good governance. The 73rd Constitutional Amendment Act, 1992 which came into effect on April 24, 1993 has created an opportunity for a larger segment of vulnerable and weaker section women, Scheduled Caste (SC) and Scheduled Tribe (ST) population, to provide leadership to the institutions of decentralized governance at the village level.

Peoples' participation is the crux of the democratic system and tool for effectiveness of PRI. The vulnerable and socially excluded communities experience social exclusion from participation in the social, economic and political life of the mainstream society. In the Indian context, Scheduled Caste, Scheduled Tribe, women are discriminated and not given the full freedom to participate. To safeguard the interest of the weaker section and bring social inclusion by ensuring the participation of weaker segments of the population, and, in particular, to ensure that they get their fair share of public goods was a big concern. To alleviate this concern, the reservations of seats for the Scheduled Caste, Scheduled Tribe and women in the 73rd Constitutional Amendment Act made *panchayat* truly a representative body of the so far marginalized section of the society. The representation of the weaker sections in all three tier of *panchayats* set-up have enable them to be involved in the democratic processes and in decision-making for development programmes. The 73rd Constitutional Amendment thus, sought to correct the prolonged marginalization of the poor, marginalized and under representative people such as women, Scheduled Tribes (STs) and Scheduled Castes (SCs). The objective of the enhanced representation in the executive bodies of PRI is likely to remove isolation of women, SCs and STs from development and political process of village polity.

The new Panchayati Raj System gives the country a whooping 22.5 lakhs elected representatives with reserved seats for SCs and STs in proportion to their population and women who are allotted 33.3 per cent representation in all the three layers of the system. Twenty-nine areas of development have been identified in which the elected panchayats have a free hand in planning and disbursement of funds. These include land reforms, agriculture, small scale industry, animal husbandry, education up to secondary level and health care (Sinha, 2004).

Reservation for women and weaker section has opened the door to revolutionary changes of a political, social and cultural nature. India can truly be proud of being the first and only country in the world to have empowered through free and fair elections more than one million women who are participating in the *panchayats*. Today, 41,210 of the 96,090 seats in all levels of *panchayats*, or 42.89 per cent, are occupied by women though only 33 per cent is reserved for them. Of 17,859 representatives from the SCs, 8,222, or 46.04 per cent, are women. Of 10,311 representatives from the STs, 6,672, or 64.71 per cent, are women (Tiwari, 2009).

Constitutional Framework

After Independence the Panchayati Raj Act was well included in the Directives Principles of the State Policy, stating that state shall take steps to organize Village Panchayats and endow them with such powers a may be necessary to enable them to function as the unit of self-government.

Reservation for Weaker Section

Initiatives towards providing an opportunity to women in the form of associating them with the village panchayats were first mooted by Balwant Rai Mehta Committee in 1957. The Committee recommended that at least two women should be included in the *panchayats* as co-opted members. The Maharashtra is the first state who introduced the provision for the nomination of one or two women to each of the three local bodies under its Zilla Parishad and Panchayati Act of 1961. Later Karnataka in 1983 and Andhra Pradesh in 1986 introduced the policy of reservation of 25 seats for women in Gram Panchayats and Zilla Parishads. The State like West Bengal, Madhya Pradesh, Kerala, Himachal Pradesh, Haryana and Orissa has also made the provisions to reserve 20 to 30 per cent of the total seats for women candidates in different existing tier of local bodies in their respective seats.

Seventy-Third Constitutional Amendment Act which came into force from April 24, 1993 has proposed that not less than one third of the total number of seats to be filled by direct election in every *panchayats* to be reserved for women. This gender-based reservation policy in favour of women is made applicable even to the number of seats reserved for Scheduled Caste, Scheduled Tribe and Other Backward Class of women in all the tiers of Panchayati Raj Institutions. It was estimated that the country would have around 2,25,000 *gram panchayats*, 5100 intermediate level *panchayats* and 475 district *panchayat* elected (Meenakshi Sundaram, 1994).

Salient Features of 73rd Amendment Act, 1992

The Constitution (Seventy-third Amendment) Act, 1992 sets out in detail, in Article 243D, the manner in which reservations are to be provided to women and others belonging to the SC/STs:

(a) Reservations to elected seats are mandated by the Constitution in the following pattern:
   (i) One-third of the total numbers of seats to be filled by direct election in every panchayat are to be reserved for women. This is inclusive of the

reservation provided for women belonging to the SC/STs [*See* Article 243D (3)].

(ii) Within the reservation provided for persons belonging to the SC/STs as detailed above, not less than one-third of the total number of seats that are reserved for different categories in each *panchayat* are to be reserved for women belonging to the SC/STs [*See* Article 243D (2)]

(b) These seats may be allotted by rotation to different constituencies within a panchayat [*See* Article 243D (1) and (3)].

(c) The provision for reservation to the office of chairperson is nearly identical to the above provisions. The additional features are as follows:

(i) While providing for reservations up to a minimum level of one-third in respect of women and in proportion to the population in each panchayat for the SC/STs, the manner in which this is done is left to the legislature of a state to provide by-law [*See* Article 243D (4)].

(ii) Unlike in the case of rotation of reservation to elected seats, which is discretionary, the rotation of reservations to the office of chairperson in different panchayats is mandatory [*See* the second proviso to Article 243D (4)].

The President of India in her address to the Parliament on 4.6.2009 had mentioned the intent to provide fifty per cent reservation for women in Panchayats as women suffer multiple deprivations of class, caste and gender. Accordingly, the Constitution (One Hundred and Tenth Amendment) Bill, 2009 for enhancing reservation for women in Panchayats at all tiers from one-third to 50 per cent in the total number of seats was moved in Parliament on 26th November by the Minister of Panchayati Raj. Thereafter, the said Bill has been referred to the Parliamentary Standing Committee on Rural Development for examination.

The proposed amendment have increased reservation for women in, (i) the total number of seats to be filled by direct election,

(ii) offices of Chairpersons, and (iii) in seats and offices of chairpersons reserved for Scheduled Castes (SCs) and Scheduled Tribes (STs) to 50 per cent in all tiers of Panchayats. This, Amendment to Article 243-D of the Constitution envisages enhanced reservation for women in PRIs leading to greater participation of women in the public sphere and also making Panchayats more inclusive institutions.

Towards Social Inclusion

The biggest success of Panchayati Raj in India is that it has politically and socially empowered women. Of the 26,00,000 *panchayat* representatives in the country, 9,75,000 are women, 8,50,000 of them from the Scheduled Castes and Schedule Tribes (Tiwari, 2009).Though under the Panchayati Raj System only 33 per cent of seats are reserved for women, Bihar took the bold step of pushing up the figure to 50 per cent in 2006. Elected women representatives (EWRs) now occupy 54 per cent of the seats in Bihar's *panchayats*. Bihar's example was followed by Sikkim, which increased its reservation for women to 40 per cent and held elections in January 2008. Chhattisgarh, Madhya Pradesh, Rajasthan and Uttarakhand have also passed laws increasing the reservation for women in *panchayats* to 50 per cent, These measures have brought political and social exposure to women from among the dalits, tribals, the backward, the poor, and the illiterate. As greater representation of the other weaker sections of the society *viz.* Scheduled Castes (SCs) and Scheduled Tribes (STs) would enhance their voice in democratic bodies and promote inclusive governance which is critical to inclusive growth.

A recent survey, commissioned by the Ministry of Panchayati Raj and executed by AC Nielsen-ORG MARGA in 2007 under the guidance of an academic advisory committee, provides many new insights into the social and political empowerment of women in PRIs major constraints faced by women in participating in Panchayat elections. This nation-wide survey covered 23 States, 114 Districts, and 228 Blocks and 1368 *Gram Panchayats* had a total sample size of more than 20,000, including EWRs, elected male representatives (EMRs), former EWRs, and official

The findings of a study of the working of panchayats in six states conducted by PRIA reveals that: "...25 per cent women notice and remark on the visible change in their status within their family after they have been elected...about 60 per cent of women said that they would encourage women to stand for election. The same percentage (60%) is contemplating to contest PRI election again" (PRIA, 2000).

Kultikri: An All Women Panchayat: An all women *panchayat* was constituted in Kultikri Gram Panchayat in West Midnapore district under Sankrail block, Jhargram Sub-division in West Bengal in 1993. The trend has continued in subsequent *panchayat* election held in 1998, 2003, and 2008 (Gupta, *et al.*, 1999).

functionaries. of which 907 were women headed *Gram Panchayats*. Nearly three-fourths of the EWRs in the sample belonged to the SC/STs and other backward communities, and were evenly divided above and below the poverty line.

The social background of the Elected Women Representatives (EWRs) surveyed indicates that the majority of them are from Scheduled Castes (SCs), Scheduled Tribes (STs) or Other Backward Classes (OBCs) groupings showing thereby that political representation of women in Panchayats is not confined to the elite.

Illiteracy is the most pertinent hurdle that prevents the entry of rural women into mainstream politics. The AC Nielsen ORG-

Table 8.1: Showing the Social Background of Elected Women Representatives (EWRs)

(Percentage)

The social background of the EWRs surveyed is as under:	General	SC	ST	OBC
EWRs Fenale Pradhan	28.3	24.3	15.3	32.1
Female Ward Members	28.4	25.8	12.0	33.8

Source: Government of India (2008), *Study on Elected Women Representatives in Panchayati Raj Institutions*, New Delhi: Ministry of Panchayati Raj.

MARGA study commissioned by the Ministry of Panchayati Raj among elected representatives of PRIs showed that about one fifth of them were illiterates. However, the gender gap was significant (women—24%; men 6%). The general educational attainment was up to middle school or above among elected representatives (48%). Pradhans had higher educational attainment than the Ward Members.

Table 8.2: Showing the Educational Status of Elected Women Representatives (EWRs)

(Percentage)

EWRs	Illiterate	Upto Primary Level	Upto Middle School	Middle School and Higher
Female Chairperson (Pradhans)	11.4	19.8	16.4	52.4
Female Ward Members	26.6	19.2	17.1	37.1

Source: Government of India (2008), *Study on Elected Women Representatives in Panchayati Raj Institutions*, New Delhi: Ministry of Panchayati Raj.

A majority of the EWRs had contested only one election (87%) and the proportion of first timers in politics was therefore high (86%). Around 14 per cent were re-elected more than once at the *gram panchayat* level. Further, analysis showed that a majority of former EWRs could not get re-elected because their seats had been de-reserved when the poll came around.

Table 8.3: Proportion of Elected Representatives that Contested PRI Elections Across Three Rounds

(Percentage)

	Contested only one election	Number Surveyed	Contested two elections	Number Surveyed	Contested three elections	Number surveyed
Elected Women Representatives	87.8	4880	9.9	4880	2.3	4880
Elected Male Representatives	71.9	1838	18.7	1838	9.4	4880

Source: Government of India (2008), *Study on Elected Women Representatives in Panchayati Raj Institutions*, New Delhi: Ministry of Panchayati Raj.

In the case of EWRs, prior association with any form of politics

Table 8.4: Comparison of Change Experience by SC, ST and All Women Elected Representatives (EWRs)

Empowering Changes after Election	% SC/ST	% All EWRs	Note on EWR data from Report
Internal Reason for poor Participation—poxy status, fear, low self-confidence, Knowledge, compliance to traditional gender roles	72	22.9	Table 4,8, pg. 56
Greater self-Confidence	55	78	Table 7.1, pg. 131
Increased Leadership Skill	31	69.8	
Family share responsibility for looking after children	39.8	62.4	
More role allowed in decision-making	39.8	68.75	
More respect after the election	58.4	79	
Able to speak up in their households and gram sabha more freely	34.3	67.9	
Greater self-esteem exhibited by SC/ST representatives	32.5	77.1	
Officials accepted invitation to visit panchayat	39.3	43.1	
Officials supported in implementing schemes	36.8	40.8	
Officials took prompt action on women request/complaints	34.2	40.8	

Source: Nupur Tiwari (2012) Women and Panchayati Raj, *Yojana*, June 2012, Vol. 56.

was low, and for most, the act of contesting the first election signaled their entry into active politics. Whatever, prior association they had was of a limited nature. A significant proportion of EWRs said that they were earlier associated with groups or committees and that this association had helped them. While 21 per cent of the representatives claimed to have been self-motivated, about 22 per cent said their spouses had inspired them. This was higher in the case of EWRs (30%). Interestingly, participation in community groups such as *Mahila Mandals*, self-help groups (SHGs), youth clubs and cooperatives seemed to have played an important role, with 22 per cent of the elected representatives reporting that this had motivated them to take the plunge into electoral politics. However, 8 per cent of the elected representatives, mainly in West Bengal, Sikkim, Tripura and Kerala, disclosed that political parties had motivated them. Husbands (30%) and other family members

Table 8.5: Comparative Involvement of Women SC/ST Representatives and all EWRs (President/Sarpanch/Pradhan)

Aspects of Involvement	% SC/ST Women	% All EWRs	Note on EWR data from Report
Able to work/discharge the official responsibilities with freedom and independence	Only one-third of total 119 presidents surveyed		
Attended Panchayat meeting during their term	52.4		
Called Panchayat meeting	35.3	86	Pg. 75 refer to Gram Sabha
Chaired Panchayat meeting	31.9	93.6	As above
Voluntarily signed resolution	27.7	34.4	5.22 pg. 91
Played significant role in the distribution of the development schemes	18.5	55.9	Table 5.23, pg. 92
Vocal in raising issues	26	94.1	Table 5.11 pg. 83 refers to Gram Sabha
Ward Members			
Raised issues in Panchayat meeting	52.2	94.1	Table 7.10 pg. 137
Issues discussed and considered	Few Times	79.7	As above

Source: Nupur Tiwari (2012) Women and Panchayati Raj, *Yojana*, June 2012, Vol. 56.

(12%) were reported to have played an important role in motivating EWRs to contest elections for the first time (Tiwari, 2012).

The economic status of more than half the elected representatives (54%) was above the poverty line (APL). There were a higher proportion of APL individuals among pradhans (72%), as compared toward members (50%). Almost two-fifths (38%) of all EWRs were reportedly BPL, the majority being ward members (41%) rather than pradhans (24%). This indicates, overall, that pradhans are better off than other *panchayat* members.

That reservation has been critical to the representation of disadvantaged groups was confirmed by the fact that 88 per cent of them had been elected from reserved seats. Approximately 86 per cent of all the representatives surveyed were first timers in *panchayats*, while 14.3 per cent had been elected for a second or third term. While 15 per cent of the women *pradhans* had been re-elected twice or more, the corresponding figure for male *pradhans* was 37 per cent (Tiwari, 2009).

Conceptually, providing representation to women in Panchayati Raj System could be accepted as an important planning approach regarding minimizing the traditional feeling of people about the status of the women in our society particularly in terms of keeping women under the subjugation of men, imposing restrictions by the households and the society against them in the availment of certain opportunities and participating in several socio-cultural and economic activities and traditional boundations disfavouring them for improving their life style and status is existing social and economic setting.

Representation *Versus* Participation of Weaker Section

However, there is big difference between representation and participation. It is easier to legislate representation, but it is rather a complex and difficult task to create conditions for participate. the adequate representation does not automatically lead to proper participation. It is important that they are in position to influence decision-making and prepare and implement the schemes for economic development and social justice (Tiwari, 2009).

Despite various provisions including 73rd Amendments made in the Constitution to safeguards members of SC and ST from exploitation, not much has changed. Yet, despite their constitutional rights, representatives of SC and ST community are often denied attendance to *Gram Panchayat* and *Gram Sabha* meetings because of caste based power dynamics, illiteracy, and dominance of upper castes, Communication problem, lack of exposure, lack of information and knowledge. This has forced them to make compromises in their role as elected representatives of local bodies. A large number of men and women come from SC and ST communities in political spaces, and most of them are playing that role for the first time.

In a case study of Madhya Pradesh found that in most of the cases women are housewives, first time entrants into politics and most of them are illiterate or educated up to primary level Rashmi Arun (1997). Nirmala Buch (2000) revealed the profile of the new

> The proxy participations and proxy role performance of the Elected Women Representatives (EWRs) are common picture across several states in India. Husbands or Sons of the Elected Women Representatives perform the daily roles. However, studies show that a majority of EWRs are not proxies of their male relatives any more. The decision to contest elections was taken on their own by 58 per cent of them. Alongside this big achievement, 15 per cent of women *pradhans* were able to win elections a second time. Women belonging to the 21-35 age groups performed better than those belonging to the 35 years and above age group. Women members of active committees at the village level were more successful at the *panchayat*.
>
> *Source*: *Study on Elected Women Representatives in Panchayati Raj Institutions*, Government of India, 2008 and Tiwari, 2012).

women in post 73rd Constitutional Amendment panchayats showed that majorities were illiterate and large percentages were from families in the lower socio-economic strata. They were comparatively younger than the earlier entrants and were predominantly first generation entrants to the public political life.

Indian Institute of Social Science (2000) in a study of Panchayati Raj in Haryana has reviewed the progress of some hundred elected women in four districts; majorities of the elected women *Sarpanches* including younger women were illiterate when elected to office. After two years in office, they demanded literary skill and generally feel the need of education for their daughter.

Union Minister of Panchayati Raj, Mani Shankar Aiyar expressed that "the rotation term of reserved posts for women should be extended up to two or three terms because generally the first term for women representatives has proved to be a period of learning and only in the second and third terms do women representatives start showing their real performance" (Cited from Nupur Tiwari, 2009).

There are many instances of EWRs in *panchayats* taking a keen interest in grassroots level issues. It has often been observed that women prioritise those developmental needs that seem to be more pressing from their perspective. Women are seen to be more involved in monitoring the presence of teachers and medical staff in schools and health centres, and inspecting nutrition centres under the Integrated Child Development Scheme. They have also taken the lead in making efforts to acquire smokeless stoves, build crèches and community halls, and rectify family problems, including counselling abusive or alcoholic husbands. Sometimes, women-headed *panchayats* have experienced a dramatic increase in revenues by auctioning village ponds, community forests and village markets for the larger welfare of the community (Tiwari, 2009).

Banerjee, A. (2011) revealed in his article Women in Panchayat: A Review the Performance of Women in PRI.

- Since, Women Panchayat representatives consistently demand for adequate supply of Drinking Water, Housing and social welfare programmes and expenditure on these count are relatively higher in women headed *panchayat*.
- Women headed *panchayats* score brownie points in construction of roads, up keep of drinking water facilities and administering government loan scheme. However, their performance is not effective in ensuring irrigation avenues.
- Women headed panchayats generally take more interest in negotiating social evils like child marriage, indiscriminate sale of liquor and witch hunting and such other problem.

Participation of women in Village General Body meeting (*Gram Sabha*) increase, while the chairperson is a woman. It highlights that political communication improves when the citizen and leaders are of the same sex (Chattopadhyay and Duflo, 2004).

S. Govinda Gowda and others (1996) in their study of Karnataka women elected *panchayat* leader found that the women members of developed *taluks* were found to play a better developmental role that their counterparts in the backward *taluks*. The study reveals that among the socio-economic attributes such as age, education, caste, annual household income and land holding of women leaders, only education and annual household income had a highly significant and positive relationship with their developmental role performance. The findings of the study state that women members of the Panchayati Raj Institution could play an effective developmental role if they are given adequate recognition and encouragement.

The book under review *Inclusion and Exclusion in Local Governance: Field Studies from Rural India* has a nationwide perspective to an extent. It is the product of a national-level study conducted in 42 *panchayats* across 12 states to see how democratic decentralization is working in Indian villages. This is done through stories of empowerment as well as discrimination against women, the scheduled castes and scheduled tribes. The main objective of the study is to find out the degree of inclusion of the excluded groups and categories like women, SCs and STs in the rural power structure. Being able to influence decisions in the *panchayats* is considered proof of empowerment of these groups and a sign of their being included, overcoming their earlier state of exclusion. It analyses the social, political, and economic forces influencing variations in the degree of empowerment of the SCs, STs and women and looks at the likely future developments. The study finds that creations of employment avenues for weaker sections are necessary to effectively include them in the PRIs.

Inclusion and Exclusion in Local Governance: Field Studies from Rural India edited by B.S. Baviskar and George Mathew (New Delhi: Sage), 2009; pp. xiv + 453, Cited from Nupur Tiwari (2011): "How Inclusive Are Panchayati Raj Institutions", *Economic and Political Weekly*, April 9, Volume XLVI, No. 15.

Raghabendra Chattopadhyay, Esther Duflo (2004) in their research project on local decentralisation conducted in two districts of West Bengal and Rajasthan analysed that reservation introduced as a tool to ensure adequate representation also assists in adequate delivery of local public goods to disadvantaged groups.

Their key findings were

- Women elected representatives invest more in goods that are relevant to the needs of local women: like water and roads in West Bengal; water in Rajasthan. They invest less in goods that are less relevant to the needs of women: non-formal education centres in West Bengal; roads in Rajasthan.
- It also shows that SC *Pradhans* invest a larger share of public goods in SC hamlets than do non-SC *Pradhans*.

This research thus shows that some of the fears expressed regarding decentralisation are not founded: Local leaders seem to have some effective control over decisions, even when they are women or SCs. Moreover, it indicates that the oft-heard anecdotal evidence regarding women being entirely controlled by their husbands when in office should not be given too much weight.

They concluded that reservations of electoral seats may therefore be an effective tool to safeguard the interest of the weaker groups. This chapter has shown that reservation for SCs and women in the Panchayati Raj makes a difference: Both women and SCs invest more in what women and SCs seem to want (water for women, goods in SC hamlets for SCs). This underscores the power of the elected panchayat leaders and, by implication, the importance of the 73rd Constitutional Amendment. These results also suggest that, given the difficulty of targeting public transfers to specific groups in an otherwise decentralized system; reservation may be a tool to ensure not only adequate representation but also adequate delivery of local public goods to disadvantaged groups.

The successful EWR now acts as a role model to others. The increased proportion of EWRs has ensured that the principles of justice between the sexes prevail and this has certainly led to the fulfilment of certain interests of women, which may otherwise have been neglected. It is for sure that without the system of reservation women would have had no role to play in grassroots politics in India.

Way Forward

Scheduled Caste (SC) and Scheduled Tribe (ST) women members suffer from extreme social, educational and economic backwardness, arising out of the age-old practice of social exclusion, untouchability, landlessness and geographical isolation. There is thus an emerging and urgent need to enhance their leadership roles. Strengthening SC and ST leadership especially women in Panchayats required capacity building of SC and ST elected leaders. Also efforts should be made on two aspects; one is knowledge and skill enhancement of elected leaders so that they can perform their mandated role and another is strengthening their sense of identity.

Banta in his essay "Women in Panchayati Raj Institution: Beginning of a New Era" (2009) outlines the various provisions of the 73rd Constitutional Amendment act that accord prominence to women's' rights and obligations. Banta observed that a mere devolution of power to women representatives is not enough. In order to enhance their competitive competence, there should be organized continuous training programmes focusing on rural development schemes, gender sensitization, training of trainers and effective administration skills. Political empowerment must be backed by a high level of administrative competence.

Pandey (2009) makes a plea that government policies must address the need of empowering women and vulnerable communities in their professional career, Political Leadership, media relation, and resource generations, opportunities to women for formal education and training, greater mobilization of women in governance and development at all levels and heightened awareness of women of their potential role in socio-economic and political transformation.

The principal component of the trainings should be orientation on rural development programmes, management development of chairperson and leaders, gender sensitisation of the leaders, administrators and communities to change attitudes and beliefs; and training of trainers.

The existing network of village-level workers, training centres, extension training units, field training centres of non-governmental organizations (NGOs) could be utilized for the purpose of the training.

In order to encourage the political participation by women in Panchayati Raj Institutions (PRIs), the Ministry of Panchayati Raj conceptualized a scheme titled Panchayat Mahila Evam Yuva Shakti Abhiyan (PMEYSA) targeted at Elected Women Representatives (EWR) and Elected Youth Representatives (EYRs). The scheme has two facets, namely: (i) Panchayat Mahila Shakti Abhiyan (PMSA), and (ii) Panchayat Yuva Shakti Abhiyan (PYSA).

The Village general meeting (*Gram Sabha*) must be deeply involved in implementation at all levels because it is the best form of social audit, both pre-implementation and post-implementation. This is also the most effective way of cutting down corruption and nepotism and ensuring transparency and accountability, as well as functioning democracy. It was also recommended by Planning Commission to provide remuneration in terms of honorarium, monthly/daily allowances, sitting fees, TA/HRA etc. to Elected Women Representatives. The available data shows that the remuneration given to Members of Gram Panchayats in most of the States is just nominal. To encourage participation of women, SC and ST in *panchayat* activities, special honorarium needs to be given to them. The ongoing experiments and experiences suggest that periodical training; orientation and sensitization can help the women leaders to perform the assigned role in a better way.

Conclusion

Political space is provided for marginalized groups and women in *panchayats* and for subsequent exposure to decentralized governance, planning development, and capacity building to some extent through imparting training. Besides, exposure to local governance by NGOs has given them some confidence in taking up leadership challenges in preparing and executing plans for economic development and social justice at the grassroots-level. The working group on decentralized planning and PRIs observed on this issue that "One of the significant achievements of the provisions of the 73rd Constitutional Amendment Act concerning reservation of seats and political offices in favour of women and the disadvantaged sections of the rural community is that it had improved their awareness and perception-levels and has created an urge in them to assert their rightful share in the decision-making process at the local level" (GoI, 2001).

Thus, the affirmative action for these groups in local governance has resulted in social identities and political awareness among them and created an urge to become part of mainstream political, economic and social life. With initial clashes between 'higher' castes and 'lower' castes, there are indications of social cohesion at local levels. The political space given to marginalized sections has to some extent dealt a blow to the asymmetrical social structure at the local level and given greater space for their participation and involvement in decision-making (Mahi Pal, 2001).

Moreover, gender equity and inclusiveness will lead to better delivery of public services, such as health, sanitation, early childhood care, drinking water etc. that affect women's lives and make the PRIs more accountable to the rural populace. Reservation for women in the third tier of governance including in leadership positions in PRIs was itself a unique innovation in the governance area. Enhancement of the reservation for women in PRIs to 50 per cent will further accelerate this process and make PRIs uniquely inclusive institutions. With the proposed Constitutional Amendment, the number of Elected Women Representatives is expected to rise to more than 14 lakhs from the present 10 lakhs. Collective empowerment through representation and democratic process will give them voice, feelings of solidarity and democratic politics. Affirmative action will build a critical mass of local leadership of such groups will be active participants in the strategic decision-making.

References

Aiyar, M.S., 2002, "Panchayati Raj: The Way Forward", *Economic and Political Weekly,* August 3.

Alsop, R.J., Krishna, A. and Sjoblom, D., 1999, *Inclusion and Local Elected Governments: The Panchayati Raj System in India*. USA: South Asia-Social Development unit, The World Bank.

Arun, R., 1997, "Role of Women in Panchayati Raj", *Administrator,* Vol. 12, April-June.

Arora, R.K. and Hooja, M., 2009, *Panchayati Raj, Participation and Decentralozation.* Jaipur: Rawat Publications.

Banerjee, A., 2011, "Women in Panchayat: A Review", *Yojana,* 55(2).

Banerjee, R., 2013, "What Ails Panchayati Raj?" *Economic and Political Weekly,* 48(30).

Chattopadhyay, R., *et al.,* 2004. "Impact of Reservation in Panchayati Raj: Evidence from a Nation-wide Randomised Experiment", *Economic and Political Weekly*, February 28.

Gochhayat, A., 2013, "Political Participation of Women in Gram Panchayat Elections in Odisha: A Case Study of Hindol Block", *International Journal of Humanities and Social Science Invention,* 2(2).

Government of India, 2007, *Impact of Bottom Up Planning Under PRIs and Women Participation Therein in the States of Madhya Pradesh, Orissa, Chhattisgarh, Gujarat, Jharkhand and Maharashtra,* New Delhi: Planning Commission.

Gowada, S.G., *et al.,* 1996, "Developmental Role of Women Members of Panchayati Raj Institutions: A Study in Karnataka", *Journal of Rural Development*, 15(2): 249-259.

Joshi, R.P. and Narwani, G.S., 2005, *Panchayati Raj in India: Emerging Trends Across the States,* New Delhi: Rawat Publications.

Lakshi, A., 1993, *Women and Politics—A Study in Political Participation*, Hyderabad: Book Link Corporation.

Mehata, G.S., 2002, *Participation of Women in the Panchayati Raj System*, New Delhi: Kanishka Publishers and Distributors.

Mohanty, B., 1995, "Panchayati Raj, 73rd Constitutional Amendment and Women", *Economic and Political Weekly*.

Pal, M., 2004, "Panchayati Raj and Rural Governance: Experiences of a Decade", *Economic and Political Weekly*.

Pal, M., 2003, *Gap between Needs and Resources of Panchayats in India*, New Delhi: Mittal Publications.

Sinha, A.K., 2004, *Panchayati Raj and Empowerment of Women*, New Delhi: Northern Book Centre.

Tiwari, N., 2009, "Rethinking the Rotation Term of Reservation in Panchayats", *Economic and Political Weekly*.

Tiwari, N., 2011, "How Inclusive are Panchayati Raj Institutions", *Economic and Political Weekly*, 46 (15).

Tiwari, N., 2009, "Rethinking the Rotation Term of Reserved Seats for Women in Panchayati Raj", *Commonwealth Journal of Local Governance*, (3).

Tiwari, N., 2011, "Women and Panchayati Raj", *Yojana*, 56.

Vyasuli, P. and Vyasulu, V., 1999, "Women in Panchayati Raj Grassroot Democracy in Malgudi", *Economic and Political Weekly.*

9

Community Development and Rural Livelihood

An Empirical Study of the Pastoral Community of Kutch District, Gujarat

Ankur Saxena

There has been gradual shift of emphasis in the natural and social sciences from the impact of environment upon mankind during the past years. In one sense disaster represents an extreme class of human, environmental or ècological phenomena. According to Meleti, "Community development seeks the determinants of human behaviour in the natural environment and the process that facilitates human adjustments to the physical world through social organizations." Community development is a skilled process and part of its approach is the belief that communities cannot be helped unless they themselves agree to this process. Community development has to look both ways: not only at how the community is working at the grassroots, but also at how responsive key institutions are to the needs of local communities.

Pastoral Community of Kutch

The Pastoral system is characterized by mass migration of animal and people throughout the year in search of water and fodder. The onset of monsoon and distribution of rainfall mainly dictate the pattern of the movement of nomadic herders and around the months march or April, these households moves towards surrounding irrigated areas forced by rising temperature in the desert and deer eased feed and water resources. The incentives for this movement are temporary employment opportunities within the irrigated farming communities, grazing of the livestock, drinking water for human and animal use and readily available markets for and live stocks by products. This community returns back around July or August with the news of the first monsoon showers and the distance travelled by them during the migration is around 100 kms. or more and in the desert vegetation is the main source of feed for grazing livestock and all the livestock's are indigenous breeds well suited to the environment. The lives of the pastoralist revolves around the water and factors like low rainfall, high rate of water infiltration into the sands, high evaporation rate prevent the natural accumulation of surface water.

Physical Characteristics

These are lean of child, noble in bearing, their oval faces uniquely expressive with well shaped, deep set eyes, which at times are green or blue in colour. Obesity is rare among them. And rich in their smiles in sharp contrast to the harshness of the land that they inhibit. The physiognomy of the faces the freshness and vitality of youth and the tensionless wrinkles of ripped age reflect inner harmony which is the gift of holistic living and are very hardworking community. The houses of this community are well kept clean; the interior of the huts are remarkable in their spotlessness and orderliness. The harsh physical environment has kept the life simple, fulfilling only essential needs which include their aesthetic need an life for them is always dignified and one does not gets the impression of the grinding poverty of material and moral degradation of the individual and in this community cognitive system man, animal and nature are viewed as unity. The livestock's especially camels heeps and goats are inseparable inmates of the family system, forest hill and desert do not divided their life an don the contrary nature unites them in their aesthetic appreciation, artistic manifestation and ceremonial performances.

Significance of the Study

Increasing awareness about the environmental issues have brought to the fore several issues faced by the communities like tribal, fisher, folks, hilly people etc. whose livelihood depends upon the natural resources. It has resulted in struggles, campaigns and constructive initiatives undertaken by these communities for the livelihood. Unfortunately, this community have largely remained depend on the natural resources.There has been unknown work on the nomadic pastoral community of Gujarat, which constitutes a fairly significant proportion of the total population of the state. This study both empirical and academically hence and most importantly useful to the pastoral community, the social scientists to understand study the self-reliance of the pastoral community for sustaining their livelihood on their own.

Objectives

1. To study the livelihood pattern with reference to the availability of resources.
2. To study the effect of the disasters on the livelihood of the community.
3. To study the living pattern of the respondents.
4. To study the coping strategies for the livelihood existence.

Research Methodology

This study is exploratory cum descriptive in nature and an in- depth study has been undertaken with the help of qualitative and quantitative research methodology. The Universe of the study is the Pastoral Community belonging to the rabari caste of the Maldhari community. The sample is selected by purposive sampling method to seek an insight into the attributes of effective practices of livelihood during the crisis. Case study method was used, Focus group discussions, and the open and close ended questions were also used including the interview schedule.

Data Analysis

Table 9.1: Age-wise Distribution of the Respondents

Age in Years	No. of the Respondents	Percentage
01 to 25	03	12
26 to 50	18	72
51 to 75	04	16
Total	25	100

Source: Primary data collected from the field for the present study.

From Table 9.1 it can be interpreted that out of total 25 respondents, 18 (72%) of the majority respondents are in the age group of 26 to 50 years, 04 (16%) of the respondents are in the age group of 51 to 75 years, while rest of the respondents are in the age group of 01 to 25 years.

Table 9.2: Occupation-wise Distribution of the Respondents

Type of occupation	No. of respondents	Percentage
Labour work	12	48
Agriculture	08	32
Animal husbandry	05	20
Total	25	100

Source: Primary data collected from the field for the present study.

Form Table 9.2 it can be interpreted that 12 (48%) respondents depends on labour work to earn their livelihood, whole 8 (32%) respondents are based on agriculture as their livelihood. And only 5 (20%) respondents are dependent on Animal Husbandry. From Table 9.2 it can be concluded that majority of the respondents belongs to the labour group as their occupation while very few belongs to the Animal, herders group because of which these people have developed their separate identity. So, these results clearly reflects the shift of livelihood pattern of these people.

From Table 9.3 it is clearly seen that 15 (60%) of the respondents are having only one earning member in their family, while 9 (36%) of the respondents are having two earning members. Under the one earning members column, 7 (28%) respondents

Table 9.3: Relation between Family Members and Earning Members of the Respondents

Total family members	Earning members			Total
	One	Two	Three	
1 to 3	7 (28)	3 (12)	—	10 (40)
4 to 6	8 (32)	5 (20)	—	13 (52)
Above 6	—	1 (4)	1 (4)	2 (8)
Total	15 (60)	9 (36)	1 (4)	25 (100)

Note: Figures in Brackets shows percentage.
Source: Primary data collected from the field for the present study.

belongs to family consisting 1 to 3 members and 8 (32%) respondents belongs to family consisting 4 to 6 members. Similarly, under the two earning members column, the family consists 1 to 3 members includes 3 (12%) respondents, while the family consist 4 to 6 member includes 5 (20%) of the respondents. While it also clearly seen in Table 9.3 that there is only 1 (4%) respondent fall in to the column of three earning members and it is also seen that it is the only family consisting more than 6 family members out of the total respondents. While it is also clearly seen in Table 9.3 that there is only 1 (4%) respondent fall into the column of three earning members family members out of the total respondents.

Table 9.4: Relation between Type of Livelihood Sources and Migration of the Respondents

Type of Livelihood Sources	Destination after Migration			Not Migrating	Total
	Within Kutch	Other Parts	Outside Gujarat		
Coal mine work	5 (20)	—	—	—	5 (20)
Salt pan work	2 (8)	—	—	—	2 (8)
Animal herding	1 (4)	4 (16)	—	—	5 (20)
Agricultural labour	1 (4)	—	—	2 (8)	3 (12)
Quarry workers	—	8 (32)	—	—	8 (32)
Any other labour work	—	1 (4)	1 (4)	—	2 (8)
Total	9 (36)	13 (52)	1 (4)	2 (8)	25 (100)

Note: Figures in Brackets Indicate percentage.
Source: Primary data collected from the field for the present study.

From Table 9.4 it can be interpreted that 13 (52%) of the respondents are migrating within Gujarat but outside the Kutch to sustain their livestock as well as to find the various alternatives to earn their livelihood, out of which 4 (16%) respondents are migrating in search of the forage for their livestock, while 8 (32%) are migrating to earn their livelihood by working in quarries. Similarly, 9 (36%) of the respondents are migrating within Kutch, out of which majority of the respondents 5 (20%) goes for labour work in coal mine processing work, while 2 (8%) are joins salt pan work as 'agaria'. It is also seen in the table that 2 (8%) respondents are not migrating while only 1 (4%) respondent is migrating outside the Gujarat. From Table 9.4 it can be concluded that as most of the respondents rely on labour work of varied kinds and very few relies on their traditional livelihoods, such as agriculture and cattle rearing. The adverse effect of continuous and frequent draught and water scarcity forced them to change their priorities of livelihood sources.

Table 9.5: Effects of Frequent Disasters on Respondents

Types of effects	Disasters		Draught
	Cyclone	Earthquake	
Loss of livelihoods	2 (8)	8 (32)	20 (80)
Uncertainty of life	—	6 (24)	14 (64)
Damages of houses	10 (40)	—	—
Total loss of shelter	—	25 (100)	—
Water scarcity	—	—	24 (96)
Loss of livestock	7 (28)	4 (16)	10 (72)
Food insecurity	—	14 (56)	10 (40)
Increase in dependency	4 (16)	18 (72)	8 (32)
Availability of medical facilities	4 (16)	25 (100)	—
Availability of temporary employment	—	15 (60)	10 (40)
Any other	—	—	

Note: Figures in Brackets indicate percentage.

Multi-response table.

Source: Primary data collected from the field for the present study.

This is a multi-answered Table 9.5 where in the respondents viewed one or more effects of the particular disaster. From Table 9.5 it is clearly derived that all of the respondents 25 (100%) have been affected negatively in terms of total loss of shelter and positively in terms of availability of medical facility as a result of earthquake-2001. It is also clearly seen in this table, that cyclone of Kandla-98 has note created much serious effects to these respondents. The most severe effect due to cyclone was damage of houses in which to 10 (40%) of the respondent's houses were damaged.

Similarly, in the column of effects due to earthquake, it is seen that 14 (56%) of the respondents feels that they may suffer from extreme food insecurity in future which is justify from the response given by the respondents regarding increases in dependency wherein 18 (72%) agreed upon it that the excessive flow of direct and temporary help in form of relief assistance after earthquake led them towards dependency.

While looking at the adverse effects of the draught, which is ongoing since, last three years, affected many of the aspects of the lives of the people. Table 9.5 shows that 20 (80%) of the respondents felt that they lost their livelihood sources, 14 (64%) are not sure of their future and 24 (96%) of the respondents felt water scarcity in all from *viz.* domestic use, for the livestock and for agricultural purpose only due to continuous draught. It is also seen that 18 (72%) respondents felt that whatever loss they have in their livestock's is also due to draught.

From Table 9.5 findings it can be concluded that people becomes extremely vulnerable because of draught while the earthquake in being highlighted as the sole reason of devastation of the Kutch, due to which appropriateness of the assistance and long-term planning might be improper.

Table 9.6: Views of Respondents on Appropriateness of Various Livelihood Sources after Disaster

Various livelihood sources	Views about appropriateness	
	Effective	Not effective
Animal husbandry	—	14 (56)
Agriculture	1 (4)	10 (40)
Labour work	16 (64)	4 (14)
Artisan activities	—	20 (80)

Note: Figures in Brackets indicate percentage.

Multi-response table.

Source: Primary data collected from the field for the present study.

This is also a multi-answered Table 9.6 where in the views of the respondents is seen regarding appropriateness of the livelihood sources after frequent disasters. From Table 9.6 it is seen that 14 (56%) of the respondents are of the view that animal herding is no more effective livelihood source. While out of total respondents 20 (80%) of the respondents felt that artisan activities are not serving the purpose of earning livelihood. And 10 (40%) of the respondents also viewed that agriculture is also becomes non-productive livelihood source. From the above findings, it can be concluded that most of the traditional and primary livelihood sources to which people are used fo are gradually becoming invisible from these people's live.

Table 9.7: Total Livestock of the Respondents

Type of cattle	Total No. of Cattle	No. of Respondents
Sheep	371	11 (44)
Goat	180	4 (16)
Bullock	1	1 (4)
None	—	5 (20)
Total	552	21 (84)

Note: Figures in Brackets indicate percentage.
Source: Primary data collected from the field for the present study.

From Table 9.7 it can be seen that out of the total respondents 11 (44%) respondents have sheep consisting total 371 numbers, while 4 (16%) are having total number of 180 goats. And only 2 (8%) are having total 2 camels. Similarly, it is also seen that 5 (20%) of the respondents do not have the livestock. From the above findings, it can be concluded that the shift in traditional livelihood pattern is taking place because earlier Rabari caste from which all the respondents belongs to was identified on their livestock composition and each family have hundreds of cattle. Belongingness was also identified on their livestock composition and each family had hundreds of cattle.

Table 9.8 show the effects of the disasters on livestock of the respondents, which once upon a time considered as a primary source of livelihood of this community. This is a multi-answered table. This table shows that out of the total respondents 10 (40%)

Table 8.8: Effects of Disasters on Livestock of the Respondents (Multi-answered)

Effects	Disasters		
	Cyclone	Earthquake	Draught
Death of Livestock	10 (40%)	6 (24%)	—
Selling of Livestock	—	4 (16%)	13 (52%)
Physical damage to Livestock	6 (24%)	2 (8%)	—
Health Problems and Death of Livestock Due to Prosodies Juliflora	—	—	12 (48%)

Note: Figures in Brackets shows percentage.
Source: Primary data collected from the field for the present study.

of the respondents responded that they have lost their livestock during 0 cyclone and 6 (24%) of them replied that there was physical damage to the livestock during cyclone. It is seen in this table along with human beings, draught severely attacked on the livestock. 13 (52%) of the respondents responded that they have to sell the livestock to sustain their own existence and because of their inability to provide proper forage and fodder to their livestock. Similarly, the *Prosopis juliflora* becomes the enemy of the livestock because its fruits caused various health problems and lastly death of the livestock, in this respect 12 (48%) of the respondents replied that it affected their livestock and continues on the mission. From the above findings it can be concluded that *Prosopis juliflora* proved as a man-made disaster added to all frequent disasters particularly for this community, because it affects severely to their primary source of livelihood.

Table 9.9: Sources of Loan of the Respondents (Multi-answered)

Source	No. of Respondents	Percentage
Bank	2	08
Government	—	—
Co-operative Society	10	40
Moneylender	3	12
Relatives	6	24
Friends	2	08
Caste people	13	52
Rich people of the Village	3	12

Source: Primary data collected from the field for the present study.

From Table 9.9 it is seen that only 2 (8%) of the respondents are using government sources for their economic needs. It is also seen that the co-operative society is one of the recent source developed through (Non-working in this area) is on much use to meet the economic needs which justify from the fact that 10 (40%) of the respondents are using this co-operative.Similarly, majority 13 (52%) of the respondents relies on their own caste members for economic assistance. From the above findings, it can be concluded that higher education level can broaden the vision of the people to utilize locally available respondents such as Bank various Government Schemes.

Findings

- 18 (72%) respondents are of the age of 26 to 50 years.
- 3 (12%) respondents are in the age group of less than 25 years.
- 24 (96%) respondents are illiterate, while only 1 (4%) respondent is literate.
- 12 (48%) respondents depend on labour work to earn their livelihood.
- 8 (32%) respondent's primary occupation is agriculture.
- 4 (16%) respondents viewed that they have to engage their children in sharing their livelihood.
- 13 (52%) respondents are migrating within Gujarat out of Kutch out of which 4 (16%) migrates in search of fodder for their livestock, while 8 (32%) migrates to earn their livelihood by working in quarries.
- 9 (36%) respondents migrates within Kutch out of which 5 (20%) joins coal processing units and 2(8%) joins salt pan work units as a labour.
- 20 (80%) of the respondents felt that they lost their livelihood sources due to draught.
- 24 (96%) of the respondents felt water scarcity in all form *viz.* domestic use, for livestock and for agriculture purpose due to draughts.
- 14 (56%) respondents feel that animal herding is no more effective livelihood source.

- 20 (80%) of the respondents viewed that artisan activities are not serving the purpose of earning livelihoods.
- 16 (64%) respondents responded that at present labour work is the only effective source of livelihood for them.
- 11 (44%) respondents have sheep consisting total 372 numbers.
- 5 (20%) of the respondents do not have the livestock.
- 10 (40%) respondents lost their livestock during cyclone and 6 (24%) respondents lost their some livestock during earthquake.
- 13 (52%) respondents said that they have to sell their livestock to sustain their existence.
- 12 (48%) respondent's livestock affected due to *Prosopis juliflora*.

Conclusions

- The shift in livelihood pattern is clearly reflected which is justify from the fact that very few respondents depends on animal husbandry as their occupation which is since ages knows as the traditional primary livelihood source of these people.
- The more the members in the family, lesser the food security, so willingly or unwillingly other family members have to join the head earners to share the family livelihood.
- The conclusion can be that being small farmers and landless labourers, people have to face extreme vulnerable living condition. Sometime, it may lead such groups towards demoralization or hopelessness when no livelihood source is effective.
- The conclusion can be that as most of the responds relies on labour work instead of their traditional livelihoods sources is the result of continue and frequent draught resulted extreme water scarcity; under such circumstances the traditional livelihood source becomes invisible.
- People become extremely vulnerable because of draught while the earthquake is being highlighted due to which appropriateness of the assistance and long-term planning might be improper.

- Strengthening and providing alternative livelihood sources can be the foremost priority to maintain the existence of the victims of the disasters.

Suggestions

- A research study can be done on in-depth study of impact of NGO on the Maladhari (Rabari) customs, traditions, decision-making, livelihood, artisans and education of the Maladhari (Rabari) community.
- Literacy efforts of the Government should be the social responsibility.
- A focus attention from all angles for development of Maladharis should be given according to the strategies developed separately for each village (Micro-planning exercise).
- It is recommended that in any developmental programme the local people, Government agencies, NGOs and private sector be engaged right from planning, implementation to supervision and monitoring stage.
- It is suggested that top propriety should be given to repair wells, irrigation facilities, dams etc. to restore livelihood resources, employment and traditional occupations.
- Fodder Bank should be developed.
- Developing Mobile Veterinary Services at the Block-level.
- Strengthening the capacity of the local Panjarapol to reduce the vulnerability during the drought.
- Developing alternative source of livelihood like small-scale industries related to milk and its by-product can reduce migration.

References

http://gujaratquake.gov.in/final/indiaeq.html.
http://www.gujaratindia.com/
http://www.ifrc.org/
http://www.reliefweb.int/
http://www.southasiadisaaster.net/
www.irm.ernet.in

10

Persons with Disabilities, Challenges for Community Development and Social Work Intervention

P.J. Kochurani

Introduction

Disability is a longstanding issue of policy, planning and academic concern. A comprehensive legislation was passed by the Government of India in the session of the Parliament in the year 1995. In this Act the "Disability" means blindness, low vision, leprosy cured, hearing impairment, locomotor disability, mental retardation, and mental illness. Moreover, the National Trust Act 1999, include the name of disabled cerebral palsy, autism, multiple disability and mental retardation. Census 2001 has revealed that over 21 million people in India are suffering from one or the other kind of disability. This is equivalent to 2.1 per cent of the population. Among the total disabled in the country, 12.6 million are males and 9.3 million are females. It is an accepted fact that people with disabilities constitute nearly 4-5 per cent of our population and it is estimated that people with moderate to severe disabilities constitute 2-4 per cent. Having mentioned this, it is found to state that there is no authentic data on disabilities (Government of India, Office of the Registrar General and Census Commissioner, India, New Delhi).

For ensuring social equality and welfare, the uplifting of the poor and marginalized in the society is required. Disabled people are most deserving group among them. Now-a-days the welfare measures for the disabled are delivered through the Local Self-Government Institutions, Government Organizations and NGOs. For the successful planning and implementation of the welfare measures a correct baseline assessment data are required. At present the data available with the Government are incomplete, partial and not comprehensive. The researcher's last 12 years experience in the field of social work and disability, many of the Government organizations of Gram Panchayats did not achieve the targets and the welfare measures did not reach to the deserving candidates. These days the three-tiers panchayat system has resources to rehabilitate the PWDs however; they lack accurate data regarding the incidence of PWDs. The researcher also proves its of vital importance in the field of social work especially the field of the differently abled people.

There is a considerable gap between the data available from the local self-government institutions and the actual data collected by the researchers. Only a small portion of the disabled are included in the list available with the Gram Panchayat authorities. And also the data available with the authorities contain narrow and very vague informations like name, age and the nature of the disability. This limited information does not help us in the planning and implementation of the developmental strategies.

Objectives of the Study

1. To identify the data available with the Local Self-Government for Planning and Implementing welfare measures for the disabled;
2. To obtain a baseline assessment data from the ten Gram Panchayats;
3. To identify the gap between the actual data and available data from the Local Self-Government; and
4. To identify the total number of people with disability, nature of disability and to compare the available data with the collected data of disabilities in the target area.

Rationale of the Study

A study on this topic has great importance in the present day situation. In India Planning Services for the handicapped have been hampered by the absence of complete statistical data. The absence of the baseline data has created a great impact on the rehabilitation or self-reliance of the Persons with Disabilities. For planning and implementation of welfare measures, a comprehensive data regarding the disabled in the target population is required.

The researcher's experience as a social worker made a realization that there exists disparity between the available official data and collected door to door data, regarding persons with disabilities. This disparity can reduce the effect of the welfare and intervention provided to persons with disability.

This exploratory study is an effort to understand the disparity between the available Government data to that of the data being collected through door to door survey. This scientific work also helps increasing awareness among the Government institutions, NGOs and social workers about the inadequacy in the available data and also about the need for a comprehensive baseline assessment of the target area before planning and implementing the welfare measures.

The researcher also highlights the importance of accurate data of persons with disability for implementing and providing the necessary social services. This study may become a means of eye opening to the social workers, officials, rehabilitation specialists, and other agencies working in the field of disabilities.

Methodology of the Study

The present study is conducted at 10 Gram Panchayats of Ernakulam district, in Kerala State. The researcher has collected the data from the records kept at the Gram Panchayats and also conducted detailed unstructured interviews with the Officials. For collecting the factual data, the researcher conducted a door to door survey in the targeted 10 panchayaths. The researcher and the Community Based Rehabilitation (CBR) staff of the NGO had visited all the houses for identifying the persons with disabilities and collected the information with the help of a socio-demographic schedule.

There are 88 Gram Panchayats in Ernakulam district. Out of these 88 Gram Panchayats, the researcher selected 10 Gram Panchayats and conducted the detailed study in these 10 Gram Panchayats where the researcher involves in CBR works.

In the present study, the researcher has prepared a socio-demographic schedule for collecting the information about the persons with disabilities. This schedule contains 21 items. The researcher along with the CBR staff visited each and every house in these 10 Gram Panchayats and collected informations about the PWDs with the help of the Socio-demographic Schedule. The researcher collected the primary data through door-to-door survey and the secondary data from Gram Panchayat, Primary Health Centre, Integrated Child Development Scheme and Anganwadies. As a result of unstructured interviews with the officials of the 10 Gram Panchayats, it could be identified that the only available data regarding the persons with disabilities are collected from the pension list which is the only evidence concerning the same.

Results and Discussion

I. Data Available with Gram Panchayats

This section is to explore the available or existing data in 10 Gram Panchayats. To collect these data an unstructured interview was conducted with the staff of Gram Panchayat.

According to the data given by Gram Panchayat, the total number of people with disability ranged from 57 to 105 people. The official data revealed that the Thuravoor Panchayat had maximum number of persons with disability whereas the least was found in Paingotoor (Table 10.1 and Fig. 10.1).

II. Data Obtained in Baseline Assessment Study (Door-to-door Survey)

In the second section of the study, a door-to-door survey was conducted by the NGO staff. They visited to all houses in the 10 Gram Panchayat and had identified the number and nature of Disability.

The number of people with disability and the type of disability are discussed in sub-sections IIa and IIb respectively.

Table 10.1: Male, Female and Total Number of PWDs in 10 Gram Panchayats

Sl. No.	Name of the Gram Panchayat	Number of PWDs		Total
		Male	Female	
1.	Pothanicad	56	42	98
2.	Pallarimangalam	43	18	61
3.	Nellikuzhy	54	38	92
4.	Poothrikka	46	41	87
5.	Mazhuvannoor	39	30	69
6.	Paipra	28	30	58
7.	Ayyampuzha	42	37	79
8.	Mookkannoor	32	48	80
9.	Thuravoor	49	56	105
10.	Paingottoor	44	13	57

Source: Data collected from the field for the present study.

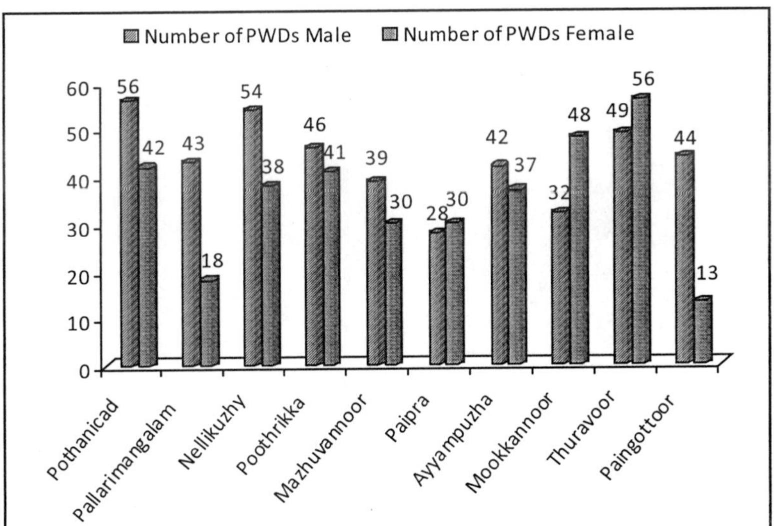

Fig. 10.1: Number of Males and Females with Disability in 10 Gram Panchayats

Source: Data collected from the field for the present study.

II (a): The Total Number of Persons with Disabilities

Table 10.2 and Fig. 10.2 provides data regarding the number of PWD in the 10 Gram Panchayats through door-to-door survey.

Table 10.2: Male, Female and Total Number of PWDs in 10 Gram Panchayats

Sl. No.	Name of the Gram Panchayat	Number of PWDs		Total
		Male	Female	
1.	Pothanicad	138	121	259
2.	Pallarimangalam	86	76	162
3.	Nellikuzhy	142	137	279
4.	Poothrikka	79	58	137
5.	Mazhuvannoor	94	72	166
6.	Paipra	103	107	210
7.	Ayyampuzha	88	83	171
8.	Mookkannoor	112	96	208
9.	Thuravoor	103	101	204
10.	Paingottoor	92	86	178

Source: Data collected from the field for the present study.

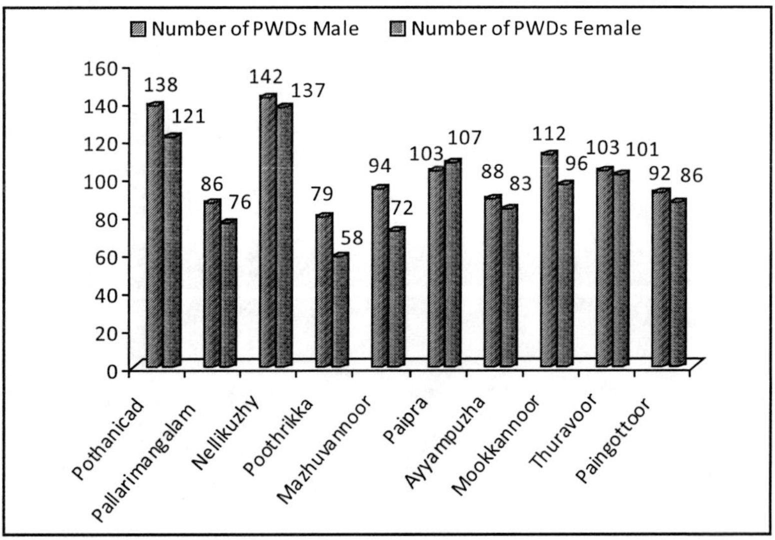

Fig. 10.2: Number of Males and Females with Disability in 10 Gram Panchayats

Source: Data collected from the field for the present study.

Table 10.2 and Fig. 10.2 indicates that the males are more prone to disability than females. This goes concurrent with the data published by the Government of India which indicated that, out of the total number of individuals with disability in India, 12.6 million are males and 9.3 million are females (Government of India, office of the Registrar General and Census Commissioner, India, New Delhi (2001). This trend was observed across all the 10 targeted Gram Panchayats. On door-to-door survey it was also identified that Nellikuzhy Gram Panchayat had highest disability count of 279 and Poorthuka Gram Panchayat had the least with a count of 137 PWD.

From section I and II it can be deducted that; when the available lists and the collected lists were compared there existed a drastic difference in the number of persons with disability across all the 10 Panchayats.

II (b): The Nature/Type of Disability

Table 10.3 and Fig. 10.3 below indicates the type of disability across the 10 panchayts. The type of disabilities considered according to the PWD Act, 1995 and National Trust Act, 1999 are blind, low vision, hearing impairment, orthopaedic handicap, mental illness, mental retardation, autism, cerebral palsy, multiple disability.

From Table 10.3 and Fig. 10.3, it is explicit that persons with orthopaedic disability is maximum across all panchayaths, followed by mental retardation and by hearing impairment and the least count was found for Autism across all Gram Panchayats. It can be substantiated that, the welfare strategies should be modified in a manner where it caters the needs of the orthopaedic handicap maximally, i.e. the needs of individuals with orthopaedic handicap needs to be addressed more and the requirements such as wheel chairs, crutches, walkers, tricycle etc. and other income generation programmes should be implemented.

A study conducted by National Sample Survey Organization (NSSO) indicated that there are 18.53 million people with disabilities in India as per July to December 2002 estimates, which form 1.8 per cent of total population in which the prevalence of locomotor disability is the most common form of disability (NSSO, 2001). The present study goes hand in hand with the findings of the NSSO, 2001.

Table 10.3: The distribution of the Type/Kinds of Disability in 10 Gram Panchayats by Door-to-door Survey

Sl. No.	Name of the Gram Panchayat	Blind	Low Vision	Hearing Impaired	Orthopaedic Handicap	Mental Illness	Mental Retardation	Autism	Cerebral Palsy	Multiple Disability	Total
1.	Pothanicad	9	13	45	68	19	68	1	4	32	259
2.	Pallarimangalam	2	4	32	41	12	34	0	4	33	162
3.	Nellikuzhy	11	11	45	74	19	69	4	4	42	279
4.	Poothrikka	8	13	20	42	8	30	0	2	14	137
5.	Mazhuvannoor	9	10	29	73	4	35	0	0	6	166
6.	Paipra	7	16	38	68	21	46	2	4	8	210
7.	Ayyampuzha	3	6	11	82	18	35	1	1	14	171
8.	Mookkannoor	4	4	15	89	26	41	6	7	16	208
9.	Thuravoor	2	6	17	85	32	31	4	15	12	204
10.	Paingottoor	11	2	22	71	10	30	1	3	28	178

Source: Data collected from the field for the present study.

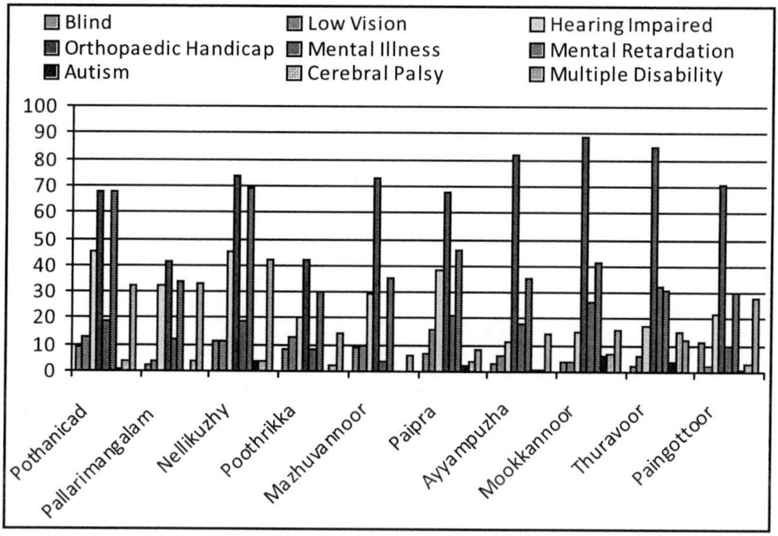

Fig. 10.3: The Distribution of the Type/kinds of Disability in 10 Gram Panchayats by Door-to-door Survey.

Source: Data collected from the field for the present study.

III. Comparison of the Data Obtained from the Gram Panchayats and from the Baseline Assessment Study

In section III, the existing data in 10 Gram Panchayats are being compared with the procured data from the same population. Table 10.4 and Fig. 10.4 compares the official and obtained data regarding the number of PWD in the 10 Gram Panchayats.

The data represented in Table 10.4 and Fig. 10.4 indicates that the data provided by the Government organization is incomplete, and not comprehensive. In all the 10 Gram Panchayats, from where the data was obtained, a considerable difference between the collected data and the data provided by the Gram Panchayats were observed. It can be observed that the number of PWD are doubled and tripled in 10 Gram Panchayats. This drastic difference in the number of PWD can be a threat in planning and implementing the welfare and developmental strategies for individuals with Disability. It is worth noticing that with the official data, only a small portion of individuals with disability are included and hence

Table 10.4: Existing and Procured Data of 10 Gram Panchayats Regarding PWDs

Sl.No.	Name of the Gram Panchayat	Data from Gram Panchayat Record	Data from Door-to-Door Survey
1.	Pothanicad	98	259
2.	Pallarimangalam	61	162
3.	Nellikuzhy	92	279
4.	Poothrikka	87	137
5.	Mazhuvannoor	69	166
6.	Paipra	58	210
7.	Ayyampuzha	79	171
8.	Mookkannoor	80	208
9.	Thuravoor	105	204
10.	Paingottoor	57	178

Source: Data collected from the field for the present study.

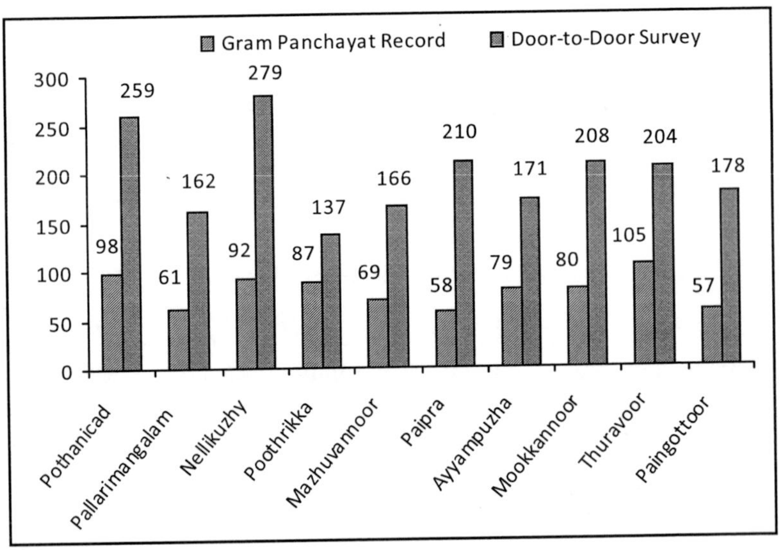

Fig. 10.4: *Comparison of Existing and Procured Data of 10 Gram Panchayats*

Source: Data collected from the field for the present study.

a large number of deserving candidates are deprived of the benefits and funds provided by Government and non-governmental organizations.

The procured/collected data plays a pivotal or crucial role in deciding the intervention; especially in the field of disability. This study highlighted that, the official data are not accurate and reliable for working with the persons with disabilities. So, to find out the original data is always a challenge for the social worker.

IV. Data Related to Paingottoor Gram Panchayat

In this section a complete data of PWD is demonstrated where the total number and nature of disability is identified for Paingottoor Gram Panchayat. This data gives the clarity of the nature and characteristics of the distribution of the disabled in Paingottoor Panchayat. An effort is also made to compare data obtained through door to door survey to that of other primary or existing data/lists of PWD given by the panchayats.

Table 10.5 and Fig. 10.5 represents the age-wise distribution and nature of disability. This enables us to identify which age group has more disability and also can help in deciding the welfare strategies.

Table 10.5: Age Distribution of Disability in Paingottoor Gram Panchayat

Sl. No.	Kinds of Disability	Paediatric (Below 10 Years)	Adolescent (11-18 Years)	Adulthood (19-55 Years)	Geriatric (Above 55 Years)	Total
1.	Blindness	1	0	9	6	16
2.	Low vision	0	0	2	0	2
3.	Hearing Impaired	0	2	11	2	15
4.	Orthopaedic Handicap	3	7	40	13	63
5.	Mental Illness	0	0	7	3	10
6.	Mental Retardation	9	15	2	13	39
7.	Autism	1	0	0	0	1
8.	Cerebral Palsy	1	4	0	1	6
9.	Multiple disability	5	9	7	5	26
	Total	20	37	78	43	178

Source: Data collected from the field for the present study.

From Fig. 10.5 it can be observed that the individuals belonging to adulthood (18-55 years) has more incidence of disability followed by Geriatric (above 55 years). Orthopaedic Handicap was most prevalent in adulthood whereas Mental Retardation outnumbered all the other disabilities in pediatric and adolescent group. Among Geriatric population, orthopedic disability and mental retardation had equal prevalence.

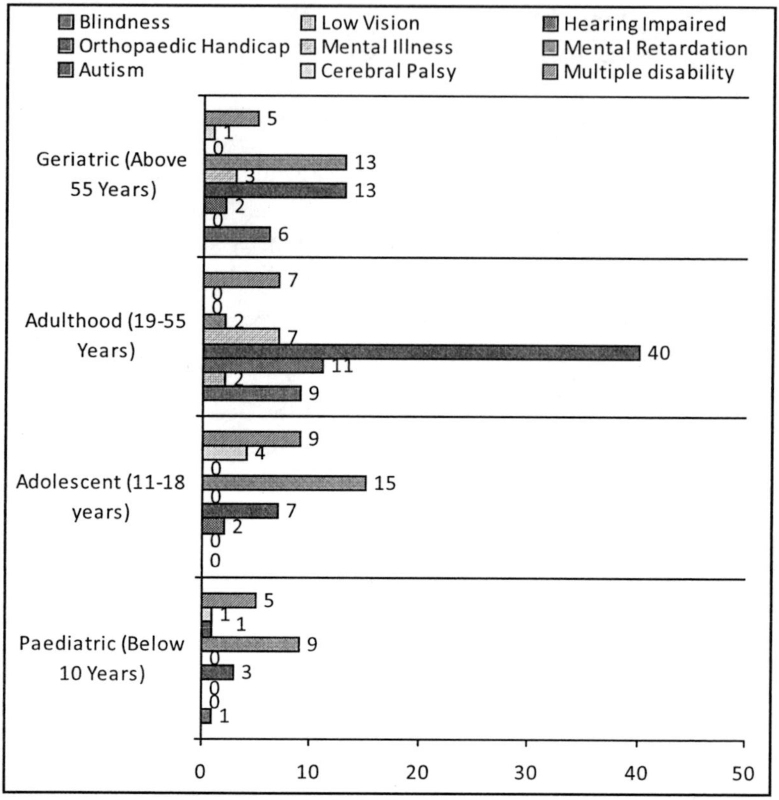

Fig. 10.5: Age Distribution of Disability in Paingottoor Gram Panchayat.

Source: Data collected from the field for the present study.

Various organizations have published their disability standards and the values are given in Table 10.6. The data obtained on door to door survey is also included in Table 10.6. For the administrative purpose of Paingottor Gram Panchayat is divided into 13 wards and have 16 anganwadies. The Primary Health Centres has been keeping records of PWDs since 2004, however they lack information on age, nature and extent of disability. The data obtained from ICDS office is also mentioned.

Comparisons between the data collected by 16 Anganwadies, ICDS office, PHC, Gram Panchayat office and door-to-door survey reveals that there existed a broad difference in the number of

Table 10.6: Comparison of Various Data Available Regarding the Disability Status in Paingottoor Gram Panchayat

Sources	Number of People with Disability
16 Anganwadies	125
ICDS Office	25
PHC	126
Gram Panchayat Office	57
Door-to-Door Survey	178

Source: Data Collected from the field for the present study.

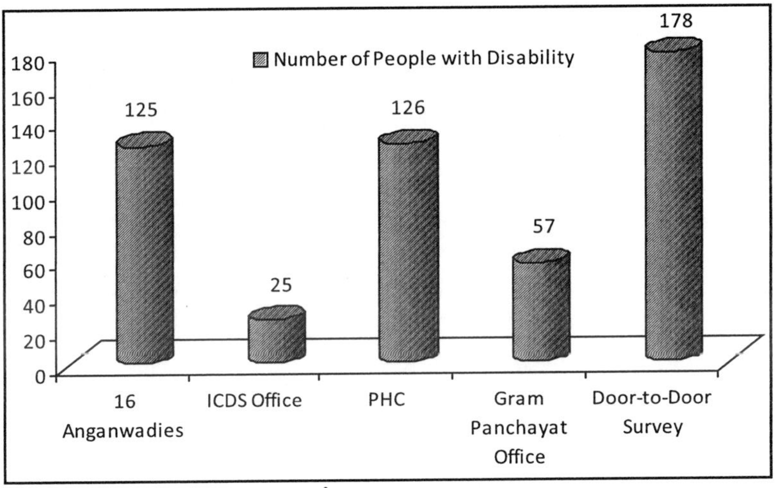

Fig. 10.6: Comparison of Various Available Sources

Source: Data collected from the field for the present study.

persons with disabilities. The data collected on door to door survey revealed the highest count of 178 PWD whereas all the other available secondary data showed a lesser count. Thus, it can be concluded that the data provided by Governmental and non-governmental organizations are incomplete and deficient. Hence, it is also advisable to collect an accurate count of the sample before the welfare strategies are implemented.

Conclusion

The magnitude of the problem of disability is vast and its impact is very severe on the individual, families and the community. So, it is important that we should have accurate data regarding people with disability. In this context the researcher has made an effort to compare the data provided by the panachayats and data collected by door-to-door survey in 10 *panchayats* of Ernakulam district, Kerala. Also the researcher analysed the data in terms of gender, age and type of disability.

The findings obtained shows that there exists a significant difference in the number of persons with disabilities when the two data sets were compared. The data obtained from the door to door survey showed that more number of males had disability than females. Also persons with orthopedic disability outnumbered all the other disabilities. It could be due to the summation of congenital (Cerebral Palsy) and acquired disabilities due to accidents and infections.

The age-wise distribution of disability showed that, maximum individuals with disability belonged to adulthood and hence, the welfare and supportive strategies need to be planned, by giving priority to this population.

So, finding out accurate data is necessary and it is a challenge for social workers who are involved in intervention programmes for PWD. Detailed household surveys are required for social work intervention and social development programmes, however, it is expensive and time consuming.

References

David, W., 1987, *Disabled Village Children: A Guide for Community Health Workers, Rehabilitation Workers and Families*, New Delhi: Voluntary Health Association of India.

Douglas, R., and Nancy, M.R., 1986, *Readings in Muscular Dystrophy*, London: Longman.

Government of India, 2001, *Disability Population in India*. New Delhi: Registrar General and Census Commissioner Office.

Mark, B.L., 2000, *Children with Disabilities* (4th Ed.). Baltimore: Paul H. Brookes Publishing Co.

Panneerselvam, R., 2009, *Research Methodology*, New Delhi: PHI Learning Private Limited.

11
Strengthening Mid-Day Meal Scheme through Social Work Intervention

Kaushalendra Pratap Singh

Introduction

A cooked mid-day meal makes the school attractive for the child and along with enrolment and attendance it impacts the learning process. It can help in improving the concentration levels, attentiveness and memory, particularly in the context in which children come to school on an empty stomach in the morning. This reduces the likelihood of children leaving school early because of hunger. The additional benefit of the Mid-Day Meal (MDM) is its significant social impacts. Children learn to sit and eat together often contributing to breaking barriers of caste and class. The mid-Day meal in a public space can also ensure equal access for girls. Thus, the scope of the study has the greater sense in its effective findings and bridging the gap of implementation in MDM. The scope can be seen in the following areas such as serves as an incentive for regular attendance, promoting social equity, providing income support to poor households, acts as a form of nutrition education, tackles hunger and can contribute all nutrients required.

Review of Studies

Independent evaluation studies on the Mid-Day Meal (MDM) have been conducted by different agencies in various parts of the country, which find *inter alia* enhancement in enrollment and attendance. The studies include:

- "Cooked Mid-Day Meal programme in West Bengal—A Study of Birbhum district". Professor Amartya Sen's Pratichi Research Team (2005). The study shows that Mid-Day Meal has made positive intervention in universalisation of primary education by increasing enrolment and attendance. The increase has been more marked with respect to girls and children belonging to SC/ST categories. The study also points out that Mid-Day Meal scheme has contributed to reduction in teacher absenteeism and a narrowing of social distances.
- "Situation Analysis of Mid-Day Meal Programme in Rajasthan". University of Rajasthan and UNICEF (2005): states that the introduction of menu based mid-day meal has positively impacted enrolment and attendance of children. It has contributed to social equity, as children sit together and share a common meal irrespective of caste and class. It has further contributed to gender equity in that it has provided employment to women.
- "Mid-day Meal in Madhya Pradesh": Samaj Pragati Sahyog, 2005: Undertook a survey in 70 most backward villages. The findings show that there was a 15 per cent increase in enrolment, which was more marked in the case of SC and ST children (43%).
- "Mid-Day Meals: A Comparison of the Financial and Institutional Organization of the Programme in Two States", Farzana Afridi; April *EPW* (2005): The implementation of the programme is improving, but a lot more needs to be done. The new initiative of 'Suruchi Bhojan' is more attractive than the earlier '*Daliya*' programme.
- "Mid-Day Meal Scheme in Delhi—A functioning programme" Anuradha De, Claire Noronha and Meera Samson; CORD; (2005). Surveyed 12 MCD schools—school children in all schools were receiving food; impact of attendance more likely on girls, who often come to school without breakfast.

- "Report on Akshara Dasoha scheme of Karnataka", Dr. Rama Naik; University of Dharwad (205). Has reported sharp rise in enrolment, particularly in rural areas. The programme has had an impact on teacher absenteeism: 64 per cent schools stated that teacher absenteeism has been reduced.
- National Council of Educational Research & Training's latest Report (2005)—Learning Achievement of Students at the End of Class-V has inferred that children covered under mid-day meal have higher achievement level than those who were not covered under it.
- "Mid-Day Meal Scheme in Karnataka—A study" by National Institute of Public Cooperation and Child Development, Annual Report 2005-06: Mid-Day Meal improved the school attendance in majority of the schools and reduced absenteeism. It has fostered a sense of sharing and fraternity and paved the way for social equity.
- "Mid-Day Meal Scheme in Madhya Pradesh—A study-2007" by National Institute of Public Cooperation & Child Development, Indore: School enrolment indicated marked improvement in enrolment pattern of children in primary school. Mid-Day Meal Scheme undoubtedly resulted in increased school attendance and facilitated in retention of children in school for a longer period. The Scheme has played a crucial role in reducing dropout, especially among girls. Parents viewed that the mid-day meal had reduced the burden of providing one time meal to their children and considered it as a great support to their families. Teachers opined that mid-day meal aided in active learning of children, which indirectly improved their academic performance. The Scheme has played a significant role in bringing social equity.

Objectives of the Study

The present study in three primary schools of district Lucknow was originally instituted to evolve some strategies to strengthen MDM scheme for the upliftment of the community, to improve the primary education, and to improve nutritional status of children. The specific objectives of the study are given below:

- to assess the existing situation of MDM in the selected schools, and
- to highlight the role of social work intervention in strengthening MDM scheme.

Methodology

A research design is a systematic plan to study a scientific problem. The design of a study defines the study type. In this study descriptive research design was used. Descriptive research is used to describe characteristics of a population or phenomenon being studied (Shields, Patricia and Rangarajan, 2013). Three primary schools namely P.S. Kila Mohammed Nagar, P.S. Tode Kheda and P.S. Aurangabad from Lucknow district were selected as a sample unit of the study by applying purposive sampling method (Table 11.1). As the study was an independent without any funding so for avoiding extra expenditure, nearest schools were selected.

Table 11.1: Covered Schools

Sl. No.	Particulars	1. School	2. School	3. School
1.	District	Lucknow	Lucknow	Lucknow
2.	School Code	09270900306	09270916076	09270911116
3.	School Name	P.S. Kila Mohammed Nagar	P.S. Tode Kheda	P.S. Aurangabad
4.	Block	Nagar Shaitra	Nagar Shaitra	Nagar Shaitra
5.	Cluster	Aurangabad	Aurangabad	Bhapta Mau
6.	Village	Ward 3	Kila Mohammdi	Ward
7.	Boys	45	80	51
8.	Girls	51	93	75
9.	Total Students	96	173	126
10.	Male Teacher	—	1	1
11.	Female Teacher	2	2	3
12.	Total Teachers	2	3	4
13.	Pupil-teacher Ratio	48	58	32
14.	Student-Classroom Ratio	48	87	25

Source: http://www.schoolreportcards.in/

A combination of various methods of data collection was adopted at each level-structured interview schedule supported by focused group discussion and firsthand observation formed part of primary assessment. Whereas, a wide range of secondary materials were accessed, reviewed and analyzed to support the hypothesis of the study. Interview Schedule was administered to undertake probe at the level of—(a) teachers, (b) families of students, (c) stakeholder providing MDM to schools, (d) Government officials those are responsible for implementation processes, and (e) NGOs that play crucial role in facilitating MDM. A crucial part formed in the primary investigation is probing with students.

Brief Description about the Schools

School–1: P.S. Kila Mohammed Nagar (*Ref. Map 11.1: Coverage Area*)

The school was established in 1960 and it is managed by the Department of Education. It is located in urban area. It is situated at a distance of about 5 km. from the Block Resource centre. It is located in Nagar Shaitra, Lucknow block of Lucknow district of Uttar Pradesh. The school consists of Grades from 1 to 5. The school is co-educational and it does not have an attached pre-primary section. The school is non-residential in nature and is not using school building as a shift-school. It had no academic inspection and was not visited by the CRC and BRC Coordinators during the previous academic year. Hindi is the medium of instructions in this school. This school is not approachable by all weather roads.

School–2: P.S. Tode Kheda (*Ref. Map 11.1: Coverage Area*)

The school was established in 2000 and it is managed by the Department of Education. It is located in urban area. It is situated at a distance of about less than 1 km. from the Block Resource centre. It is located in Nagar Shaitra, Lucknow block of Lucknow district of Uttar Pradesh. The school consists of Grades from 1 to 5. The school is co-educational and it does not have an attached

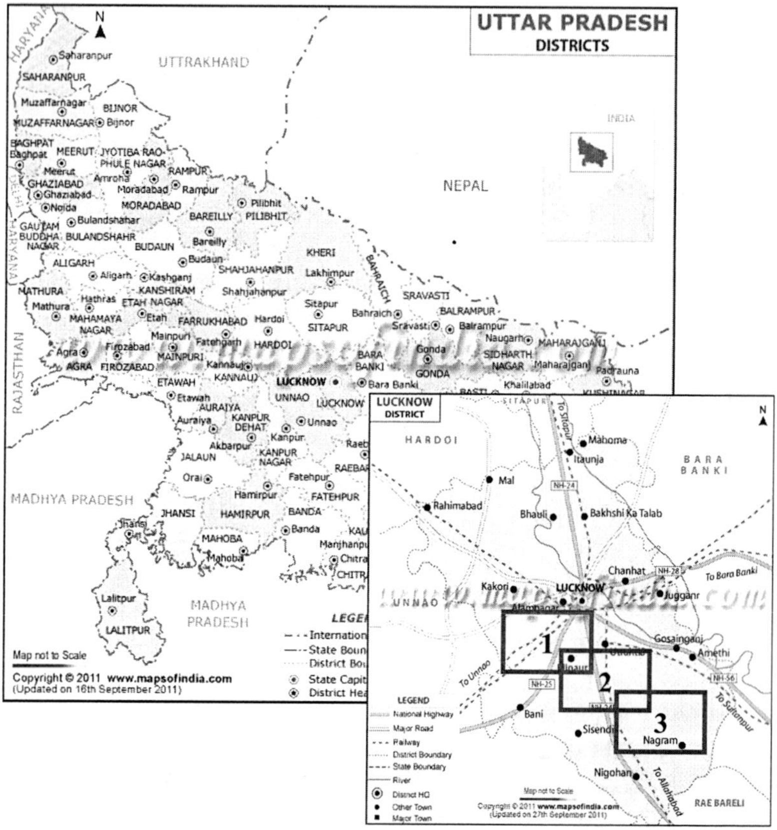

Map 11.1: Coverage Area.

pre-primary section. The school is non-residential in nature and is not using school building as a shift-school. It had no academic inspection and was not visited by the CRC and BRC Coordinators during the previous academic year. Hindi is the medium of instructions in this school. This school is not approachable by all weather roads.

School–3: P.S. Aurangabad (Ref. Map 11.1: Coverage Area)

The school was established in 1972 and it is managed by the Department of Education. It is located in urban area. It is situated at a distance of about less than 1 km. from the Block Resource center. It is located in Nagar Shaitra, Lucknow block of Lucknow district of Uttar Pradesh. The school consists of Grades from 1 to 5. The school is co-educational and it does not have an attached pre-primary section. The school is non-residential in nature and is not using school building as a shift-school. It had no academic inspection and was not visited by the CRC and BRC Coordinators during the previous academic year. Hindi is the medium of instructions in this school. This school is not approachable by all weather roads.

Key Findings

Table 11.2: Basic Information about the Study Area

Schools	Facilities in School	Teachers	Enrolment
(1)	(2)	(3)	(4)
School–1: P.S. Kila Mohammed Nagar	The school has no building block. It has got 2 classrooms for instructional purposes. All the classrooms are in good condition. It has no other room for non-teaching activities. The school does not have a separate room for Head Master. The school has got no boundary wall. The school does not have electricity connection. The source of Drinking Water in the school is hand Pump. The school has a playground. The school does not have a library. The school did not arrange medical check-up for its students during the previous	The school does not have a regular Head Master. The school has 2 regular teachers in position against a sanctioned strength of 4 posts. All the teachers of school are female teachers. It has no Contract Teacher. The school does not have non-teaching staff. All teachers of school are having graduate and above degrees. On the other hand, all teachers have professional certifica-tion(s)/ degree(s). The Pupil-Teacher Ratio (PTR) of the school is 48:1 and the Student-	The total enrolment of school is 96, out of which boys' enrolment is 45 (46.9 per cent) and girls' enrolment, 51 (53.1 per cent). The SC enrolment is 62 (64.6 per cent), ST enrolment, zero and OBC enrolment, 25 (26.0 per cent). No student repeated primary grades during the previous academic year. The school has 2 disabled children.

(*Contd.*)

(1)	(2)	(3)	(4)
	academic year. It has got ramp for the disabled children. The school has got 2 blackboards for the use of teachers and 3 blackboards at the ground level for the use of children. The school does not have a computer. The school hasn't received the one time kitchen devices grant.	Classroom Ratio (SCR), 48:1. On an average, about 48 students sit in one classroom which sounds bit uncomfortable.	
School–2: P.S. Tode Kheda	The school has no building block. It has got 2 classrooms for instructional purposes. All the classrooms are in good condition. It has no other room for non-teaching activities. The school does not have a separate room for Head Master. The school has got pucca boundary wall. The school does not have electricity connection. The source of Drinking Water in the school is Hand Pump. The school has a playground. The school does not have a library. The school did not arrange medical check-up for its students during the previous academic year. It has got ramp for the disabled children. The school has got 2 blackboards for the use of teachers but it does not have	The school has 2 regular teachers in position against a sanctioned strength of 2 posts. In addition, the school has got 1 contract teacher. The school does not have non-teaching staff. All teachers of school are having graduate and above degrees. The Pupil-Teacher Ratio (PTR) of the school is 58:1 and the Student-Classroom Ratio (SCR), 87:1. On an average, about 87 students sit in one classroom which sounds un-comfortable.	The total enrolment of school is 173, out of which boys' enrolment is 80 (46.2 per cent) and girls' enrolment, 93 (53.8 per cent). The SC enrolment is 53 (30.6 per cent), ST enrolment, zero and OBC enrolment, 38 (22.0 per cent). No student repeated primary grades during the previous academic year. The school did not have disabled children.

(*Contd.*)

(1)	(2)	(3)	(4)
	blackboard at the ground level for the use of children. The school does not have a computer. The school hasn't received the one time kitchen devices grant.		
School–3: P.S. Aurangabad	The school has no building block. It has got 5 classrooms for instructional purposes. All the classrooms are in good condition. It has no other room for non-teaching activities. The school does not have a separate room for Head Master. The school has got no boundary wall. The school does not have electricity connection. The source of Drinking Water in the school is hand Pump. The school has a playground. The school does not have a library. The school did not arrange medical check-up for its students during the previous academic year. It has got ramp for the disabled children. The school has got 5 blackboards for the use of teachers but it does not have blackboard at the ground level for the use of children. The school does not have a computer. The school hasn't received the one time kitchen devices grant.	The school does not have a regular Head Master/ Teacher. The school has 3 regular teachers in position against a sanctioned strength of 3 posts. In addition, the school has got 1 Contract Teacher. The school does not have non-teaching staff. Precisely, 1 teacher of school is having graduate and above degrees. On the other hand, all teachers have professional certification(s)/ degree(s). The Pupil-Teacher Ratio (PTR) of the school is 32:1 and the Student-Classroom Ratio (SCR), 25:1. On an average, about 25 students sit in one classroom which sounds comfortable.	The total enrolment of school is 126, out of which boys' enrolment is 51 (40.5 per cent) and girls' enrolment, 75 (59.5 per cent). The SC enrolment is 31 (24.6 per cent), ST enrolment, zero and OBC enrolment, zero. No student repeated primary grades during the previous academic year. The school did not have disabled children.

Source: Author's Study Area.

Management of MDM

The Central guidelines allow State Governments to manage the MDM through a designated nodal department such as school education, rural development, women and child development, or social welfare, Non-Governmental Organizations (NGOs) have also been permitted to be involved in the provision of MDM. There are significant variations in management system among these three schools. Various management issues have emerged in recent studies, e.g., irregular supplies, inadequate monitoring, incomplete reimbursement of fuel or transport costs, low and delayed remuneration of cooks and helpers, etc. Aside from disrupting MDM, these hurdles create incentives for corruption. For example, inadequate transport funds create a temptation to recover the costs by selling some of the rice meant for children.

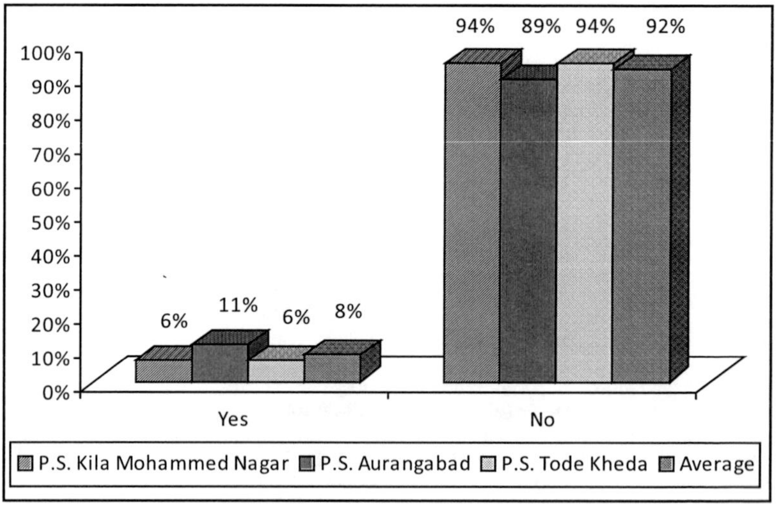

Fig. 11.1: Do Students get Meal if they Want to Take Second Time?

Source: Primary data collected from the fields for the present study.

In urban areas, a common approach is to cook the meals in centralized kitchens and transport them to the schools. Also, NGOs often provide the meals on a contract basis. This approach seems to work reasonably well in some cases. There is anecdotal evidence (e.g., from media reports) of serious problems in the provision of

Mid-day Meals in many urban areas, partly due to crowding, inadequate infrastructure and lack of hygiene. Public-private partnerships are fraught with potential dangers, including the perverse influence of commercial lobbies and the possible use of mid-day meals as a platform for the pursuit of private agendas. These relatively new initiatives are spreading rapidly, but require close scrutiny and evaluation. Monitoring mechanisms vary across states. While some have tried to involve the community, it seems unlikely that monitoring by the community (generally the mothers) will be sufficient.

- MDM is being conducted by the Village Education Committee (VEC), there is no role of SHG and other kind of organization to conduct mid-day meal.
- MDM helpers are mostly being appointed by the Gram Pradhans.
- Wheat and rice for MDM is being arranged through Sarvjanik Vitran Pranali, Kotedar and Pradhan as well.
- On an average 92 students do not get the meal if they want to take second time. Highest 11 per cent students get second time meal if they want. (Ref. Fig. 11.1: Do students get meal second time?)

Status of MDM in the Project Area

Enrolment, Retention and Attendance

By all available accounts, the MDM has led to a substantial increase in the enrolment of children in primary schools. In fact, several micro-studies point to major increases in enrolment immediately after the introduction of mid-day meals.

Even more encouraging than the overall increase in enrolment figures is the in-crease in enrolment of girls. Dreze and Kingdon (2001) found convincing evidence for this based on household data pertaining to primary schooling in 1996. They found that the provision of mid-day meals, on average, halves the proportion of girls excluded from the schooling system (*Ibid.*, 20). In most of the studies reviewed here, girls' enrolment records a much higher increase than overall increase in enrolment.

Similarly, there is a greater impact on the enrollment of children from disadvantaged families, dalits, scheduled tribes, and the poor. This is as one would expect since those are the families that need MDM most. Poor working mothers are particularly happy with the programme as it frees them from the burden of feeding children during the day. Many of these studies also hint at an improvement in attendance rates as well as retention rates. However, since both are difficult to measure, the evidence remains inconclusive.

Food Supervision

On an average 78 per cent food supervision in all selected schools is missing. Maximum 29 per cent in P.S. Aurangabad MDM is being supervised by the concerned authorities (Ref. Fig.11.2: Food supervision).

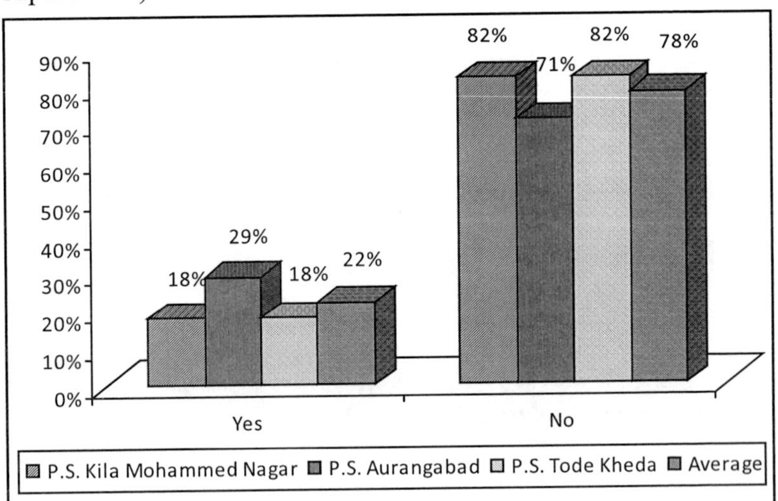

Fig. 11.2: Food Supervision

Source: Primary Data Collected from the Fields for the Present Study.

Nutritional and Health Impact

The nutritional impact of mid-day meals depends both on the quality and the quantity of food provided at school. These in-turn depend *inter alia* on the budget, which affects the menu as well as cooking practices (e.g., safety and hygiene). According to the Supreme Court order, the school meal is supposed to provide 300 kCal and 8-10 gm of protein. On the quantity of food provided, there are two key issues: (a) whether the SC order is being complied with; and (b) whether the quantities prescribed by the SC order are adequate. Some studies have noted that the amount of food provided by schools does not meet the SC norms.

The quality of the meal is the main remaining challenge as far as the MDM is concerned. Reports of children being taken ill after consuming the mid-day meal have occasionally made headlines in various parts of the country. Besides these occasional incidents, nutritive value of the meal needs to be monitored carefully. This depends on the menu as well as cooking practices in schools.

Provision of micro-nutrients (such as iron, vitamin A and iodine) and deworming tablets are other simple and low-cost health interventions that can be fruitfully combined with the MDM. The issue of micro-nutrient supplements, however, needs further discussion in so far as nutrient such as zinc are concerned.

Socialization and Educational Benefits

The socialization benefits of MDM can also be substantial, though these seem to have taken a backseat as the nuts and bolts of putting the system in place have been the main preoccupation of the administration. Good MDM also encourage education activities at school to the extent that they make the school environment more inviting for children.

Infrastructure Issues

A good MDM programme requires sound infrastructure. This includes physical infrastructure such as water supply, kitchen sheds and storage facilities. Adequate staff is also needed for organizing and cooking the meal as well as for serving it to the children. The lack of adequate infrastructure undermines the objectives of the MDM in two ways: one, by causing obstructions in the teaching activities in school and two, by reducing the nutritive impact of the meal. Adequate infrastructure is also very important for safety and hygiene.

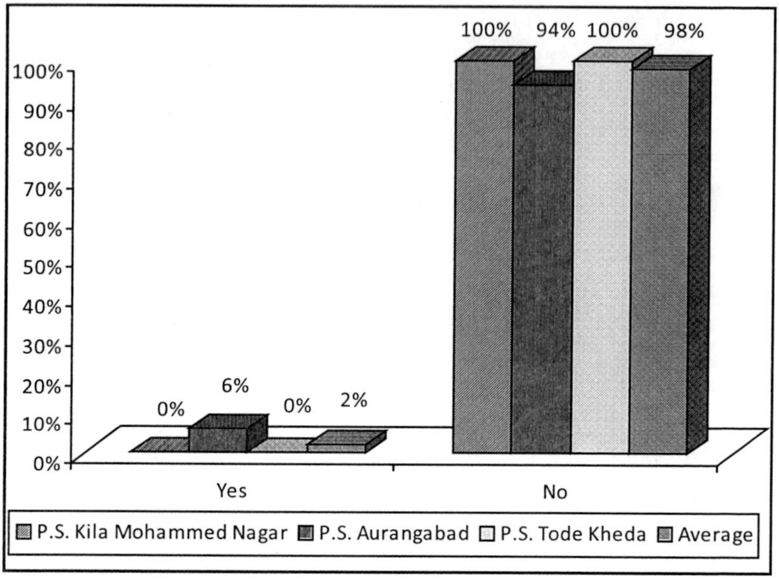

Fig. 11.3: Do Parents Know about this Scheme?

Source: Primary data collected from the fields for the present study.

Awareness of MDM Scheme to Parents

Mostly parents are not aware about the technicalities of the MDM scheme. About 98 per cent on an average parents are not aware, maximum 6 per cent of P.S. Aurangabad's students' parents are slightly aware about the scheme but not in intensity (Ref. Fig. 11.3).

Social Work Intervention

The experience so far clearly shows that mid-day meals have much to contribute to the well-being and future of Indian children. As things stand, mid-day meal programmes have many flaws, but the way to go is forward and not backward. With adequate resources and quality safeguards, mid-day meals can play a major role in improving school attendance, eliminating classroom hunger and fostering social equity. Having said this, qualitative improvements are urgently required if mid-day meals are to achieve their full potential. The survey findings suggest a number of priorities for action. First, financial allocations need to be raised. With the programme in place, additional expenditure is likely to be very effective in enhancing the quality of the mid-day meals. Second, the mid-day meal infrastructure calls for urgent improvement. All primary schools need a cooking shed, and most cooks need a helper. Schools also require better utensils, storage facilities, water supply, and related facilities. Adequate infrastructure is particularly crucial to avoid the disruption of classroom processes, and also to ensure good hygiene. Third, the monitoring system needs to be overhauled. Close supervision and regular inspections are essential to achieve higher quality standards. Better monitoring would also help to eradicate petty corruption, such as the pilferage of food by various intermediaries. Fourth, the socialization value of mid-day meals can be enhanced in various ways. Instances of social discrimination at school have to be firmly dealt with. Clear guidelines for the selection of cooks need to be issued and enforced. And the lunchtime routine can be used to impart various good habits to children, such as washing one's hands before and after eating. Fifth, the issue of dalit cooks calls for specific attention. Yet this is also an opportunity to break traditional prejudices and foster social change. Sixth, there is a case for more varied and nutritious lunch menus. Seventh, there is much potential for linking mid-day meals with related inputs such as micronutrient supplementation, health services and nutrition education. As discussed earlier, some of these complementary inputs (e.g., deworming combined with iron supplementation and vitamin A) can make a major difference to children's nutrition at negligible cost.

The central focus of social work has been to help the helpless to help themselves. On the basis of its central theme social workers try to help individuals, groups, and communities. Social work has wide range of activities such as social reforms at one end and at the micro-level it helps individual in need. Social Workers are imbibed with social work values and principles such as respect for the dignity and uniqueness of an individual, and recognition of client's self-determination, principle of acceptance, individualization, confidentiality, etc. as a matrix of social work practice with different clients. Social work has six unique methods to solve the various problems at individual, group and community level. The primary methods are social case work, group work and community organization. The social worker engaged in the welfare of the community uses casework method coupled with group work and community organization. Social worker uses scientific method to solve the problem of society and applies problem solving approach. Firstly, social worker identifies the problems and assessed it, later on worker provides treatment against the existing problems, and finally evaluates the entire process. During this entire process worker follows values of dignity and worth of the individual and applies the principles of acceptance, confidentiality and non-judgmental attitude. In working with community, a social worker assumes a variety of professional roles, which are primarily (i) enabler, (ii) broker, (iii) analyst, (iv) catalyst, (v) advocate, and (vi) expert etc.

Therefore, Social intervention is highly suited in strengthening the mid-day meal schemes because it has various sections and stakeholders to whom social worker can easily tackle. Following strategies can be used to strengthen MDM through social work intervention.

- By strengthening and capacitating to concerned staffs and authorities.
- Through creating awareness among community and other stakeholders.
- Using the holistic approach of implementation.
- Regular monitoring and evaluation.
- Transparency in buying food grains.
- Avoiding discrepancy among children.
- Sensitizing parents, children and school staff members.
- By maintaining hygiene, sanitation and drinking water facilities.
- System approach and integrated social work approach, and generic method approach would be very effective in practicing the above strategies.
- By appointing social work professionals so that they can regularize the scheme in order.

Thus, we have seen that there is huge potential in MDM scheme to promote primary education but still there are some gaps at the end of different stakeholders which can be fulfilled through social work intervention by appointing social work professionals in this scheme. Social Work professionals are equipped with skills and knowledge and can play a vital role as an expert, researcher, enabler, advocate, executer in strengthening mid-day meal scheme for the better future of the nation.

References

Afridi, F., 2005, "Mid-Day Meals: A Comparison of the Financial and Institutional Organization of the Programme in Two States", *Economic and Political Weekly*, 40(15): 1529-34.

De, A., Noronha, C. and Samson, M., 2005, "On the Brink of Adulthood: Glimpses of Schooling and Work in the Lives of Adolescents", *Draft Report Submitted to DFID*.

Dreze, J. and Goyal, A., 2003, "Future of Mid-Day Meals", *Economic and Political Weekly*, 38(44): 4673-4683.

Khera, Reetika, 2006, "Mid-Day Meals in Primary Schools—Achievements and Challenges", *Economic and Political Weekly*, 41(46): 4742-4750.

Naik, R., 2005, *Report on Akshara Dasoha Scheme of Karnataka*, Dharwad: University of Dharwad.

Samaj Pragati Sahyog, 2005, *Mid-Day Meal in Madhya Pradesh*, For details, visit: http://www.samprag.org

Sen, A. and Pratichi Research Team, 2005, *Cooked Mid-Day Meal Programme in West Bengal—A Study of Birbhum District*, Delhi: Pratichi (India) Trust.

Shields, Patricia and Rangarajan, N., 2013, *A Playbook for Research Methods: Integrating Conceptual Frameworks and Project Management*, Stillwater, OK: New Forums Press.

Singh, S.B., 2004, "Future of Mid-Day Meals", *Economic and Political Weekly*, 39 (9): 998-1000.

www.nipccd.nic.in/res.htm

12

Tribal Development through Poverty Alleviation Schemes
Perception and Attitude

Sujit Kumar Paul and *Kakali Paul Mitra*

Introduction

Tribal society is normally conceptualized as clan-lineage based segmentary system characterized by mechanical solidarity. Beteille (1977), described the tribe as a society; further society based on kinship, where social stratification is absent. Broadly tribe is an aggregate of people sharing social values, common dialect, territory and culture. But in a restricted sense, tribe means "a group of people under a chief and maintaining distinct cultural traits". The ways of livelihood of Indian tribe are several and it is true that they cannot be exclusively placed in a particular typology in its strict sense. They use all available means to eke out its subsistence and make complex economy, though the tribesmen of India have their primary means of economy that grading from hunting and gathering stage to settled agricultural stage according to varied environmental circumstances of the country. Thus, over 8 per cent of India's total population, the tribals have a variety in their culture, lifestyle and above all different customs and worldview of their own. Today despite their adaptation and exposure to the culture of larger society, modernization, industrialization; live in a world of dynamic isolation that helps the tribal to maintain its distinct socio-cultural identity.

Since Independence, considering the general socio-economic backwardness of the tribal communities, Government of India has been planning and launching programmes to develop and integrate them with the mainstream of Indian national life. To sustain the Constitutional safeguards given to them, Government adopted so many programmes through the Plan periods. The Fifth Five-Year Plan is considered as the turning point in the history of tribal development in the post-Independent India for the launching of Tribal Sub-Plan. Initially, it was an area development programme. But in the subsequent plan periods it was becoming a target group approach where individual family were to benefit specifically for the programme to build-up their economic base. The objective of assisting the targeted number of tribal families is to cross the poverty line and to increase the access to health, education and employment opportunities and thereby to improve their quality of life.

In the course of tribal development approaches in the post-Independent India the Fifth Five-Year Plan may be mentioned as the turning point for the launching of Integrated Tribal Development Programme (ITDP). ITDP was launched in the year 1972. During Sixth Plan, emphasis was placed more on family oriented programmes than on infrastructure development. Thus, from the Sixth Plan period it was becoming a target group approach where individual families were to benefit specially from the programme. During the Seventh Plan Tribal Development with ITDP pattern was continued without any basic changes in the approach, pattern or structure. In this plan period thirty lakhs tribal families were assisted to build-up their economic base. The Eighth Five-Year Plan gave emphasis on development of essential infrastructure facilities to achieve the objective of assisting the targeted number of tribal families to cross the poverty line and to increase their access to health, education and employment opportunities. These families were selected on the basis of their absolute economic status, the poorest being given the first preference.

In Birbhum District of West Bengal, ITDP was introduced in the year 1983. If the number of beneficiaries in the study area is considered, it is found that 30.53 per cent of the total tribal population is under these schemes. Various kinds of schemes have introduced for the tribal people. Some of the schemes are meant for agriculture; some are employment and income generating schemes. From the primary field investigation, it was noticed that some beneficiaries are conducting the schemes successfully and in some cases schemes are become failure. However, there remain some factors for non-feasibility of the loans.

From the very beginning of the tribal development it was realized that no development activity could be of benefit to the tribal population unless their exploitation was prevented and an integrated credit-*cum*-marketing services developed in the sub-plan areas. Hence, elimination of exploitation was given priority in objectives of Tribal Sub-Plan. Priority was also given to do away with middlemen and the moneylenders. But elimination of exploitation has limited success. Inspite of financial assistance though ITDP loans, private sources are also being used by the tribal people side by side. Private sources are still standing between the development agencies and the beneficiaries as an alternative.

It is necessary to evaluate the tribal development programmes in the micro-level for identifying the emerging issues, problems and changes after its long-run implementation for the upliftment of the tribal people to integrate them in the mainstream. It is however, essential to know the economic, social and cultural needs of the people's own, to fill-up the gaps between their actual needs and incentives offered by the Government. The scope of family benefit schemes is quite large, but this kind of institutional credit covers only a part of the poor tribal people's huge canvas of needs. More precisely, it may be said that the institutional credit deals with the situations which have some limitations.

From this point of view, an attempt has been made to study the perception and attitude of the tribal beneficiaries about the poverty alleviation schemes those are running under this project. It was also been made to understand their own perception about their actual need.

Study Area

The present study has been conducted in 16 ITDP mouzas of Bolpur-Sriniketan Block of Birbhum district of West Bengal. These ITDP mouzas are located in 2 Panchayats. Total 264 households were identified. Four tribal groups are present in the study area. They are the Santal, the Mahali, the Kora and the Oraon/Sardar. Out of 264 beneficiary households, 223 households (84.47%) are the Santals. Eighteen households are the Mahalis (6.82%). Eighteen households are Oraons who call themselves as Sardars. Only five households are the Koras, i.e. 1.89 per cent. Total population of 264 beneficiary households is 1474, of which 772 (52.37%) are male and 702 (47.63%) are female. The total population of Santal beneficiary households is 1249. It is highest among the four communities of the study area.

The Schemes

From the field investigation, we found 16 different schemes in the study area. These are distributed among the beneficiaries either single scheme or two different schemes at a time as an integrated scheme and considered as a single scheme. In Tables 12.1 and 12.2, different schemes and their acceptance pattern by 264 beneficiaries are found according to their land size.

Here, it is noticed that some schemes are directly related to agriculture, some schemes are rearing animals and poultry birds, some for business purposes and some for Rickshaw and Rickshaw-van pulling. Besides, these schemes, bamboo work is a scheme introduced in this area especially for Mahalis, the traditional basket-makers. All these schemes are of two categories, one is crop loan, given for short-term, generally for six months. It is primarily for seasonal agricultural operations. It includes providing seeds, fertilizer, pesticides etc. Besides short-term crop loan, all others are medium-term loans and financed partly by subsidy and partly by bank loans and margin money. The capital cost of the projects are subsidized by 50 per cent, 20 per cent is margin money which is a share of State Government and rest 30 per cent is bank loan financed by Commercial Gramin Banks. Bank loan should be

Table 12.1: Acceptance Pattern of Schemes: According to the Land Size

(More than one Schemes)

Sl. No.	Name of the Scheme	Land Size (in Acre)					
		Landless	0.1 - 2.50	2.51 - 5.00	5.01 - 7.50	Above 7.50	Total
1.	Calf rearing + Goatary	13 (50.00)	26 (50.00)	1 (5.00)	1 (50.00)	—	41 (41.00)
2.	Calf rearing + Sheep	4 (15.38)	1 (01.92)	2 (10.00)	—	—	7 (7.00)
3.	Calf rearing + Rice Processing	3 (11.54)	6 (11.54)	2 (10.00)	—	—	11 (11.00)
4.	Rickshaw + Rice Processing	1 (03.85)	—	—	—	—	1 (1.00)
5.	Veg. Vending + Calf rearing	2 (07.69)	2 (03.85)	—	—	—	4 (4.00)
6.	Duckary + Calf rearing	1 (03.85)	1 (01.92)	—	—	—	2 (2.00)
7.	Rickshaw + Calf rearing	—	1 (01.92)	—	—	—	1 (1.00)
8.	Van + Calf rearing	1 (03.85)	1 (01.92)	—	—	—	2 (2.00)
9.	Bullock Cart + Short-term	—	3 (05.78)	11 (55.00)	—	—	14 (14.00)
10.	Calf rearing + Milch cow	—	1 (01.92)	—	—	—	1 (1.00)
11.	Calf rearing + Short-term	—	—	1 (5.00)	—	—	1 (1.00)
12.	Bullock cart + Bamboowork	—	1 (01.92)	—	—	—	1 (1.00)
13.	Short-term Agriculture+Bamboo work	—	1 (01.92)	—	—	—	1 (1.00)
14.	Grocery + Calf rearing	1 (03.85)	4 (07.69)	—	—	—	5 (5.00)
15.	STW Pump-set + Short-term	—	—	1 (5.00)	—	—	1 (1.00)
16.	Bamboo work + Calf rearing	—	3 (05.78)	—	—	—	3 (3.00)
17.	Bullock cart + Duckary	—	1 (01.92)	2 (10.00)	1 (50.00)	—	4 (4.00)
	Total	26 (100.00)	52 (100.00)	20 (100.00)	2 (100.00)	—	100(100.00)

Source: Field survey done for the present study.

Table 12.2: Acceptance Pattern of Schemes: According to the Land Size (*More than one Schemes*)

Sl. No.	Name of the Scheme	Land Size (in Acre)					
		Land-less	0.1 - 2.50	2.51 - 5.00	5.01 - 7.50	Above 7.50	Total
1.	Bullock with cart	—	20 (13.07)	14 (22.22)	—	—	34 (12.87)
2.	Calf rearing	4 (10.26)	16 (10.46)	3 (4.76)	1 (16.67)	—	24 (9.09)
3.	STW with Pump-set	—	4 (2.61)	10 (15.87)	1 (16.67)	2 (66.67)	17 (6.43)
4.	Duckary	—	1 (0.65)	—	—	—	1 (0.37)
5.	Heifer rearing	2 (5.13)	10 (6.54)	—	—	—	12 (4.55)
6.	Rickshaw	1 (2.56)	2 (1.31)	—	—	—	3 (1.14)
7.	Piggery	—	1 (0.65)	—	—	—	1 (0.37)
8.	Goatary	—	2 (1.31)	—	—	—	2 (0.75)
9.	Rice Processing	1 (2.56)	2 (1.31)	1 (1.59)	—	—	4 (1.52)
10.	Milch Cow	2 (5.13)	11 (7.19)	—	—	—	13 (4.92)
11.	Carpentry	—	4 (2.61)	1 (1.59)	1 (16.67)	—	6 (2.27)
12.	Fishery	—	1 (0.65)	—	—	—	1 (0.37)
13.	Bamboo work	—	3 (1.96)	—	—	—	3 (1.34)
14.	Business	2 (5.13)	2 (1.31)	—	—	—	4 (1.52)
15.	Grocery	1 (2.56)	10 (6.54)	2 (3.17)	—	—	13 (4.92)
16.	Short-term Agriculture	—	12 (7.84)	12 (19.05)	1 (16.67)	1 (33.33)	26 (9.84)
17.	More than one	26 (66.67)	52 (33.99)	20 (31.75)	2 (33.33)	—	100 (37.88)*
	Total	39 (100.00)	153 (100.00)	63 (100.00)	6 (100.00)	3 (100.00)	264

* *Details breakup shown in separate table.*

Source: Field survey done for the present study.

returned with 12 per cent interest and margin money with 4 per cent interest within the stipulated period of 3 to 5 years. In case of margin money if the due period of 5 years is crossed the rate of interest increased to 10 per cent.

Attitude of the Beneficiaries for Accepting Further Loans

To analyze the attitude and perception of the beneficiaries about these schemes an attempt has been made to know either the beneficiaries are willing or unwilling to accept the schemes further. It was found that 58.33 per cent of the total tribal beneficiaries are willing and 41.67 per cent of total beneficiaries are unwilling to accept the Government loan again (Table 12.3). It was noticed that 58 per cent of total tribal Santal beneficiaries are willing and 42 per cent are unwilling to take any loan from Government. In case of Mahali beneficiaries, 72.22 per cent are willing and 27.78 per cent are unwilling. Out of five beneficiaries of Kora community two are willing beneficiaries and three are unwilling. Among the eighteen Sardar beneficiaries, ten are willing and remaining eight are unwilling. Thus, in every community most of the beneficiaries have a desire to take further financial assistance from Government for their economic upliftment.

Table 12.3: Attitude of the Beneficiaries for Accepting Further Loans

Name of the Tribe	Willing		Un-Willing		Total
	No.	(%)	No.	(%)	
Santal	129	57.85	94	42.15	223
Mahali	13	72.22	5	27.78	18
Kora	2	40.00	3	60.00	5
Sardar	10	55.56	8	44.44	18
Total	154	58.33	110	41.67	264

Source: Field survey done for the present study.

It is found that most of the unwilling beneficiaries are marginal farmers (Table 12.4). Sixty-three per cent marginal farmers and twenty-five per cent landless beneficiaries were identified as unwilling and reluctant to take the Government assistance further. This is true for every community. Beside this, Twelve Santal small

Table 12.4: Unwilling Beneficiaries for Accepting Further Loan (by Land Size)

Land Size (in Acre)	Santal		Mahali		Kora		Sardar		Total	
	No.	(%)	No.	(%)	No.	(%)	No.	(%)	No.	(%)
Land Less	23	24.47	1	20.00	1	33.33	2	25.00	27	24.55
0.1 - 2.50	57	60.64	4	80.00	2	66.67	6	75.00	69	62.73
2.51 - 5.00	12	12.77	—	—	—	—	—	—	12	10.91
5.01 - 7.50	—	—	—	—	—	—	—	—	—	—
Above 7.50	2	2.13	—	—	—	—	—	—	2	1.82
Total	94	100.00	5	100.00	3	100.0	8	100.0	110	100.00

Source: Field survey done for the present study.

farmers and two Santal large farmers were also found to reluct to receive loans for the second time. To get a Government scheme every tribal individual has to communicate regularly with the Panchayat, Block office, Cooperative Society, and Bank to satisfy all the official procedures. It seems that majority of the marginal farmers and landless beneficiaries are disinterested to loss one manday instead of a day spending for a loan which have no surety to get and also have no assurance of economic upliftment.

Reasons of Unwillingness

The marginal farmers and the landless beneficiaries are *afraid about the repayment in cash* by installment. From their previous experience they lost their faith upon themselves. Some of them are still defaulter. But the beneficiaries, who have repaid fully, bring in their difficulties of paying the loans in cash. Cash among these people is considered scarce, and is preferred. Thus, instead of cash they feel it more convenient to pay back any debt in terms of kind or labour. But there is no scope for paying the bank loans in kind or labour. Sometimes beneficiaries have the experience that when they receive the bank notice for payment of installment at a time then it becomes quite impossible for them to pay after fulfilling all the immediate requirements for their families.

Sometimes it was noticed that the beneficiaries have *a bad experience of inadequacy in financial assistance*. They were given the unit according to sanctioned project always in kind not in cash. But then they did not get any financial assistance to obtain and maintain the assets economically. All the responsibilities were devolved on the beneficiaries after the acceptance of the scheme. They have to procure all the required feed and fodder and also the required infrastructure for the animal husbandry scheme privately. In case of other scheme also they have to provide some money for its successful implementation and maintenance. Sometimes, the landless and the marginal farmers were too poor to subsidise their schemes privately.

They also have a *bad experience of sub-standard quality* of assets, from which they did not generate income but remain indebted to Government forever.

From the previous experience some beneficiaries are *frustrated about the long-term official processes and formalities*. It reported by the beneficiaries that they have to spend a number of days in the official process of getting papers ready for having a loan. The entire exercise in this connection may even fail to materize. They thus think that if they work on those days, they can earn some money instead of wasting time this way.

Some beneficiaries are reluctant to take it again due to a *long-term repayment procedure*. In such cases, the loans have to be paid in installments within a time schedule of three years. The installments have to be paid with interest and the repayment would start after two years from the date of receipt. The loans are subsidised, and the repayment installments are ascertained excluding the subsidised amount; the beneficiaries, however, do not understand this long-term procedure of repayment nor do they fill free with a burden of indebtedness to the Government such a long time. Some of the beneficiaries were also found to observe that they do not, in reality, get any subsidy and the entire amount of loan with interest is realized from them through this system.

A few beneficiaries also think that they *do not need any further assistance*. They are able to make their family secured by the first time assistance. Their perception is that, generated income from the first time assistance is sufficient to make their family income secure. No doubt these beneficiaries could effectively run the schemes and able to raise their income level. But due to their limited want they think it sufficient instead of taking the opportunity to make the income level more high. Side by side it is also to be mentioned here that sometimes these beneficiaries are defaulters and only chiefly interested in grabbing the assistance.

Preference of Schemes of the Willing Beneficiaries

An attempt had been made to know what kinds of schemes the willing beneficiaries prefer for their further acceptance (Table 12.5). It reflects the perception and attitude of the beneficiaries about the schemes of these existing developmental projects for them. If the preferable schemes of the beneficiaries are analyzed it is found that two landless preferred calf rearing scheme, one preferred business, five for Milch cow and another two have preferred calf and goatary scheme. Most of these schemes belong to the animal husbandry sector. Though there are instances of failure in these schemes, and the beneficiaries had faced problems in the past in running the projects effectively, they preferred these schemes to others. They say that they have knowledge in animal husbandry compared to the schemes of other sectors. To speak otherwise, it seems that the beneficiaries feel somewhat at ease with schemes of animal rearing, which is quite in conformity with their traditional habit and schemes. The problems they have to face now is primarily the increasing lack of communal resource base in terms of grazing land, natural water pools and the infrastructural facility for farm of birds. The lack of adequate veterinary facilities to the new variety of birds and animals about which the people seem to have little or no knowledge is also a problem they have to face.

Besides these, one landless expressed that he is willing to accept any kind of loan. Another two landless beneficiaries said that they do not know what kind of schemes will be suited for them and for what scheme they have sufficient skill and capabilities for its effective implementation. Thus, it is to be said that these kinds of beneficiaries are chiefly interested in grabbing the assistance rather than running the scheme.

The marginal farmers prefer almost all types of schemes. But the most preferable scheme is short-term agricultural scheme. Twenty-nine willing marginal farmers are found to prefer this

Table 12.5: Willingness of Beneficiaries for Accepting Further Loans (by Land Size)

Sl. No.	Name of the Scheme	Land Size (in Acre)					
		Landless	0.1 - 2.50	2.51 - 5.00	5.01 - 7.50	Above 7.50	Total
1.	Short-term Loan	—	29(34.94)	26(50.98)	2(33.33)	—	57(37.01)
2.	Milch Cow+Short-term	—	—	1(1.96)	—	—	1(0.65)
3.	Goatary + Sheep	—	1(1.20)	—	—	—	1(0.65)
4.	STW with Pump-set	—	2(2.42)	5(9.80)	2(33.33)	1(100.00)	10(6.49)
5.	Calf Rearing	2(15.38)	8(9.65)	5(9.80)	—	—	15(9.74)
6.	Bullock with Cart	—	2(2.42)	1(1.96)	—	—	3(1.95)
7.	Bullock Cart +Short-term	—	1.(1.20)	3(5.88)	—	—	4(2.60)
8.	Craft	—	7(8.43)	—	—	—	7(4.55)
9.	Business	1(7.69)	—	1(1.96)	—	—	2(1.30)
10.	Craft+Short-term	—	1(1.20)	2(3.92)	—	—	3(1.95)
11.	Duckary	—	—	1(1.96)	—	—	1(0.65)
12.	Milch Cow	5(38.46)	9(10.85)	3(5.88)	1(16.67)	—	18(11.69)
13.	Goatary + Short-term	—	1(1.20)	—	—	—	1(0.65)
14.	Rice Pro. + Short-term	—	1(1.20)	—	—	—	1(0.65)
15.	Grocery	—	1(1.20)	—	—	—	1(0.65)
16.	Grocery + Calf rearing	—	1(1.20)	—	—	—	1(0.65)
17.	Calf + Sheep	—	2(2.42)	—	—	—	2(1.30)
18.	Calf + Goatary	2(15.38)	3(3.61)	1(1.96)	—	—	6(3.90)

(Contd.)

Table 12.5: (*Contd.*)

19.	Fishery	—	1(1.20)	—	—	—	1(0.65)
20.	Rice Processing	—	—	1(1.96)	—	—	1(0.65)
21.	Pump-set + Short-term	—	—	1(1.96)	1(16.67)	—	2(1.30)
22.	Goatary	—	1(1.20)	—	—	—	1(0.65)
23.	Rickshaw	—	1(1.20)	—	—	—	1(0.65)
24.	Poultry	—	1(1.20)	—	—	—	1(0.65)
25.	Thatching	—	1(1.20)	—	—	—	1(0.65)
26.	For Improvement of Grocery	—	2(2.42)	—	—	—	2(1.30)
27.	Any kind of Loan	1(7.69)	2(2.42)	—	—	—	3(1.95)
28.	Do not know	2(15.38)	5(6.02)	—	—	—	7(4.55)
	Total	13(100.00)	83(100.00)	51(100.00)	6(100.00)	1(100.00)	154(100.00)

Source: Field survey done for the present study.

scheme. On the other hand, one marginal farmer prefers this scheme with another agriculturally associated scheme Bullock with cart. Another two have preferred this scheme, one with a Goatary scheme and another with rice processing. Marginal farmers are not interested to take medium-term loan, though they are eligible for it. From their previous experience they learnt that it was a problem for them to repay the medium-term loan in the prescribed manner, though there is a scope to get 50 per cent subsidy on his project cost. Short-term scheme has no subsidy at all, and the entire loan is to be paid immediately after six months. From their previous experience or by sharing the experience of the neighbours they have learnt that it is comparatively easy to get loans under this and achieve an immediate gain. They can use chemical fertilizers, HYV seeds, necessary for good harvest without any own investment and stored-up their crops for the lean period. Another advantage of this scheme is that they have to repay a smaller amount of loan, which is comparatively easy to them. Next preference of the marginal farmers is the animal husbandry and poultry bird scheme. Only one beneficiary is there who want to take the grocery scheme again and other one, the short-term scheme with calf rearing. There is one marginal farmer who does not want to take any scheme further. Instead he would like to have some financial assistance for thatching his huts. While talking of his own preference he also observed that every year they have to bear a heavy expenditure for repairing their huts specially before the rainy season. To fulfil this requirement most of the time they have to take loans from private sources like their landowner, professional money-lenders, and *aratdars*. He therefore, feels some provision of loan for this kind of work would be of more use to them.

Two marginal farmers who have taken the scheme of Grocery and effectively implementing it have felt an inadequacy for its maintenance. They want to get financial assistance of the project for improvement of their grocery rather than any new scheme.

Like the landless beneficiaries two marginal farmers are also identified who donot know what types of schemes they can take again for their economic betterment but he is willing to take it definitely.

To the small farmers the most preferable scheme is also the short-term agricultural loan. Fifty-one per cent of them are found willing to take this scheme again and again. Their next preference is Shallow Tube-well with Pump-set by which, they think; they would be able to minimize their cost of expenditure for cultivating the Boro Paddy. It is a common experience to them that they could not cultivate their land in the Boro season due to inadequacy of money for irrigation. They also have an experience that after acquiring money they could not able to irrigate his land in a proper time, as they have to depend upon others for irrigation purpose. Five willing small farmer beneficiaries however, expressed their eagerness to obtain this essential equipment of modern agricultural practices. Another five small farmers prefer calf rearing scheme to others. One of them is willing to acquire a Bullock with cart, as he does not have it. He wants to acquire this by a loan with 50 per cent subsidy. Three beneficiaries are willing to take the same scheme as well as the short-term agricultural scheme. Besides these, only one small farmer is willing to take the scheme of business, two opt for craft and short-term scheme, one, for duckary, three, for milch cow, one, for calf and goatary and another one, for rice processing scheme.

Out of six willing medium farmer beneficiaries two are willing to take the short-term agricultural loan and two, for Shallow Tube-well with Pump-set scheme. One has a desire to obtain a milch cow and the other, wants to take a pump-set as well as short-term scheme. There is only one large farmer, who is willing to take Government scheme again. His willingness is for obtaining a shallow tubewell with pump-set without own investment and with the facility for fifty per cent subsidy.

Thus, from the above discussion it is revealed that the majority of landless beneficiaries and a part of marginal farmers prefer the animal husbandry schemes for the next time. A good number of marginal farmers and most of the small farmers prefer the scheme in terms of a short-term loan. A few of these two categories preferred to take a medium-term scheme of shallow tube-well with pump-set for the next time. Medium farmers have the desire equally for short-term and medium-term scheme, obviously for irrigation purpose. Lastly, the large farmers are desirous only for the medium-term scheme of irrigation. The landless and marginal farmers are more in number, they are also poorer than other beneficiaries. They are willing to have benefits of the schemes, all of which are not accessible to them. Moreover, they are afraid of the long-term complicated system of cash repayment. Whereas, the large farmers are willing to utilize the opportunity of 50 per cent subsidy of a Government scheme and acquiring a valuable asset like shallow tube-well with pump-set without any own investment. They do not bother about the procedure of repayment and amount of the project cost of the scheme. To the landless and marginal farmers the canvas of needs is so broad. Sometimes, it is found that they themselves are not clear about their actual need. In many cases they are ready to receive any scheme they offered. But to the landholders need, expectation and want is clear and restricted.

Since 1983, various family benefit schemes of Integrated Tribal Development Project are actively running in the District of Birbhum as well as in the study area. From the entire study it reveals that the schemes could not make similar impact on the beneficiary households. The families with the same type of scheme could not have the same economic benefit. It involves activities and responsibilities both of the project functionaries and the beneficiaries themselves.

Conclusion

The problems of tribals have attracted special attention of social reformers and political leaders since the attainment of Independence of India. Therefore, planned efforts have been made and series of innovative plans, programmes, structure and institutions have been created with a view to bring about a desired change in the life of the tribal people. The tribal people having their own sprit, world view and community feeling sometimes confused with the planned approaches of development programmes. Generally, they are found to participate in the developmental programmes, avail the opportunities gladly but if they feel that the programme is going against the sprit of their society, it hurts their conscience and solidarity; they refuse to participate in the programme whole-heartedly. Tribal people are very much conscious about their group solidarity and always try to maintain it. They have their own perception about the programmes, about their own society and even some aspiration regarding their own development. In fact, ethics has a greater role to play for such a tradition bound society which is culturally and ideologically different from others. Planning a project for tribals which involves directly some cultural changes; the planners have to find out what the normal and local channels of influence and infiltration are in population. It is extremely valuable when deciding how to introduce a programme of change for the tribals. Mystery of success of any programme for planned change is entrusted largely on whether the targeted population wants and likes to adopt the proposed programme and to what extent the targeted population is aware or prepares to accept the benefits of the proposed change.

References

Beteille, A., 1977, "The Definition of Tribe", in Ramesh. T. (Ed.): *Tribe, Caste and Religion in India*, Delhi: The MacMillan Company of India Limited.

Deogaonkar, S.G., 1994, *Tribal Administration and Development,* New Delhi: Concept Publishing Company.

Dube, S.C., 1998, "Development Designs and Tribal People in Antiquity to Modernity", in Dube, S.C. (Ed.): *Tribal India,* Vol. I, New Delhi: Inter-India Publications.

Mahalingam, S., 1988, "Tribal Development Programmes: A Review", *Kurukshetra,* 36 (4).

Mitra, K. and Paul, S.K., 2003, "LAMP: A Flame for the Tribals", in Haldar, A.K. and Bhowmick, P.K. (Ed.): *Social Justice for Tribal,* Narayangarh, Bidisa: The Institute of Social Research and Applied Anthropology.

Mitra, K. and Paul, S.K., 2004, *Development Programmes and Tribals – Some Emerging Issues,* New Delhi: Kalpaz Publications.

Patel, M.L., 1994, *Tribal Development without Tears,* New Delhi: Inter India Publications.

Ramaiah, P., 1988, *Issues in Tribal Development,* Allahabad: Chugh Publications.

Roy Burman, B.K., 1995, *Tribal Situation and Approach to Tribal Problems in India: A Preliminary Appraisal,* New Delhi: Rajiv Gandhi Institute for Contemporary Studies.

Verma, M.M., 1996, *Tribal Development in India: Problems and Perspective,* New Delhi: Mittal Publications.

Vidyarthi, L.P. and Rai, B.K., 1985, *The Tribal Culture of India*. New Delhi: Concept Publishing Company.

13

Child Sexual Abuse of Boys

Role of Community in Encouraging Disclosure

Srenwantee Bhattacharjee

Introduction

Child sexual abuse is an intimate and intricate form of abuse. The anger that victims, the family of the victim, and their communities are likely to feel in response to child sexual abuse is deep and comprehensible. It is only in the last few decades that society has begun to recognize it as a significant problem, to portray the trauma of sexual abuse in the media, and to seek ways to prevent and eliminate sexual violence. Despite the centuries of silence and denial that have surrounded the sexual abuse of children, the attention of the last 30 years has begun to change the ways in which victims can access help, family and community members can intervene before a child is harmed, and society can work toward solutions to the problem of child sexual abuse. While it has manifested itself in varied forms, the similarity that emerges out of all cases of child sexual abuse is that disclosure becomes a major problem. Child abuse is not an arbitrary incident. Society is the driving force that creates or impedes circumstances that lead to abuse but family is the most important factor of all.

According to the World Health Organization (WHO), "The involvement of a child in sexual activity that he or she does not fully comprehend is unable to give informed consent to, or for which the child is not developmentally prepared, or else that violate the laws or social taboos of society. Children can be sexually abused by adults or other children who are – by virtue of their age or stage of development—in a position of responsibility, trust, or power over the victim." The National Centre on Child Abuse and Neglect defines sexual abuse as "any childhood sexual experience that interferes with or has the potential for interfering with a child's healthy development." A simplistic approach to understanding it is, child sexual abuse is the use of a child for the sexual gratification of an adult (Tower, 1999). The Standing Committee on Sexually Abused Children (SCOSAC) in 1984 has defined Child Sexual Abuse (CSA) as: "Any Child below the age of consent may be deemed to have been sexually abused when a sexually mature person has by design or by neglect of their usual societal or specific responsibilities in relation to the child engaged or permitted engagement of that child in activity of a sexual nature, which is intended to lead to the sexual gratification of the sexually mature person. This definition pertains whether or not it involves genital or physical contact, whether or not initiated by the child and whether or not there is discernible harmful outcome in the short-run" (Bajpai, 2006).

Child Sexual Abuse (CSA) typically includes unwanted and inappropriate sexual solicitation of, or exposure to, a child by an older person. It may include fondling of the child's genitals (or getting the child to fondle the perpetrator's genitals); masturbation (with the child as either observer or participant); oral sex (either fellatio or cunnilingus); vaginal or anal penetration by a penis, finger, or any other object; fondling of breasts; voyeurism (regular observation of the child) or exhibitionism. Child Sexual Abuse can vary along a number of dimensions including frequency, duration, age at onset, and relationship of victim to perpetrator. However, the most common dimension used to define CSA is the 'type of abuse'. Three categories that evolve out of existing literature are: (i) non-contact abuse encompasses a range of acts and includes inappropriate sexual solicitation or indecent exposure; (ii) contact abuse, which includes touching or fondling; and (iii) intercourse, which includes oral, anal or vaginal intercourse.

Factors Influencing Severity of Negative Impact of Child Sexual Abuse

Sexual abuse is also physical, mental, emotional and sexual abuse. Children and adolescents who have been sexually abused often face a range of psychological and behavioural problems, from mild to severe, in both the short and long-term. The initial or short-term effects of abuse usually occur within 2 years of the termination of the abuse. These effects vary depending upon the circumstances of the abuse and the child's developmental stage but may include regressive behaviours (such as a return to thumb-sucking or bed-wetting), sleep disturbances, eating problems, behaviour and/or performance problems at school, and non-participation in school and social activities. Long-term effects of child sexual abuse are self-destructive behaviours, such as alcoholism or drug abuse, anxiety attacks, situation-specific nervous disorders, and insomnia. Many victims also encounter problems in their adult relationships and in their adult sexual functioning.

Sexual abuse is not naturally occurring or accidental. It is the result of purposeful human behaviour. Every person reacts to his victimization in his own way, based on the personality and personal resources. Hunter (1990) tries to understand the intensity of the negative impact based on the following factors:

- *How coercive, threatening, intrusive and violent the abuse was*—Vicious and violent sexual assault over a period of time tends to be more traumatic. It has been found in numerous studies that intrusive and deviant acts of sexual abuse, the greater the negative impact on the child. Atrocities impact the children immensely and it also affects disclosure of the abuse.
- *The age at which the abuse began*—Hunter mentions one study that looked at the emergency room records of boys admitted due to sexual abuse found that their ages ranged from 3 years to 16 years, with an average age of 9.7 years. According to him another similar study found that boys as young as six months were admitted for medical treatment

as a result of sexual abuse. Finkelhor reports that the greater the age difference between the victim and the offender, the more negative the impact. When a boy is exposed to abuse at a younger age, it tends to set him up as susceptible to repeated abuse from others, both within and outside family.

- *How long the abuse lasted*—The more prolonged the abuse history, the more profound the effect. The more frequent and persistent the sexual abuse, the more stages of development that can be interfered with.
- *How frequently the abuse took place*—Every incident of abuse is damaging. Hunter talks about Russell's finding wherein 48 per cent of the children had faced abuse between ten and twenty times while in 10 per cent of the cases the abuse took place over twenty times. Repeated acts of violence affect the child's ability to talk about the abuse thus delaying disclosure.
- *How many adults took part in the abuse*—The greater the number of adults who took part in the act of abuse the more traumatic the experience for the child. The child's sense of powerlessness subdues his want to disclose about the abuse and he is apprehensive of the presence of safe adults in his life.
- *The child's relationship with the offending adult*—The more closely related the abuser is to the child the more disturbing the abuse. A common myth about sexual abuse is that it is perpetrated by strangers who lure children away, but it has been found that majority of sexual offences towards children are committed by someone the child knows and trusts. Summit puts it as "A child is three times more likely to be molested by a recognized, trusted adult than by a stranger." Parent figures are particularly powerful when you take into consideration the vulnerability of the child and the difficulty a child faces to disclose about abuse by a family member.
- *How adults other than the abuser(s), respond to the abuse*—The response a child gets following the abuse by

> significant care-givers affects the child significantly. The children who are fortunate to have supportive people available to them disclose of abuse and are better equipped to cope with the trauma. Children have a difficult time verbally disclosing about abuse and neglect of the parents to notice such abuse is "second injury" to the victim. The child feels deserted and it affects the child's health and his demeanor. If the offender is a family member or someone else who has easy access to the child, that child has a great deal to lose if he discloses the abuse. If he is ignored and his abuse neglected, it exposes the child to greater risk of abuse.

The impact of sexual abuse varies from minor consequences to very severe consequences. Experiences of abuse during childhood can have lasting impact on a child's physical, emotional, psychological and cognitive development. A child sexually abused develops coping mechanisms to deal with the abuse experience. Research shows that the ability to cope and bounce back depends on the victims close relations and his/her opportunity to disclose about the abuse to a loved one. Disclosure is crucial as denial or suppression of abuse results in low recognition of the problem which leads to lesser initiatives to deal with it.

Understanding Disclosure

Disclosure is not a simple clear-cut concept, as children do not always purposefully tell about abuse. Disclosure (of child abuse) is the word used when it is revealed that child sexual abuse has occurred. Existing research leans to treat disclosure in a narrow sense: a singular episode that happens in an official context, such as recounting the incidence of abuse to the Police or a social worker, or in an official forensic interview. Disclosure of CSA is a socially-embedded act, not only involving the child, but also the individuals and systems receiving the disclosure, including family members, the child protection system, the criminal justice system, and the perpetrator (Myers, *et al.*, 2002). According to Grossman, Kia-

Keating and Sorsoli, disclosure is conceptualized as conveying or attempting to convey the experience of being sexually abused to another person, regardless of whether official reports were made to authorities. Brown (1991) stated that "disclosure is almost always an ongoing process. It may begin with an initial quite dramatic first step, or it may manifest itself as a series of tentative revelations, hints and explorations" (Buck, M., Ceci, J.S., London, K. and Shuman, W.D., 2005).

Children's abuse disclosures have been described as being: (a) purposeful or accidental; (b) spontaneous or prompted/elicited; and (c) explicit or vague. These descriptors correspond to the three dimensions of disclosure: *intent, spontaneity* and *detail*. In reality, disclosure may happen in different situations and in different ways: 'accidental disclosure' is the term frequently used in the research to refer to situations when the abuse is found out by someone else through observation or through medical examinations. In contrast, 'purposeful disclosure' occurs when a child *intentionally tells* someone about the abuse, perhaps with the aim of stopping it. Paine and Hanson (2005) on study of previous research find age related differences in disclosure dimensions of intent and detail. Researchers like Bybee and Mowbray found that 70 per cent of children less than 5 years of age provide explicit details whereas only 34 per cent of children above the age of 5 can provide detailed description of abuse.

According to Doyle (2006) complex concepts, embarrassing incidents, confusing experiences make it difficult for children to articulate the abuse verbally. Small children who attempt to communicate of the abuse often cannot fully understand the consequences and describe it spontaneously, but this can go unnoticed as these children do not have the words to express their experience. Older children are communicative but are aware of possible consequences thus hesitation sets in. Finally, the term "prompted/elicited disclosure" is used to describe situations when authorities, professionals, parents, care-givers or other adults encourage a reluctant child to tell about the abuse (Alaggia, 2004). Children may disclose sexual abuse by directly telling someone about it. They may also disclose less directly, sometimes unintentionally, over a period of time, through a variety of behaviours and actions, including discussions and indirect non-verbal cues.

Doyle (2006) has pointed out that not all communication is verbal. When children's gestures, facial expression, demeanor or other movements are incongruent with their words there is a cause for concern. Alaggia (2004) and Lindblad (2007) include non-verbal cues as part of the disclosure process. In Alaggia's (2004) qualitative study of 24 abuse victims, she found that half of the participants did not fit into the already established categories of disclosure types described above: some exhibited certain behaviours and attempted to tell someone about the abuse indirectly; some intentionally withheld their disclosures; while other disclosures came to light after being triggered by recovered memories.

There are physical indicators of abuse, injuries, bruises or lesions in different parts of the body that do not fit the explanation. Also indication of discomfort or indirect indication of injury may be an effort to disclose of the abuse. Sexual abuse may also manifest itself through games with other children or toys. They may show signs of increased arousal, sleeping difficulties, irritability, outbursts of anger, difficulty concentrating, over-vigilance and an exaggerated startle response. Eating disorders or self-destructive behaviour also often stem from sexual abuse.

Children are most liable to tell their peers or their mothers about experiences of abuse and least likely to tell a professional. Abraham's (1996) study highlighted that the reason many children who do disclose choose a best friend or their mother is that they have chosen the person(s) they think will believe their account rather than disparage their abuse experience as fantasy. Another study found that informal contacts such as a family doctor, faith group representative or mental health professional were important as potential confidants when disclosing, but much less so than close friends. Close friends were the most common confidants, followed by mothers, other relatives and non-familial members of the community. Paine and Hansen (2002) noted that "A child's self-disclosure of sexual abuse is a critical component in initiating intervention to halt the abuse, address its immediate effects, and decrease the likelihood of negative long-term outcome. Professionals working with perpetrators, families, and victims of child sexual abuse (CSA) have identified numerous internal and external factors that inhibit children from disclosing their abuse."

Barriers to Disclosure for Boys

Close scrutiny of various studies on child sexual abuse has affirmed the hypothesis of this study that disclosure of child sexual abuse is difficult for boys. While majority studies on Child Sexual Abuse focused on the effects of abuse on children, few crucial researches were found which delved into the understanding of disclosure patterns of children based on age, gender and brutality of abuse. There is a whole range of reasons why children give partial disclosure, delay or deny sexual abuse. The literature highlights the importance of understanding how individual and contextual factors may inhibit or encourage disclosure of abuse in a child's life. Often the victim is threatened by their perpetrator, they are fearful of facing blame, the victim may lack the verbal or mental capability and some children do not realize that abuse is taking place. Often children expect parents to figure out the aberrations by becoming ill-disciplined which will attract their attention and discipline.

There are distinct types of personal obstacles to disclosure, including lack of cognitive awareness, intentional avoidance, difficulty approaching the topic or articulating the thoughts and emotions involved, emotional readiness and safety, and shame. Beyond cognitive difficulties, emotions are often a predominant premise among the personal reasons for silence—whether the emotions originated from the experience of disclosure itself or as reactions to anticipated responses of others. Childhood choices not to disclose also involved a sense of shame and potential blame, such as knowing "it was wrong," and feelings of "being bad," at "fault," or "weak." Shame, although more prominent in narratives of why they did not tell during childhood, was also salient in adulthood. Shame was about both the experiences themselves and the fact that they were not disclosed earlier.

Alaggia's (2005) analysis of the disclosure of child sexual abuse is exceptional because it highlights the presence of unique themes in male and female survivors' disclosure narratives. For men, the themes that inhibited or precipitated disclosure were sex or gender related—fear of being seen as homosexual, feelings of isolation due to the belief that boys are rarely victims, and fear of becoming an abuser. Women, as it appears have more difficulties disclosing abuse because of internal confusion about who was responsible for the abuse and fears of being blamed or not believed.

Male sexual abuse victims are not identified because the counsellors or therapists they meet with do not give them permission to disclose about their sexual issues and experiences. Sexual abuse is only superficially discussed because of the therapist's denial or lack of awareness of the client's behavioural and emotional clues. Another reason why victims go unidentified is that the professional definition of sexual abuse is vague and may not include what was done to the particular client (Hunter, 1990). Men remain sensitive to the notion of disclosure as it could be disruptive in the relational domain. The fear that there could be accusations, blaming, shame, depression, anxiety, anger, and other difficulties tended to outweigh their desires to disclose. They also face confusion about sexual identity due to passivity or sexual arousal during abuse which is often manifested as guilt or provocation and a potential barrier to disclosure. Yet reframing the issue of sexual responsiveness from an adult perspective is crucial to understand sensations experienced as a child are simply a physiological reaction to sexual simulation.

Hunter also points out that since there is a stereotype that all males who were sexually abused as children become child molesters themselves, hence many non-offender victims will not disclose that they were sexually abused. Also when a boy is abused by another male significantly older but not legally an adult, the younger boy is seldom seen as having victimized. Such sexual contact is merely seen as an "inappropriate sex play", a manifestation that either of the participants is homosexual. The two are mistakenly viewed as peers whereas in case a younger female is sexually coerced by a teenager it is seen as sexual abuse.

Sexual orientation validates sexual relation between men but this concept overlooks the power difference between the young boy and the older man who exploits the child. The sexual abuse is overshadowed by the occurrence of homosexuality. Gender differences were also reported in the dynamics of Child Sexual Abuse. Likewise, Finkelhor *et al.* (1994) National survey of adults showed that a higher percentage of adult men, *versus* women, reported sexual abuse experiences that they had never disclosed. Another study specifically focused on sexually abused boys, including the prevalence, characteristics, and psychological consequences of abuse, found that because of the stigma against homosexuality, boys are less likely to disclose the abuse than girls when perpetrated by a male (Valente, 2005).

Men delayed disclosure because of reluctance of being identified as a victim, and concerns about being regarded as homosexual, or becoming an abuser, especially when they were abused by male perpetrators. While Peluso's (1996) study suggests that boys who are sexually abused by males as a result fear homosexuality, another study suggests that boys who are sexually abused by females, due to social and cultural factors, may overlook sexual contact as abuse rather discounts it as sexual experience (Alaggia, 2005). In addition, certain barriers were found to prevent the likelihood of obtaining a full disclosure. These barriers are the child's development, and the fear of the outcomes of disclosure, including the potential lack of care-giver support and possible threats made by the perpetrator.

Role of Community

A major barrier in disclosure of sexual abuse of boys is the experience of shame and fear of adverse reaction from the community. There has been far less public awareness of boys facing sexual abuse in comparison to girls; this is responsible for boys invalidating their experience as an accident as they have no reason to expect social acceptance or support. The pattern of masculine socialization is a key contributor in men's reluctance to disclose childhood sexual abuse. Society casts the average male as strong and sexually dominant. Early childhood socialization of a boy within the family and immediate community reaffirms the notion of a dominant and independent male. Disclosure of sexual abuse contradicts the societal attributes that make a man hence making a boy feel "less of a man". Thus, the social construction of male is in juxtaposition to the experience of abused boys and does not encourage help seeking behaviour (Fortunato, 2005).

Our society expects males to be able to protect themselves. Successful men are depicted as never being vulnerable, either physically or emotionally. But boys are not men. They are children. They are weaker and more vulnerable than those who sexually abuse or exploit them—perpetrators use their greater size, strength and knowledge to manipulate or coerce boys into unwanted sexual experiences and staying silent. This is usually done from a position of authority (e.g., coach, teacher, religious leader) or status (e.g. older cousin, admired athlete, social leader), using whatever means are available to reduce resistance, such as attention, special privileges, money or other gifts, promises or bribes, even outright threats. Absence of social support from community and paucity of services for male victims of sexual abuse have damaging and isolating effects on boys making them believe that their abuse is a segregated case.

Communities need to provide a child-friendly environment for the holistic development of children. They have to ensure a neighbourhood free from sexual aggressors as well as provide social support to children who have faced sexual abuse. Disclosure of sexual abuse exposes a child to shame and stigma and it is here that secondary agencies of socialization like the neighbourhood, school and other social agencies reach out to the victim. Disclosure for the child post-abuse has to be made easy and trust has to be established so that instances of abuse are not masked in secrecy and trepidation. Children have to be sensitized on the subject of what to speak-up about and whom to confide into when facing any form of abuse. Sexual abuse is extremely traumatic and children are not always able to articulate their experiences due to lack of understanding or fear. Boys especially are in a dire need to understand what all encompasses as sexual abuse and how they face abuse. Faller (1989) has noted that boys' reluctance to disclose emanates from "the fact boys are socialized not to reveal doubts, weaknesses and fears, and the fact that, since most of the abusers are male, boys have the additional taboo of homosexuality to overcome if they tell."

Many boys suffer harm because adults who could believe them and help them are reluctant, or refuse, to admit that these children have been sexually abused and the harm it caused. This increases the damage, especially the shame felt by boys and men, and leads many to believe they have to "tough it out" on their own. And it makes it harder to seek help or therapy in the midst of the abuse, or even years later when help is still required. Parents and teachers have to be encouraged to be amenable to and trusting to a child's disclosure of sexual abuse. Children at the onset of abuse often exhibit various non-verbal indicators of abuse, parents and significant care-givers must be cautious and understand these symptoms. It is through trust and attention from family and communities that children who face abuse get the courage to speak up and provide a detailed verbal disclosure.

Service development should focus on innovative ways of ensuring that services address children's concerns: they could provide a forum for children and young people to talk to someone about abuse they are experiencing, while also giving them the space and time to think about their options before providing details that may cause them to lose control of the situation. Services should be well-publicised in places where children and young people spend time. This includes places like schools and youth clubs, but in view of the increasing use of technology, internet websites such as social networking sites should also be part of any awareness-raising strategy. Confidentiality is one of the key issues children raise when they are asked about why they do not disclose abuse.

This brief review of the literature has identified some of the dynamics involved in disclosure of sexual abuse, including who children tend to turn to and what inhibits children, especially boys from speaking out. Several factors play an important role that increases the likelihood of disclosure of sexual abuse. These factors are creating of child-friendly environment, societal support, and a trusting relation between the care-giver and the child. It is important to learn lessons from the research, particularly to listen to and address children and young people's concerns, so that we are able to create a safe environment for open dialogue so that children can confide of their abuse to care givers without inhibitions.

References

Abrahams, C., 1996, *Hearing the Truth: The Importance of Listening to Children who Disclose Sexual Abuse,* London: AFC.

Alaggia, R., 2004, "Many Ways of Telling: Expanding Conceptualizations of Child Sexual Abuse Disclosure", *Child Abuse and Neglect*, 28(11): 1213-27.

Allnock, D., 2010, *Children and Young People Disclosing Sexual Abuse: An Introduction to the Research*, for details, please access: http://www.nspcc.org.uk/inform .

Bajpai, A., 2006, *Child Rights in India: Law, Policy and Practice,* New Delhi: Oxford University Press.

Brown, A. and Finkelhor, D., 1986, "Impact of Child Sexual Abuse: A Review of the Research", *Psychological Bulletin*, 99.

Buck, M., Ceci, J.S., London, K. and Shuman, W.D., 2005, "Disclosure of Child Sexual Abuse: What Does the Research Tell us About the Ways That Children Tell", *Psychology, Public Policy and Law,* 11(1): 194-226.

Doyle, C., 2006, *Working with Abused Children*, New York: Palgrave Macmillan.

Finkelhor, D., 1994, "The International Epidemiology of Child Sexual Abuse", *Child Abuse and Neglect,* 18: 409-417.

Fortunato, J.V., 2005, "Re-Authoring the Story of Sexual Abuse and Gender Socialization: A Narrative Approach to Treatment for Adolescent Boys", *Ph.D Dissertation*, California School of Professional Psychology: Alliance International University.

Hunter, M., 1990, *Abused Boys: The Neglected Victims of Sexual Abuse.* New York: Fawcett Books.

Jones, M., 2012, "Influences of Disclosure among Child Sexual Abuse Victims", *Undergraduate Honours Theses, Paper 107*, For details, please access: http://digitalcommons.usu.edu/honors/107.

Paine, M.L. and Hansen, D.J., 2002, "Factors Influencing Children to Self-Disclose Sexual Abuse", *Faculty Publications, Department of Psychology*, Paper 59. For details, please access: http://digitalcommons.unl.edu/psychfacpub/59

Ramirez, S. May, 2007, "Severity of Child Sexual Abuse and Perceptions of General Support Networks in Adulthood: Examining The Role of Disclosure", *Thesis Submitted in Partial Fulfilment of the Requirements for the Master of Arts Degree*, Department of Psychology. Southern Illinois University.

Government of India, 2007, *Study on Child Abuse: India 2007*, New Delhi: Ministry of Women and Child Development.

Valente, S.M., 2005, "Sexual Abuse of Boys", *Journal of Child and Adolescent Psychiatric Nursing,* 18: 10-16.

14
Lost in Counting
India's Vulnerable and Marginalized Children

Indranil Sarkar

Introduction

The first word which comes to our mind when we think about vulnerability is risk and crisis. A child in any situation is at risk and crisis by some way or the other. Children are always dependent on the adult, they have around them and they are not able to decide, what they want to do or what things they should do when they are in crisis situation. But there are many children whom we do not take in the list of vulnerable children because we do not think about them. This document talks about the various cause and effect relation of child vulnerability, the rights which are there for the children in IPC as well as the International Conventions, it also explains the two very situations of children where they are at very risk and crisis and there will be the responses and interventions of State, NGOs, and Civil Societies. In any Country protection of children and young people is of prime importance. So, the responsibility to provide healthy atmosphere to the children to their fullest physical and mental development rests on all the civilized society (Doddawadmath, 2010).

Forms of Child Vulnerability

A high number of children in the society are at risk of being deprived of their fundamental rights. The following categories of children are considered at special risk and requiring particular protection and/or assistance: Children living in households headed by children, children in fostering care, street children, children living in centres, children in conflict with the law, children with disabilities, children affected by armed conflict, children who are sexually exploited and/or abused, working children, children affected/infected by HIV/AIDS, infants with their mothers in prison, children in very poor households, refugee and displaced children, children of single mothers, children who are married before they achieve majority.

Factors Influencing Child Vulnerability and Marginalization

The development of the Nation is exclusively influenced by the status of the Child who is one of the vulnerable groups in the society (Satbhai, 2011). There is no single known cause of child vulnerability. Nor is there any single description that captures all families in which children are victims of abuse and neglect. Child vulnerability occurs across socio-economic, religious, cultural, racial, and ethnic groups. While no specific causes definitively have been identified that lead a parent or other care-giver to abuse or neglect a child, research has recognized a number of risk factors or attributes commonly associated with maltreatment. Children within families and environments in which these factors exist have a higher probability of being vulnerable. Risk factors associated with child maltreatment can be grouped in four domains: Factors directly related to children, factors encompassing family/care-giver, community factors, and natural disaster.

Factors Directly Related to Children

Children are not responsible for being victims of maltreatment. Certain factors, however, can make some children more than others. The child's age and development—(physical, mental, emotional, and social)—may increase the chance of maltreatment.

Age: The relationship between a child's age and maltreatment is not clear and may differ by type of vulnerability. In 2000, for example, the rate of documented maltreatment was highest for children between new born and 3 years of age (15.7 victims per 1,000 children of this age in the population) and declined as age increased. The inverse relationship between age and maltreatment is particularly strong for negligence, but not as evident for other types of maltreatment (physical, emotional, or sexual abuse).

Infants and young children, due to their small physical size, early developmental needs and strive for constant care. These groups of children are particularly vulnerable for maltreatment. New born are more likely to experience certain forms of maltreatment, such as shaken baby syndrome and nonorganic failure to thrive. Teenagers, on the other hand, are at greater risk for sexual abuse.

Disabilities: Children with physical, cognitive, and emotional disabilities appear to experience more maltreatment than do other children. A national study, completed in 1993, found that children with disabilities were 1.7 times more likely to be maltreated than children without disabilities. Children who are perceived by their parents as "different" or who have special needs, including children with disabilities, as well as children with chronic illnesses or children with difficult temperaments—may be more exposed to maltreatment. The demands of caring for these children may overwhelm their parents. Children with disabilities are vulnerable to repeated maltreatment because they may not understand that the behaviours are inappropriate, and they may be unable to escape or defend themselves in abusive situations. Some societal attitudes, practices, and beliefs that devalue and depersonalize children with disabilities indirectly sanction abusive behaviour and push them towards difficulties. For instance, there may be greater tolerance of a care-giver verbally berating or physically responding to a disabled child's inability to accomplish a task or act in an expected way than there would be if similar behaviour was directed at a normally able child.

Physically and Mentally Weak: The children both physically and mentally are not as strong as they are in the stage of growth and they are not that much matured to deal with every situation. This factor makes them dependent on the adults. This dependency turns up as the inability for the children to raise the voice of the children and take the step of their will. The adults become ignorant to listen to the voice of the children too. In many situations it happens that the children really want to protest against something but they are unable to fight because of this thing and they are forced to do work against their will.

Gender: Gender plays a big role in making the children vulnerable. In India and also in the whole world there are some specific roles allotted for the genders but when they try to step out of the predetermined frame they fall into the situation which makes them vulnerable.

Child factors such as aggression, attention deficits, difficult temperaments, and behaviour problems—or the parental perceptions of such problems—have been associated with increased risk for all types of child maltreatment. These factors may contribute indirectly to child maltreatment when interacting with certain parental characteristics, such as—poor coping skills, poor ability to empathize with the child, or difficulty controlling emotions. In addition, these same child characteristics may be reinforced by the maltreatment (e.g., a physically abused child may develop aggressive behaviours that elicit harsh reactions from others) and create conditions that can lead to recurring maltreatment.

Parent or Care-giver Factors

Personality Characteristics and Psychological Well-being: No consistent set of characteristics or personality traits has been associated with maltreating parents or care-givers. Some characteristics frequently identified in those who are physically abusive or neglectful include low self-esteem, an external locus of control (i.e., belief that events are determined by chance or outside forces beyond one's personal control), poor impulse control, depression, anxiety, and antisocial behaviour. While some maltreating parents or care-givers experience behavioural and emotional difficulties, severe mental disorders are not common.

Parental Histories and the Cycle of Abuse: A parent's childhood history plays a large part in how he or she may behave as a parent.

Individuals with poor parental role models or those who did not have their own needs met may find it very difficult to meet the needs of their children.

While the estimated number varies, child maltreatment literature commonly supports the finding that some maltreating parents or care-givers were victims of abuse and neglect themselves as children. One review of the relevant research suggested that about one-third of all individuals who were maltreated will subject their children to maltreatment. Children who either experienced maltreatment or witnessed violence between their parents or care-givers may learn violent behaviour and may also learn to justify violent behaviour as appropriate.

An incorrect conclusion from this finding, however, is that a maltreated child will always grow up to become a maltreating parent. There are individuals who have not been abused as children who become abusive, as well as individuals who have been abused as children and do not subsequently abuse their own children. In the research review noted above, approximately two-thirds of all individuals who were maltreated did not subject their children to abuse or neglect.

It is not known why some parents or care-givers who were maltreated as children abuse or neglect their own children and others with a similar history do not. While every individual is responsible for his or her actions, research suggests the presence of emotionally supportive relationships may help lessen the risk of the intergenerational cycle of abuse.

Substance Abuse: Research supports the association between substance abuse and child maltreatment. For example: one and two-third of the maltreated children in the CSW is reported to come from parents who have history of substance abuse.

Attitudes and Knowledge: Negative attitudes and attributions about a child's behaviour and inaccurate knowledge about child development may play a contributing role in child maltreatment. Some studies have found that mothers who physically abuse their children have both more negative and higher than normal expectations of their children, as well as less understanding of appropriate developmental norms. Not all research, however, has found differences in parental expectations.

Age: Caretaker's age may play a key role in for some forms of maltreatment, although research findings are inconsistent. Some studies of physical abuse, in particular, have found that mothers who were younger at the time of birth of their child exhibited higher rates of child abuse than did older mothers. Other contributing factors, such as lower economic status, lack of social support, and high stress levels may influence the link between younger childbirth—particularly teenage parenthood—and child abuse.

Family Factors: Specific life situations of some families—such as marital conflict, domestic violence, single parenthood, unemployment, financial stress, and social isolation—may increase the likelihood of maltreatment. While these factors by themselves may not cause maltreatment, they frequently contribute to negative patterns of family functioning which leads to maltreatment.

Family Structure: Children living with single parents may be at higher risk of experiencing physical and sexual abuse and neglect than children living with two biological parents. Single parent households are substantially more likely to have incomes below the poverty line. Lower income, the increased stress associated with the sole burden of family responsibilities, and fewer supports are thought to contribute to the risk of single parents maltreating their children. In 1998, 23 per cent of children lived in households with a single mother, and 4 per cent lived in households with a single father. A strong, positive relationship between the child and the father whether he resides in the home or not, contributes to the child's development and may lessen the risk of abuse.

In addition, studies have found that compared to similar non-neglecting families, neglectful families tend to have more children or greater numbers of people living in the household. Chronically neglecting families often are characterized by a chaotic household with changing constellations of adult and child figures (e.g., a mother and her children who live on and off with various others, such as the mother's mother, the mother's sister, or a boyfriend).

A national survey of nearly 1,000 parents found that 7.4 per cent of children who lived with one parent had been sexually abused, compared to only 4.2 per cent of children who lived with both biological parents.

A study of 156 victims of child sexual abuse found that the majority of the children came from disrupted or single-parent homes; only 31 per cent of the children lived with both biological parents. Although, step families make-up only about 10 per cent of all families, 27 per cent of the abused children in this study lived with either a step-father or the mother's boyfriend.

Marital Conflict and Domestic Violence: According to published studies, in 30 to 60 per cent of families where spouse abuse takes place, child maltreatment also occurs. Children in violent homes may witness parental violence, may be victims of physical abuse themselves, and may be neglected by parents who are focused on their partners or unresponsive to their children due to their own fears. A child who witnesses parental violence is at risk for also being maltreated, but, even if the child is not maltreated, he or she may experience harmful emotional consequences from witnessing the parental violence.

Stress: Stress is also thought to play a significant role in family functioning, although its exact relationship with maltreatment is not fully understood. Physical abuse has been associated with stressful life events, parenting stress, and emotional distress in various studies. Similarly, some studies have found that neglectful families report more day-to-day stress than non-neglectful families. It is not clear, however, whether maltreating parents actually experience more life stress or, rather, perceive more events and life experiences as being stressful.

Parent-Child Interaction: Families involved in child maltreatment seldom recognize or reward their child's positive behaviours, while having strong responses to their child's negative behaviours. Maltreating parents have been found to be less supportive, affectionate, playful, and responsive with their children than parents who do not abuse their children.

Poverty, Unemployment of Parents: This factor creates financial insecurity for the children which directly effects in the accessibility of the children of the various resources around them. The child always remains in a very insecure manner in case of their future and side-by-side they do not have anything in their present also. They do not get the right amount of food in their growing period, they donot get the health facilities and also they become prone to child labour for the sake of supporting their family financially which results to exploitation and dropout from the school and prone to drugs and many more types of addiction.

Parental Education and Illiteracy: Due to lack of education of the parents, they do not have the proper knowledge of the child rearing and they are unable to provide the support in their education also. This factor also affects the interest of the parents towards the education of the children. The parents become very ignorant towards the education and they do not understand the importance of it in one's life.

Poor Health of Parents: There are many parents who have health problems like cancer and HIV or TB which makes them vulnerable for their health and also for many social stigmas. On the other hand, the children are isolated by the peer group because of their parents especially in case of HIV, TB and leprosy. Due to the prolonged ill-health they often tend to become abusive.

Community Factors

Environmental factors are often found in combination with parent, family, and child factors, as highlighted in previous sections of this chapter. Environmental factors include poverty and unemployment, social isolation, and community characteristics. It is important to reiterate that most parents or care-givers who live in these types of environments are not abusive.

Location (Rural/Urban, Remoteness, Slums): Location of the children in a society works a lot for making the children vulnerable or safe. If the child is in a urban location then the child is open to many resources but when the same child is in a rural area then he/she gets isolated from the many resources and very less scope to get the exposure for the resources and also less opportunity to get rid of the risky situations which they face.

Geographic Factors (Risk of Flooding, Risk of Drought): The geographic factors results too many risk factors for the children. In the places which are prone to flood, drought and earthquake creates a very risky situation for the children and these children are also in a risk of the natural disaster by birth.

High Prevalence of Malaria, HIV/AIDS and Other Diseases: The presence of any kind of communicable disease in the community makes the child prone to various kinds of health issues. If the child is reared in a place where there is no presence of diseases rather in a healthy environment than the child won't be in risk of bad health.

Infrastructure in the Community: *Roads, Schools, Health Centres, Water and Sewerage*: The absence of the different infrastructure in the community makes the child away from many facilities, just in case of any kind of health problems the child will not get proper treatment neither he will be able to go to the hospital as there is no road facility or anything.

Violent Communities: Children living in dangerous neighbourhoods have been found to be at higher risk than children from safer neighbourhoods for severe neglect and physical abuse, as well as child sexual victimization. Some concerns remain that violence may seem an acceptable response or behaviour to individuals who witness it more frequently.

Societal attitudes and the promotion of violence in cultural norms and the media have been suggested as risk factors for physical abuse. In addition, while the research is controversial, some studies show a positive relationship between televised violence and aggressive behaviours, particularly for individuals who watch substantial amounts of television.

Natural Disaster

Natural disaster is another factor which creates a sudden crisis in the human life and mostly for the children. Due many natural disasters the children has become orphans, they have lost their family and they have become homeless which makes them open to risk. Due to this particular factor the children's life change in a moment from a safe family life to a unsafe open to danger condition.

It is important to note that a single risk factor at any level does not necessarily lead to developmental impairments. Rather, it is the combination of risk factors that will make a child vulnerable. Risk factors are cumulative and interactive, and tend to reinforce each other. Identifying the children that are particularly at risk will help in ensuring that the ECD intervention will have the greatest impact because it is targeted at those that are potentially most in need.

Impact on Child

The different factor which affects to make the child vulnerable and marginalized has a range of impacts on their life and some of the children become homeless and in absence of any care-giver they get into crime or dies out of hunger, and even become street children. Child residing with a person(s) who has threatened to harm them and is likely to carry out that threat, harmed other children and hence is likely to kill, abuse or neglect the child. Children who are mentally/physically handicapped, has an illness, terminal/incurable disease and has no one to provide and care for him/her. The other impacted children: Are the orphans, who have no family to take care of him/her, or is a runaway or missing child whose parents cannot be located after a reasonable search period, the children being or is likely to be sexual, mentally, emotionally or physically abused, tortured or exploited; the children who are trafficked or abusing drug substances; the children who are abused for unthinkable gains or illegal activities; the children who are victims of arm conflict, civil unrest or a natural disaster.

Child Labour

A child chasing cows, goats, cutting grass or very young child washing dishes and looking after her little brother while cleaning her houses—are visible in rural India. On the other hand, in the urban area we can see the shoeshine boy or a little child serving tea in the tea shop and the rising number of street children. But there are innumerable girls and boys performing domestic chores, helping their parents working in the urban houses. Some of these children attain regular schools, some are irregular and some become dropouts. These are different forms of child labour and its consequence. Child labour is defined with different purposes.

A child is anyone below the age 14 years—this is, what the Constitution of India says. On the other side the United Nations Convention on the rights of the child says, anyone below the age of 18 year is a child. So, from these definitions we can understand that there are many definitions rather no fix definition is there for the children. The term Child Labour is used to describe employment of children below a certain age, which is considered illegal by law and custom.

The International Labour Organisation (ILO) states that child labour may be defined in a number of different ways, and a different definition yields a different estimate of child labour in India as well as other countries. According to ILO, children or adolescents who participate in work that does not affect their health and personal development or interfere with their schooling, is not child labour; rather it may generally be regarded as being something positive. These kinds of activities, suggests ILO, may contribute to children's developmentally, socially or morally dangerous and harmful to children, or work whose schedule interferes with their ability to attend regular school, or work that affects in any manner their ability to focus during school or experience healthy childhood.

In 2000, the ILO estimates, "246 million child workers aged 5 and 17 were involved in Child Labour, of which 171 million were involved in work that by its nature is hazardous to their safety, physical or mental health, and moral development. Moreover, some 8.4 million children were engaged in so-called 'unconditional' worst forms of Child Labour, which include forced and bonded labour, the use of children in armed conflict, trafficking in children and commercial sexual exploitation."

Child Labour is conventionally defined as a working child between age of 5 to 14 who are doing labour or engaged in economical activity either paid or unpaid. The definition of child as given under Child Labour (Prohibition and Regulation) Act of 1986 defines child means a person who has not completed his fourteen years of age so by this definition the question of Child Labour is solved (Lawz, 2011).

UNICEF defines child labour differently. A child, suggests UNICEF, is involved in child labour activities if between 5 to 11 years of age, he or she did at least one hour of economic activity or at least 28 hours of domestic work in a week, and in case of children between 12 to 14 years of age, he or she did at least 14 hours of economic activity or at least 42 hours of economic activity and domestic work per week. UNICEF in another report suggests, "Children's work needs to be seen as happening along a continuum, with destructive or exploitative work at one end and beneficial work—promoting or enhancing children's development without interfering with their schooling, recreation and rest—at the other. And between these two poles are vast areas of work that need not negatively affect a child's development."

India's Census 2001 office defines child labour as participation of a child less than 17 years of age in any economically productive activity with or without compensation, wages or profit. Such participation could be physical or mental or both. This work includes part-time help or unpaid work on the farm, family enterprise or in any other economic activity such as cultivation and milk production for sale or domestic consumption. Indian Government classifies child labourers into two groups: Main workers are those who work 6 months or more per year and marginal child workers are those who work at any time during the year but less than 6 months in a year. Working long hours, child labourers are often denied a basic school education, normal social interaction, personal development and emotional support from their family. Child labour is work which impairs the health and development of children (Lieten, 2002).

Beside these problems, children face many physical dangers—and death—from forced labour: Physical injuries and mutilations are caused by badly maintained machinery on farms and in factories, machete accidents in plantations, and any number of hazards encountered in industries such as mining, ceramics and fireworks manufacture. Pesticide poisoning is one of the biggest killers of child labourers. In Sri Lanka, pesticides kill more children than diphtheria, malaria, polio and tetanus combined. The global death toll each year from pesticides is supposed to be approximately 40,000. Growth deficiency is prevalent among working children, who tend to be shorter and lighter than other children; these deficiencies also impact on their adult life. Long-term health problems, such as respiratory disease, asbestosis and a variety of cancers, are common in countries where children are forced to work with dangerous chemicals. HIV/AIDS and other sexually transmitted diseases are rife among the one million children forced into prostitution every year; pregnancy, drug addiction and mental illness are also common among child prostitutes. Exhaustion and malnutrition are a result of underdeveloped children performing heavy manual labour, working long hours in unbearable conditions and not earning enough to feed themselves adequately. The children do not get the basic right to education fulfilled and in the macro-level the country will go short of skilled and educated labour force.

Framework of Constitutional Provision and Child Rights

In the present day world, the child has to be protected and his/her well-being has to be taken into consideration. This recognition and emphasis which has done on the child is due to the new perspectives of the rights of the child. The United Nations is a powerful body in the world because it acts as a global stage to put up issues which are emerging or issues which have gained prominence in the world. The United Nations Convention is a universally agrees set of non-negotiable standards and obligations. Thus, what UNCRC has done is that it has recognized the rights of the child and many countries have ratified the convention also. As it is a legally binding instrument, its implementation became a big obligation for the nations who have ratified this convention. India has ratified this convention on child rights. This means that India in a way has adopted the rights based framework, which is committed to protect the child rights which he/she is entitled to have. The Government of India ratified the UNCRC on 12th November, 1992. It has been almost more than two decades since India signed it but the plight of the children in our country is still miserable. Malnutrition, child labour, child sexual abuse in all these parametres India is topping the list in the world. It has become more important for our country to act for the protection of child rights.

The Indian Context

The Indian law has created many provisions and amendment also to make sure that the rights of the child are secured. But there are great flaws also which are attached to it. There are lot of contradictions as the law is entailing children for their rights but in the actual condition Indian children are the most vulnerable and marginalized. India has the huge number of child population. This increases the responsibility on the part of the Government to protect the rights of the child and ensure their well-being. Following are some of the important concerns that are faced by children and that are in contrast with the law.

Child Labour (Prohibitoin and Regulation) Act, 1986 and the Problem of Child Labour

India has the highest number of child labourers. The Child Labour Act, 1986 prohibits the employment of child labour under the age of 14 years in hazardous work places. But we find all lot of child labourers working in various situations in the different industries. Child labour has become the necessary evil of the economy of our country and a lot of money is also generated out of it.

Right to Education and Lack of Education among Children

The Right to Education act is a strong legal tool, which was brought about in the year of 2009. The nation after six decades on independence has understood the importance of education. But education is still inaccessible to lacks of children who are living in rural areas. The Sarva Shiksha Abhiyan (SSA) has not brought that results which it was ought to bring. The result of that is, there is increasing number of dropouts from the schools, and it is a very big issue which the Government is trying to address.

Right to Early Childhood Care

The early childhood care is given by the Government and is implemented through the ICDS scheme where the small infants are provided nutritious food. This scheme is running from 1975, but still India remains a hub for malnourished children. The Government has not been able to ensure the care of the children and even after so many years of Independence, the country suffers deaths of small infants from malnutrition. In India child labour can be seen in all the state but though there are laws against it there is no scope for it to stop. Selected articles of Constitution of India in this regard are presented as follows: Article-23—Prohibition of traffic in human beings and forced labour. Article-24—Prohibition of employment of children below the age of 14 years in factories, mines, or in any other hazardous employment. Article-45—Provision of early childhood care and education for children until the age of six years (86th Constitutional Amendment Act, 2002). Article-21(A)—Provision of free and compulsory education of children of the age of six to fourteen years (86th Constitutional Amendment Act, 2002). Article-51-A (k)—Fundamental duties of parent or guardian to provide opportunities for education of children between the age of six and fourteen year (Basu, 2008).

There are many loopholes in the Constitution of India also. As the Constitution has taken few of the works done by the child as child labour, those are the work which cause hazard for the child and has not considered the others works. But any work which is done by the child and which causes hamper to the psycho-social development of the child should be considered as a child labour. There are many works which creates hamper to the childhood like domestic work, patching posters, shoe shiners, vendors etc. and these works are not hazardous but they hamper the psych social development of the child. The segmentation of the labour market usually occurs in an environment in which there is a reasonably high demand for labour and a low degree of labour empowerment (Lieten, 2002). As the child is always cheap as labour and they can be easily controlled so they are hired in the different work places.

Bridging Community Development and Child Development

In the community, several issues must be looked at critically which are reinforcing vulnerability. These issues include: beliefs, tradition, care of school teachers etc. The kind of *beliefs* that the community people have towards the children and their socialization is very offensive for the children themselves. People may feel, "There is nothing wrong in the fact that the children are working in the factories and not going to the school are not very harmful for the children". The whole community gets a kind of economic support from the child that makes them feel if children are earning without any education, it's good to let them work also. In reality, this kind of belief actually effects the socialization of the children. The community is very ignorant to the fact that it is a viscous cycle which needs to be broken and the child should get a proper environment for the development.

The culture of the people, i.e. a *tradition* which is practised generation after generation, also matters a lot. The whole thing can be considered historically. The people who are staying and working in a particular place have practiced the same thing as their parents sent there. Now, they are sending children in the factories and earning money through them. In later stage when they become elder these children will start sending their children to the same place. Thus, the whole thing is going on over the generations and becoming a culture.

The *school* is another aspect which can nurture the children. According to the RTE, every child has the right to get education. In contrary, the Firozabad experience is different. The schools prevailing there are not interested to nurture children or to oppose who are working in the factories. The teachers can play a major role in the whole scenario but some are ignorant and some of them do not know how to deal with the matter as no one in the community including the parents care for this issue. To them it is a very normal thing and as the children are supporting the families and nothing is wrong in it.

In brief, I feel, as the emphasis on education has shifted and now more focus is on the development of the whole child, it is apparent that the community plays an increasingly greater role in education. The reason is obvious. The community is the local social world of the child and it is the smallest unit of the society that presents an integrated pattern of reality to which he must become adjusted. In other words, it is society in microcosm (Dodson, 1947). To provide every child the fullest opportunity possible for development of their own capabilities and potentialities, it is necessary to look into the community for the forces that thwart personality development and keep it from achieving its maximum development.

References

Basu, D.D., 2008, *Comments on the Constitution of India,* Vol. 3, Nagpur: Lexis Nexis, Butterworth's Wadhawa.

Doddawadmath, J.V., 2010, "ILO Conventions on Development of Children and Young Persons", *Legal News and Views*, 24 (10).

Dodson, D.W., 1947, "The Community and Child Development", *The Journal of Educational Sociology,* 20 (5): 264-271.

Lawz, 2011, *Child Labour Problems and Perspective*, 16-18.

Lieten, G.K., 2002, "Child Labour in India", *Economic and Political Weekly*, 37 (52). For details, please access: www.epw.yodasoft.com

Satbhai, B.S., 2011, *Child Labour in India—Issues and Responses*, For details, please access: www.legalservicesindia.com

www.ilo.org

15

Indian Aborigines Solicit Intensive Interventions for Ensuring Inclusive Growth

Subhrasil Basu

Right now, global population of aborigines has been estimated to be a little more than 300 million who are living in 70 countries across the world. General Assembly adopted "*UN Declaration on the Rights of Indigenous People*" in 2007 with a view to setting an important standard for the well-being of this stratum of people. This declaration aims at strengthening international cooperation for alleviation of crises in the areas of human rights, environment development, education and health and so on and so forth. The state of primitive communities as it transpires from the *UN Declaration* solicits special attention of all concern since they are truly in deplorable condition. Since the onset of human civilization, this stratum of people has been incessantly under subjugation by the mainstream of population.

The reference of Indian indigenous people is found in '*Vedas*' who could have been Dravidians or Pre-Dravidians. Salient characteristics of Scheduled Tribe (ST) communities stated by the Lokur Committee are thus: (i) indication of primitive traits; (ii) distinctive culture; (iii) shyness of contact with the community at large; (iv) geographical location; and (v) backwardness.

In our country, the number of individual ethnic groups notified as Scheduled Tribe is 705, but 194 sub-groups have further been notified too who are living in 9 states. All these communities constitute 8.6 per cent of the total population of the country (Fig. 15.1).

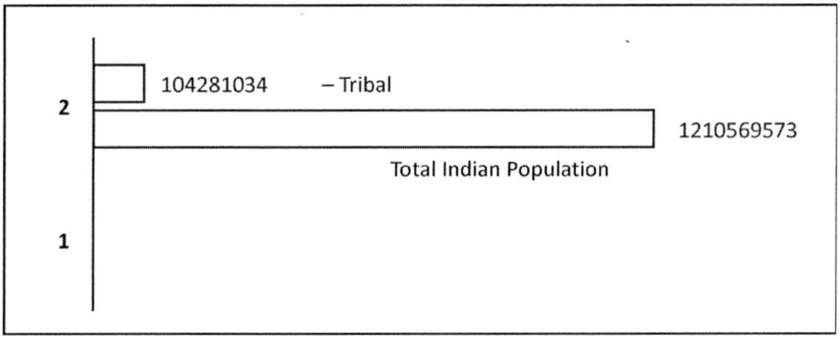

Fig. 15.1: Tribals in Relation to Indian Total Population

Source: Census of India, 2011.

As regards settlement pattern, Lakshadweep, Mizoram, Nagaland, Meghalaya and Arunachal Pradesh are thickly populated with Scheduled Tribe (ST) people ranging from nearly 70 per cent to 94 per cent and next to these States and Union Territories, there are four States viz. Chhattisgarh, Jharkhand, Odisha and Madhya Pradesh having 21 to 30 per cent ST people out of the total population of India. A few communities are almost going to extinct, e.g. Jarwas and other communities like Andamanese, Onge, Oraon, Munda, Mina, Khond, Saora having less than 1000 population. The Gond, on the other hand is large in number having a little over than 7 million. These primitive communities basically survive on hunting, wood gathering, other forest products and finally shifting cultivation. Besides them, a few aborigine groups were involved in criminal activities because of perpetual neglect by the elite sections of our society. Prior to 1953, ironically they were called as Criminal Tribes and now they are regarded as Ex-criminal Tribes or De-notified Groups. There are Nomads who are engaged in mimicry, jugglery, dancing and begging too. Obtained data revealed that 11.3 per cent of the total rural population is Scheduled Tribe while 2.8 per cent tribals of the total population in the country have become settled in urban areas (Fig. 15.2).

Constitutional Safeguards

Indian Constitution has made elaborate provisions to promote and protect the social, educational, economic and cultural interests of

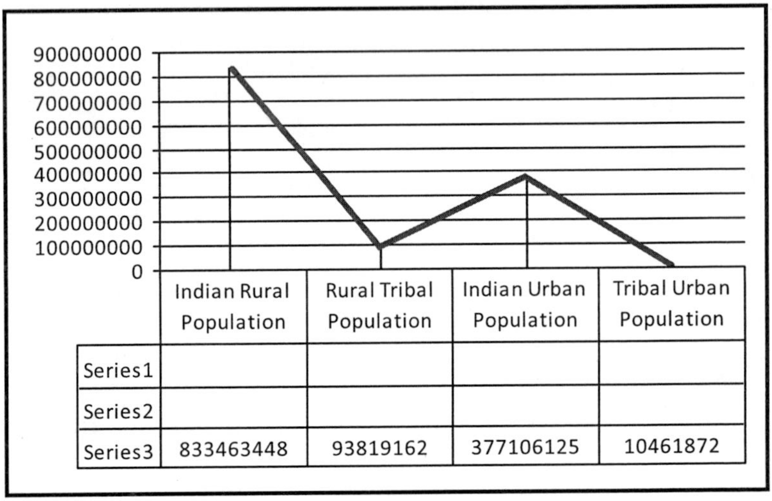

Fig. 15.2: Rural Urban Settlement of STs *vis-à-vis* Indians

Source: Census of India, 2011.

these communities in India who have been included in the *'Weaker Sections'* and the *'Backward Classses'* category. Scheduled Tribes have been defined as socially and educationally backward in our Constitution. Provisions made for them in the constitution are as follows :

Article 46 under Directive Principles of State Policy lays down that*"The state shall promote with special care the educational and economic interest of the weaker sections of the people and in particular, ... the Scheduled tribes, and shall protect them from social injustice and all forms of exploitation"*.

Article 48 of our Constitution directs the State Governments to make provisions for improving social, economic, and educational standard of these sections of people.

Article 244 lays down that the Union Government will have the power to direct the states in respect of administration of Scheduled Areas and Scheduled Tribes.

Part XVI of the Constitution concerned with Special Provisions Relating to certain Classes deals with reservations of seats for … Scheduled Tribes … in the parliament and Legislative Assemblies for a limited period and their reservation in services and posts (Articles 330 to 336).

Article 338 provides a special officer for the Scheduled Castes and Scheduled Tribes to be appointed by the President to investigate all matters relating to safeguards provided for the Scheduled Castes and Tribes ......

Article 339 has laid down that the President would appoint a Commission to report on the administration of scheduled areas and the welfare of the Scheduled tribes in the states.

Finally, the entity of Indian tribals has been established under Article 342 (i) and 342 (ii) of the Constitution of India.

Legislations

There is no dearth of efforts on the part of the Government of India for the protection of interest of the tribal people as ample progressive legislations have been enacted which are as follows:

- The Minimum Wages Act, 1948;
- The Bonded Labour System (Abolition) Act, 1976;
- The Child Labour (Prohibition and Regulation) Act, 1986;
- The Scheduled Castes and the Scheduled Tribes (Prevention of Atrocities) Act, 1989;
- The Panchayats (Extension to the Scheduled areas) Act, 1996;
- Minor Forest Produce Act, 2005;
- Recognition of Forest Rights Act, 2006;
- The Right Fair Compensation and Transparency in Land Acquisition, Rehabilitation and Resettlement (Amendment) Ordinance, 2015.

Apart from above referred legislations, *National Policy of Education* (1986 and revised Policy in 1992) suggested the following programmes for education of tribal people:

(a) Opening primary schools in Tribal Areas.
(b) Need to develop curricula of their language.
(c) Promoting schedule tribes youth to work as teachers.

(d) Ashram schools, Residential schools should be established in large scale in Tribal areas.
(e) Incentives to encourage their life style through education.

Glimpse of Development Programmes

Prior to analyzing their existing state of affairs, it may be pertinent to make an overview of the programmes in brief launched by Government of India. Tribal Sub-Plan (TSP) provides Special Central Assistance to different States and Union Territories to promote their initiatives for tribal development. The assistance is given for family-oriented income generating schemes in Agriculture and allied sectors like Horticulture, Minor Irrigation, Soil Conservation, Animal Husbandry, Forests, Cooperatives, Fisheries, Village and Small Scale Industries and Education also.

Benefits under the scheme of development for Primitive Tribal Groups (PTGs) are extended to certain tribal groups. 75 such groups have been identified on the bases of pre-agricultural level of technology, low level of literacy, declining or stagnant population and so on. Furthermore, comprehensive long term "Conservation-*cum*-Development (CCD) Plans" have also been formulated through base line survey.

In different States, 14 Tribal Research Institutes (TRIs) have been functioning and extending planning inputs to State Governments, conducting research and impact studies, data collection, codification of customary law and organizing training, seminars and workshops, museum containing tribal artifacts etc.

Besides above, Girls' and Boys' Hostel, Ashrama Schools in TSP areas, Vocational Training Centres in Tribal areas, strengthening education among Scheduled Tribe Girls in Low Literacy District, Tribal Cooperative Marketing Development Federation of India Limited (TRIFED), Coaching for Scheduled Tribes, Grant in Aid to Voluntary Organisations working for welfare of Scheduled Tribes, Post-Matric Scholarship for ST students, Up-gradation of Merit of ST students and finally Rajiv Gandhi National Fellowship Scheme (RGNFS) for pursuing higher studies like M.Phil. and Ph.D. etc. schemes and programmes have been in operation too.

Apart from Government programmes, ample NGOs have been working very intensively for the cause of this segment of people in the different parts of tribal dominated areas.

Existing Scenario

Prevailing condition of Indian aborigines happens to be very gloomy. Seventieth anniversary of Indian Independence will be commemorated just after couple of months, but surprisingly enough, an overwhelming portion of them has been socio-economically languishing behind almost polar opposite compared to the rest of the population still now. To be frank enough, their survival is almost at stake owing to their incapability of availing the scope of Government's schemes and programmes on education, alternative sources of earning, basic civic amenities and services and so on and so forth. Pace of development of Indian primitive communities is quite far from the expected growth.

In spite of the efforts taken by both Central and State Governments during the preceding seven decades, these communities have been supposed to be still struggling for their survival since they possess uneconomic land without having occupancy rights, following traditional practices, working basically as landless labourers, pursuing animal rearing on a small scale etc. Existing state of the tribal communities can legitimately be perceived if we just go through the findings of the Government's Reports also.

Tribal Settlement

As regards settlement pattern, out of the total tribal folk in our country, nearly 90 per cent live in rural area while a little more than 10 per cent came to reside in urban area. So, 1/10th of the total tribal people was almost compelled to migrate to cities for earning their livelihood which is obviously an unhealthy practice. It is a proven phenomenon that the existence of any community becomes at stake while its community members are forced to leave their native land (Fig. 15.3). Migration from native lands make the people devoid of social identity.

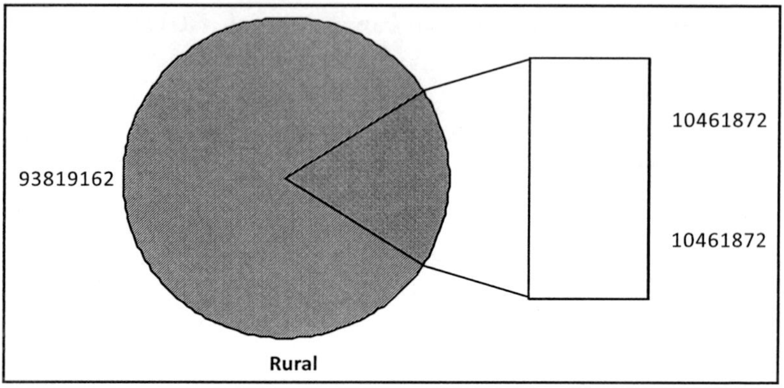

Fig. 15.3: Primitives Living in Rural and Urban Area.

Source: Census of India, 2011.

Sex-Ratio

Now, everyone admits that the unevenness in male/female-ratio is evident because of sheer negligence towards women in our society. Sex-ratio among tribal is 990:1000 and it is undeniably decent compared to over all sex-ratio of Indian population. It reflects that the attitude towards women in so-called male dominated society in plains has not been percolated to the primitive communities. But paradoxically, the sex-ratio in urban areas among them happens

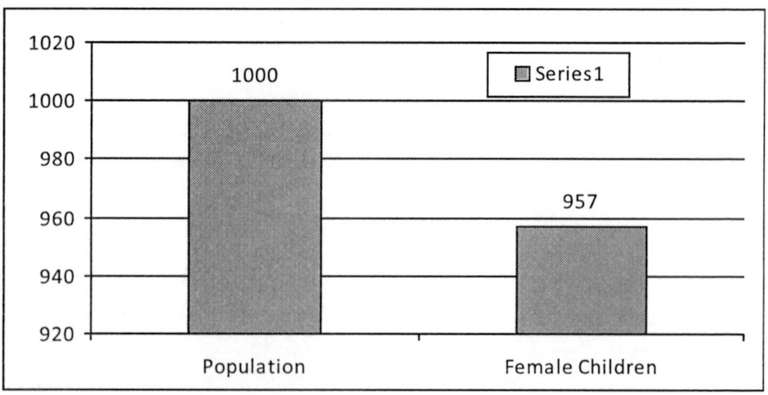

Fig. 15.4: Child Sex-Ratio among Tribals.

Source: Census of India, 2011.

to be almost same like mainstream population. Hence, this emerging negative trend certainly proves the penetration of virus of plains has enveloped the tribal people too. Existing child sex-ratio among tribal has been reported to be 957:1000 which is which is, in fact very much alarming.

Literacy

Massive illiteracy is one of the major pulling factors which inhibits the tribal people for being aware of their backwardness and at the same time, it refrains them too from getting the benefits from the available opportunities for their socio-economic well-being. As regards literacy, altogether 49.51 per cent ST people have been found literate out of their total population. Among the total tribal people, 42.79 per cent literate people live in rural area and urban literates constitute only 6.71 per cent. Furthermore, sex-wise segregation status depicts that women literates are lagging behind by 8.15 per cent from their male counterparts overall. If we take into account male female ratio out of their total population in rural and urban areas, the gender gap encompasses 7.54 per cent in the rural area while the difference is negligible, i.e. 0.6 per cent only. On the contrary, gender gap percentage between rural and urban area is only 2.32 per cent in so far as the total literates among primitives are concerned. Following table shows the literacy status of these communities:

Table 15.1: Literacy Status of Tribals

Area	Male	Female	Total
Rural	26247871	18383774	44631645
Urban	3819041	3184737	7003778
Total	30066912	21568511	51635423

Source: Census of India, 2011.

Economy

Poor economic condition always acts as the prime barrier to avail of the benefits provided in different development schemes.

"Statistical Profile of Scheduled Tribes in India 2010" published by the Ministry of Tribal Affairs, Statistics Division, Government of India depicts the dismal scenario of Indian tribals. This publication highlights that percentage of ST people living below the poverty line in urban area is 34.75 where as in rural area it is 45.86 in 1999-2000 (*Source* : Planning Commission). This poverty ratio for STs has been estimated covering all major states, a few small groups could not be covered due to some practical reasons. It would be worthwhile to mention that Planning Commission used poverty line based on per capita consumption expenditure as the criterion to determine the persons living below the poverty line.

In the sphere of total worker force in the country, ST people represent a considerable segment. People of ST communities survive especially as wage-labour. Census 2011 shows that *Work Participation Rates* among Scheduled Tribe is 48.7 per cent of the total ST population in the country and Scheduled Tribe males constitute 55.58 per cent of the total Scheduled Tribe workers while 44.41 per cent workers are females on the other. In the rural area, the difference between male and female in terms of participation rate is negligible, but the female participation rate is highly low in comparison with male workers in urban area. Perhaps, wages are

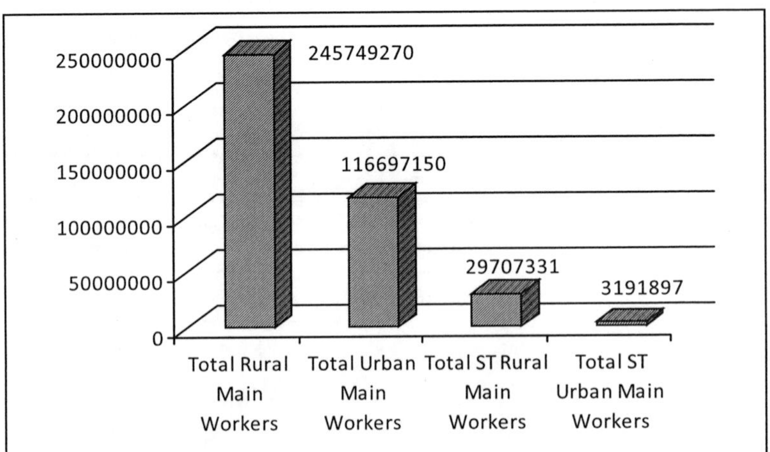

Fig. 15.5: Total Main Workers and ST Workers in India.

Source: Census of India, 2011.

better in cities hence, majority of female urban dwellers need not go for working as their male family members earn well or like mainstream population the male members do not prefer their female members to work outside. As regards marginal workers, ST occupies 35.3 per cent of the total ST workers and only 16.8 per cent ST people are cultivators. In the realm of Agricultural Labourers, ST Labourers are 26.68 per cent of the total agricultural labour force which is 44.5 per cent of the total workers in the country. As far as the Household Industry Workers and Other Workers are concerned, ST people comprise of 0.86 per cent in the former category and 9.36 per cent in the latter group of labours. All these statistical data reveal the magnitude of the wretched economic condition of the primitive communities in our country.

Health

In so far as the available services for improving the health condition of the tribal people is concerned, they have been observed unable to avail of health facilities provided by the Government. Miserable scenario is observed in the health sphere as per the findings of National Family Health Survey (NFHS-3, 2005-2006). The said report depicts that Infant Mortality amongst STs is 62.1 (per 1000), under-five mortality is reported to be 95.7 per 1000, Percentage of *Institutional Deliveries* happens to be only 17.7 and the coverage of *childhood vaccination* (full immunization) is only 31.3 per cent. *Own home* has been found to be the place of delivery in case of 70.9 per cent and only 17.9 per cent of births to ST mothers are *Delivered through health facility*. Data with regard to frequency of going to an *AWC (Anganwadi Centre) for early childhood care/ preschool education* depicts that 16 per cent goes regularly while 14.4 per cent goes occasionally. In case of Households covered under the purview of a *health scheme or health insurance* it has been reported to be only 2.6 per cent. All these statistical information revealed that ST people are neither aware nor capable of perceiving the importance of these services.

Violence

Another crucial aspect is violence against women, 47 per cent married ST women as has been evident in the aforesaid report, in the age group of 15-49 years have experienced emotional, physical or sexual violence which is higher than any other social group. The most amazing fact is that many women believe their husbands are justified in committing violence against their wives for any of the specific reasons. It reveals the poor state of understanding persisting among tribal women.

Civic Amenities

Report of "NSSO Housing Condition of Amenities in India, 2008-09" has highlighted that nearly 11 per cent of rural households and 3 per cent of urban households belong to STs. The said report also revealed that in rural areas, 56.1 per cent of ST households depended on tube-well/ hand pump as the major source of drinking water, only 18.5 per cent ST people could use tap water and the amazing scenario is that 2.7 per cent of rural ST households still use spring as source of drinking water. The most striking findings appeared that 237 households in rural areas and 157 households in urban areas per 1000 population do not get sufficient drinking water throughout the year. Electricity has not extended to majority of the ST households and ironically a sizeable portion of them still go for open defecation. Therefore, rural ST people have been found to be deprived of enjoying basic civic amenities.

Empowerment

Empowerment of ST women seems to be highly important especially as HDI (Human Development Index) has been considered to be the universally accepted indicator of development. Here, we may highlight different facets of women empowerment. The findings of Women's Report of NFHS-3 (2005-2006) have been analysed herein in brief. The report highlighted that *Women's cash earnings* happened to be always less compared to men and only 6.5 per cent ST women earned more than their husbands. *Participation in decision-making* has been evident in 37.5 per cent women belonging to the age group of 15-49 years. *Women's decision regarding use of her own cash earnings* has been found only 14.8 per cent among ST women though 47.9 per cent ST women opined to have *an equal or greater say than their husbands*. In another sphere of women empowerment, 38.2 per cent of total ST women *have money that they can decide how to use* and only 9 per cent has a bank or savings account which they themselves operate. *Women freedom of movement* is very much restricted in STs as only 30.3 per cent is allowed to *move to market, health facility and outside the village or community*. Hence, ST women are undoubtedly far away from the empowerment in the true sense of the term.

It is well known that the tribal possess rich folk culture which encompasses dance, drama and puppetry. All these have deep roots in the society as these are stuck to the tradition. The rural tribal people get immense pleasure by performing these forms of art. These obviously manifest the rich heritage of our ancient culture. But these are going on the wane due to eviction of primitives from their native lands owing to deforestation for infrastructural development projects and popularization or commercialisation of Hindi film songs as well.

Development Approach

In view of above findings, the plight of ST communities can pertinently be assessed to a great extent. With the passage of time, certain advancements have surely been taken place among them compared to their preceding condition. But any one goes for appraising the existing state of affairs keeping in view of newly emerged parametres of development, it will certainly be evident that the people of this community is still far away from the mainstream population. We may quote Korten, an eminent scholar in this sphere as he defined that "*Development is a process by which the members of a society increase their personal and institutional capacities to mobilize and manage resources to produce suitable and justly distributed improvements in their quality of life consistent with their own aspirations*". Undoubtedly, this is almost nightmare to the primitive communities as they are far off from this state rather they have been enormously struggling for their existence in the true sense of the term.

In the recent past, bottom-up approach for formulation of grass-roots-level planning through participatory development process has been initiated by the Government. NGOs happened to adopt this technique long back. As a matter of fact, NGOs have gained success to a large extent as far as their development objectives are concerned. Government functionaries have recently started Participatory Rural Appraisal/ Participatory Learning and Action (PRA/PLA) techniques for formulation and refinement of local level plan of action on the bases of the people's needs and aspirations. Every development functionary admits that motivating and getting involved the primitive communities in development programmes cannot be taken place within a short while.

It is a proven fact that mere provision of reservation cannot make them equipped to get the advantage of the existing opportunities and it happens to be bit difficult to make the rural primitive community people involved in participatory planning also. It solicits perpetual adherence to them by the development functionaries in order to empower and convince them so as to bring about changes in their quality of life by themselves only with numerous assistances available in the various schemes initiated by Governments and Voluntary organizations as well.

An empirical observation may be cited here for its enormous significance. Present writer had the opportunities, on a few occasions to have practical exposure during his visit to certain tribal infested areas of Purulia and Bankura Districts where some development programmes initiated by the Joint Forest Management (JFM), a wing of Ramakrishna Mission Lokashiksha Parishad, Ramakrishna Mission Ashrama, Narendrapur. He happened to interact with the beneficiaries too during visit which made him enlightened about the present state of affairs of the tribal community and thrust areas taken into consideration for the wellbeing of its members. Besides organising programmes on education, capacity development, JFM gave pivotal thrust on people's empowerment in terms of perceiving their perennial problems, shortcomings and also exploring the feasible remedial measures by themselves and finally, to overcome those on their own. With the passage of time, it has been evident that the forest fringe dwellers became so empowered that they happened to be the members of Forest Protection Committees and started to protect the forest areas. They successively realised the need for enriching the forest environment which ultimately proved to be an important resource of their survival and avenue of earnings. Their processed products are sold from the *Ashrama's* sales out-lets. So, the socio-economic condition of the tribal communities living in the aforesaid areas has gradually been elevated due to Ramakrishna Mission Lokashiksha Parishad's participatory development endeavour.

Swami Vivekananda's development philosophy appears to be highly plausible to be referred here as those always steer Lokashiksha Parishad's multifaceted development programmes launched in the different corners of the State covering both rural and urban areas. Swamiji was very much down to earth and he profoundly believed in people's own drive for their own well-being. He had crystal clear perception of the socio-economic hierarchy of each stratum of Indian social structure as he travelled India on foot and used to stay in the houses of both rich and poor and intensively interacted with them on various issues. During his stay in America also, he talked to the labourers and agrarian community members apart from elite sections of people. Marie Louise Burk referred above in her book, entitled "*Swami Vivekananda in the West: New Discoveries*".

Hence, the epitome of development initiatives lies in the utterance of Swamiji as he aptly conceived and opined "*you cannot help anyone, you can only serve..... Give-up the idea that by ruling over others you can do any good to them. But you can do just as much as you can in the case of the plant; you can supply the growing seed with the materials for the making-up its body, bringing to it the earth, the water, the air, that it want by its own nature: it will assimilate and grow by its own nature*".

References

Advaita Ashrama, 1970, Complete Works of Swami Vivekananda, Mayavati Memorial Edition, Calcutta.

Government of India, 2011, *Census of India 2011*, New Delhi: Ministry of Home Affairs.

Government of India, 2005-06, *National Family Health Survey-III*, New Delhi: Ministry of Health and Family Welfare.

Government of India, 2010, *Statistical Profile of Scheduled Tribes in India*, New Delhi: Ministry of Tribal Affairs, Statistics Division.

Government of India, 2008-09, *Report of NSSO-Housing Condition of Amenities in India*, New Delhi: Ministry of Statistics and Programme Implementation (MOSPI).

Mahajan, V.D., 2008, *Select Modern Government*, New Delhi: S. Chand & Company.

SECTION-III
Gender and Community Development

16
Gender Justice in India
An Overview

Rupa Biswas and *Asok Kumar Sarkar*

Women constitute nearly half of India's population and play a crucial role in social and economic development of the nation. But no society treats its women at par with its men and they continue to suffer diverse deprivations because of their sexual orientation. Widespread discrimination against women is structural and existed long before the civilization. The discrimination and atrocities reflected in several forms like striking demographic features, low literacy rate, poor health condition, under-representation in public domain such as Parliament, administration and share in the earned income. Gender-based violence is another area of concern. Women's issues were raised for the first time in India in the 19th century during the British rule. Social reformers were champion for starting crusade against the prevailing evil practices like *sati*, child marriage, widowhood, polygamy, *devdasi* etc. and at the same time emphasized the importance of women's education for their upliftment. In the following section we shall have a glimpse on the challenges encountered by women in different arenas.

Challenges Faced by Women in India

Education

Denial and low achievement in the arena of female education is a major hurdle to attain equality. Just after independence the female literacy rate was only 9 per cent. According to 2011 census data, there is a wide gender disparity in the literacy rate in India. The female literacy rate is only 65.46 per cent while the male literacy rate is 82.14 per cent respectively. About 50 per cent girls of the total number of enrolment dropout before reaching class-VI. Only 36.22 per cent girls complete secondary education. Women fought a lot for getting education. In this context the experiences of Dr. Haimavati Sen (1866-1932) need to be mentioned here (Forbes, 1998): "The outer quarters were my resort, that is where I spent all my time; during the office hours, I stayed in the school room. The teacher was very fond of me. I greatly enjoyed listening to the lessons. But I had no right to education. Though I lived like a boy in every respect, in matters of education, I remained a woman. It was a popular superstition in our country that women, if educated, have to suffer widowhood; hence, that path was entirely closed for me. But, I was inspired by an eager wish God had planted in my heart". Fortunately, a School Sub-Inspector visited the school and heard Haimavati answered the questions her brothers missed. The Sub-Inspector spoke to her father and Haimavati became a regular pupil. The Missionaries began the first Girls School which was immediately followed by the efforts of social reformers.

Politics

For obtaining the right to franchise there was a great amount of struggle which begun long before Independence. The Government of India Act of 1935 granted voting right to only 6 million women over 21 years of age and who owned property or had attained a certain level of education to general seats or reserved seats. It was only after Independence that voting rights to all the women were ensured. The 73rd & 74th Constitutional Amendment Act, 1992 reserves seats for women at the grassroot-level up to 33 per cent which created a window to be a part of governance and effecting development process. After the passage of 70 years of Independence, women's representation in the arena of politics is quite distressing. In the 14th Lok Sabha, there were only 51 women, constituting 9.51 per cent and in Rajya Sabha 23 women constituting 9.50 per cent respectively. Women's Reservation Bill, for the first time, introduced by Devegowda Government on September 12, 1996, a day just before Parliament was to be adjourned. The main criticism was that the Bill contained hardly any provision for OBCs, Dalit and the Minorities. The former bill renamed under Constitution 108th Amendment 2010 which was passed by Rajya Sabha on 9th March within amidst controversies. It proposes 33 per cent of all seats to be reserved at Lok Sabha and Legislative Assemblies. But, it is unfortunate that the Bill is yet to be passed by the Lok Sabha.

Legal Disabilities and Atrocities before Independence

During 19th century in Bengal, there was a tradition of self-immolation after the death of the husband which was known as *sati* and for which Raja Ram Mohun Roy started a crusade. This evil practice was banned by introducing legislation in 1829. The widows were bound to live a miserable life. The effort of Vidyasagar for widow remarriage was another achievement and the Widow Remarriage Act of 1856 was passed. The sacrosanct character of Hindu marriage was challenged for the first time in 1885 in the case of Rukhmabai, married at the age of 11 and refused to live with her husband. When the husband moved to Court, the Court, did not grant the plaintiff the relief, he sought. But, the Appellate Court set aside the earlier judgement. But Rukhmabai stood firm on her decision and ultimately an out of Court settlement was arrived at (Desai and Thakkar, 2001). Then, the case of Phulmani Dasi, 11 years old bride bleed to death which brought for the first the miseries of child-brides and the issue of Age of Consent. Ultimately the age of consent was fixed at 12 in 1891 (Desai and Thakkar, 2001).

Work

The lives of India's working women deteriorated under colonial rule. Jobs in the modern sector did not offset the decline of traditional industries for either men or women, but women suffered the greatest loss. Because labour was plentiful, women continued to work in the unskilled, unmechanized sectors where they were poorly paid. The new professions like teaching, law and medicines required education and family support. Even Kadambini Ganguly, first women graduate and later a doctor by profession was called a whore; unmarried women without impeccable credentials and respectable families were even more vulnerable to verbal and sexual harassment. In Ahmedabad in the early 1930 the case of Dr. (Miss) Ahalyabai Samant, the Director of the Municipal Dispensary of Nadiad, was reported in the newspapers. Dr. Balabhai Harishankar Bhatt, the Municipal Councillor abducted and assaulted her. In this regard the verdict of Lower Court went in favour of Dr. Samant whereas The Chief Justice of the High Court overturned this decision and simply fined Bhatt (Forbes, 1998). The struggle against discrimination in matters of employment surfaced in 1979, when it was discovered that the Service Rules of the Indian Foreign Service required a woman officer to obtain the permission of the Government for marriage and also to resign if in the view of the Government that such a marriage or the domestic commitments were likely to come in the way of the efficient discharge of her duties. In 1979 the Apex Court of India declared that such rules were unconstitutional (C.B. Muthamma *vs*. India, AIR, 1979, SC, 1868). In an another case Maya Devi *vs*. State of Maharashtra (1986) a requirement that a married woman obtain her husband's consent before applying for public employment was challenged and the Apex Court once again held that such consent requirement was unconstitutional (Desai and Thakkar, 2001). Then the most well-known case of sexual harassment where the woman sought legal help to punish the perpetrator was Rupan Deol Bajaj *vs*. KPS Gill. The victim fought 8 years long battle and Gill was sentenced to 3 month imprisonment along with Rs. 2.5 lakh fine. From the incidents it is quite evident that even workplace is not free from violence and also denied the right to equality. The persistent decline in female labour force participation rate (LFPR) in India in rural areas from 33.3 per cent to 26.5 per cent and for urban areas from 17.8 per cent to 14.6 per cent (NSSO, 2011) is a matter of grave concern (www.iimb.ernet.in/research/sites/default/files/WP%20No.%20364.pdf). According to the ILO's Global Employment Trends 2013 report India is placed at 120th of 131 countries in women's labour force participation.

Demography

According to the 2011 census, The sex-ratio is 940—but when it comes to child sex ratio it has declined over the years (1991—927, 2001—933, 2011—914) and a matter of great concern (Government of India, 2011). Preference is given for boys over girls and discrimination begins before she is born. Sex determination tests and female foeticide has led to the skewed sex-ratio in India. We are a nation of daughter killers which affirms India's 2011 census. For every 1000 boys there are at least about 60-70 girls under the age of 6 years who were killed before or within 6 years after birth (www.genderbytes.wordpress.com). This is the lowest gender-ratio recorded since India's Independence in 1947. So, discrimination on women starts well before she is born and continues till she breathes her last. The skewed sex-ratio generates other problems too like trafficking. Some of the India's prosperous states like Haryana (830), Punjab (846), Delhi (866), Rajasthan and Maharashtra (883), Gujarat (886) respectively shows remarkable decline in child sex-ratio. The phenomenon of lower CSR is linked with other factors too. Since, the 1970s there has been a marked increase in dowry demands and deaths. Tensions have increased in a family where a daughter has to be educated, married, and demands of the in-laws have to be met even after years of marriage. This initially used to be an urban middle class phenomenon, but now has found acceptance in the rural society as well. The family of the girl child considers her as a social and an economic burden. Thus, the deep-rooted attitude of parents, family, society lead to female infanticide and encouraged sex-detection test, female foeticide.

Child Marriage

Nearly 47.4 per cent of women aged 20-24 years were married by the age of 18 years and the states where mostly the incidences of child marriage reported are Bihar 69 per cent, Rajasthan 65.2 per cent, Jharkhand 63.2 per cent, Madhya Pradesh 57.3 per cent, Uttar Pradesh 58.6 per cent respectively (NFHS-3). The issue of child marriage has direct bearing upon their health (www.nfhsindia.org).

Table 16.1: Crime against Women in India (2002-2011)

Nature of Crime	2002	2003	2004	2005	2006	2007	2008	2009	2010	2011
Rape	16373	15847	18233	18359	19348	20737	21,467	21,397	22,172	24,206
Kidnapping and Abduction	14506	13296	15578	15750	17414	20416	22,939	25,741	29,795	35,565
Dowry Deaths	6822	6208	7026	6787	7618	8093	8,172	8,383	8,391	8,618
Cruelty at Home	49237	50703	58121	58319	63128	75930	81,344	89,546	94,041	99,135
Molestation	33943	32939	34567	34175	36617	38734	40,413	38,711	40,613	42,968
Sexual Harassments	10155	12325	10001	9984	9966	10950	12,214	11,009	9,961	8,570
Importation of Girls	76	46	89	149	67	61	67	48	36	80
Other Crimes	11922	9237	10718	12030	10607	10391	9240	8969	8576	9508
Total Reported Incidence	143034	140601	154333	155553	164765	185312	195856	203804	213585	228650

Source: Crime in India, National Crime Records Bureau, 2004, 2005, 2006, 2007, 2008, 2009, 2010 and 2011.

Health

The health of Indian women is intrinsically linked to their status in society. India has high maternal mortality rate 254/1,00,000 live births (Sample Registration System, 2004-05) (Dhar, 2012). Giving birth to children before reaching physical maturity increases the risk of MMR which is followed by depriving them from institutionalized health care. One woman dies in every 8 minutes which adds up to a loss of more than 63,000 young and productive lives every year. Most women did not receive health care during pregnancy. The high levels of maternal mortality are especially distressing because the majority of these deaths could be prevented if women had adequate health services. In India most of the birth took place at home and were not attended by trained medical personnel. Women are also suffering from anemia and malnutrition.

Violence

Women constitute the weaker sex and this fact is also borne by the number of crimes and atrocities committed against them in their life cycle. This takes the form of female foeticide, infanticide, rape, domestic violence, dowry harassment, molestation, honour killing, acid attack, sexual abuse of girl children, trafficking and so on. In 1972 at Mathura, a girl of 16 was raped in the premises of a police station and the Supreme Court set aside the judgement of the High Court and acquitted the policemen which brought the entire nation into shock. Though, the *Sati Pratha* was legally banned in 1829, the incident of *Sati* again took place in 1987 in Rajasthan where Rup Kanwar, a young and educated girl was said to have burnt herself on the pyre of her husband. The recent Delhi gang rape case on 16th December, 2012 where the victim died of injuries took the nation to shock and subsequently public protest was made against Government for not providing adequate security to women. The murder of Aarushi Talwar in 2008 in the name of family honour which held responsible her parents are awaiting trial. In Haryana, Punjab, Rajasthan girls are being killed in the respect of family honour. Table 16.1 depicts incidences of violence against women in India 2002-2011.

Government Initiatives for Gender Justice

Government of India over the years has introduced programmes, policies and legislations to address women's plight which can be categorized as follows:

Constitutional Provisions

The commitment to gender justice is well entrenched at the highest policy-making-level—the Constitution of India. A few important provisions for women are: Article-14—equal rights and opportunities in Political, Economic and Social spheres, Article-15—prohibits discrimination on grounds of sex, Article 15(3) enables affirmative discrimination in favour of women, Article 39 equal means of livelihood and equal pay for equal work, Article 42 just and humane conditions of work and maternity relief, Article 51 (A) (e) fundamental duty to renounce practices derogatory to dignity of women.

Initiatives through Five Year Plans

Efforts have also been made through Five Year planning towards securing gender justice. One of the main objectives of the First Five Year Plan was to provide adequate services to promote the welfare of women to enable them to play their legitimate role in family and community. The 2nd, 3rd, 4th, 5th Five Year Plans were more or less the same as that of the First Five Year Plan. The welfare approach guided policies and programmes. Condensed course of education and working women's hostel, short stay home introduced. The year 1974 was the landmark in Indian history as the committee on the status of women submitted a report titled "Towards Equality" which reflected distressing facts on the status of women in India for the first time. From Sixth Five Year Plan onwards a marked shift took place from welfare to development approach. The difference between these two approach lies that the former approach treated women as beneficiaries or recipients of benefits whereas the later one recognized women as participants in development and not mere as targets. During Seventh Five Year

Plan emphasis laid on employment generation opportunities and STEP was launched. The decade 1990-2000 was declared as the SAARC decade of the Girl Child. The Shramashakti Report was published in 1988. The National Perspective Plan on Women was also declared (1988-2000). During the Eighth Five Year Plan National Commission for Women a statutory body was constituted. The 73rd & 74th Constitutional Amendment Act, 1992 were also came into being. From the Ninth Five Year Plan onwards there was a shift towards the approaches, i.e. empowerment and National Policy for the Empowerment of Women was framed in 2001. The highlight of the Tenth Five Year Plan was gender budgeting.

Legislative Intervention

The Government of India over the years enacted several legislations covering almost all the issues. *Education related legislative measures*: Right to Education Act, 2009 ensures that every child of the age of 6 to 14 years shall have a right to free and compulsory education. *Work related legislative measures*: Then employment related laws like Factories Act, 1948 prohibits women's employment in hazardous tasks, Equal Remuneration Act, 1976 provides same wages in same work, Maternity Benefit Act, 1961 prohibits the termination of women from service during pregnancy as well as ensuring wages during pregnancy. Recently, the law on Sexual Harassment of Women at Workplace (Prevention, Prohibition and Redressal) passed by Lok Sabha on 3rd September, 2012. *Property-related legislative measures*: The Hindu Succession Act, 1956 amended in 2005 provides the right to parental property. *Health-related legislative measures*: Medical Termination of Pregnancy Act, 1971 under which a woman can go for abortion on the ground of physical and mental health. *Violence-related legislative measures*: Protective legislations like Dowry Prohibition Act, 1961 declares that giving and taking of dowry an unlawful activity, Protection of Women from Domestic Violence Act, 2005 provides remedies to the women and victims of domestic violence, The Immoral Traffic Prevention Act, 1956 gives protection to women from trafficking and regulate sex work, The Pre-Conception and Prenatal Diagnostic Techniques (Prohibition of Sex Selection)

Act, 1994 also formulated to ban female foeticide. The Commission of *Sati* (Prevention) Act, 1987 came into being. The Sexual Harassment of Women at Workplace (Prevention, Prohibition, Redressal) Act, 2013 seeks to protect women from sexual harassment at their place of work. The recent Delhi gang rape case laid the foundation of Justice Verma Committee for amendments to Criminal Law and the Criminal Law Amendment Ordinance, 2013 was promulgated by the President. *Legislative measures for ensuring political participation*: The 73rd and 74th Constitutional Amendment Act, 1992 provides opportunity to participate in the decision-making process at all levels of the Panchayati Raj. The Women's Reservation Bill, 2010 was passed in Rajya Sabha, on 9th March, 2010 which proposes to provide 33 per cent of all seats in the Lower House of Parliament and State Legislative Assemblies reserved for women. But till March 2013 the Lower House has not yet voted on the bill. *Other Legislative measures*: The Hindu Marriage Act, 1955 prohibits polygamy and child marriage and ensures equal rights to divorce. The Family Court Act, 1984 provides justice to women who get involved in family disputes. The Indecent Representation of Women (Prohibition) Act, 1986 prohibits the vulgar presentation of women in the media. The Hindu Adoption and Maintenance Act, 1956 give a childless woman the right to adopt a child and to claim maintenance from the husband if she is divorced by him. Prohibition of Child Marriage Act, 2006 enacted to deal with child marriage.

Programmatic Interventions

The commitment of Government towards ensuring gender justice reflected in the formation of a separate Ministry, i.e. Ministry of Women and Child Development which started functioning from 2006. Health-wise the Supplementary Nutrition Component of ICDS aims at eradicating malnutrition among women, National Rural Health Mission launched in 2005 with a strong commitment to reduce maternal mortality and universal access to public health services. Then Janani Suraksha Yojana (JSY) was also launched in 2005 for promoting safe motherhood and institutional delivery among the poor pregnant women. Beside Rajiv Gandhi Scheme for Empowerment of Adolescent Girls (RGSEAG), SABLA for the overall development of adolescent girls (11 to 18 years) was initiated from November 2010. Another health related measure taken in the form of Janani Shishu Suraksha Karyakrama from June 2011 onwards and under this scheme all women delivering in public health institutions will have absolutely free of cost services including medicines, food, diagnostic, free transport from home and back and even blood required. 2180 residential Kasturba Gandhi Balika Vidyalaya have been sanctioned and are providing elementary education to 1,82,000 out of school girls. Balika Samriddhi Yojana was also launched in 1997 to promote girl's education. Rashtriya Mahila Kosh was set-up in 1993 to extend credit facilities to poor and needy women in the informal sector. Indira Gandhi National Widow Pension Scheme, which comes under the National Social Assistance Programme for extending financial support to widowed women, came into being. Swadhar Scheme was launched for providing shelter and rehabilitation to women in difficult circumstances. Then there is Women Helpline, a 24 hour phone emergency outreach programme for women and girls in distress initiated. *Ujjawala*, the scheme meant for comprehensive care for the victims of trafficking in 2007. The National Policy for Empowerment of Women also came into being in 2001 for bringing about the advancement, development and empowerment of women.

Institutional Mechanisms

Besides this, a National Commission for Women, a statutory body was set-up in 1992 to safeguard the rights and interests of women.

Policy Framework Needed

India's status as the world's largest democracy is undermined if the atrocities and plight against women are not addressed:

- Mere banning on foeticide is not enough. Efforts needed to correct the skewed sex-ratio through awareness drive and more and more incentives for the girl child specially the worst affected states is needed.

- Free uniform, free bicycles, mid-day meal scheme, gender sensitive school will contribute much to counter the problem of dropout and the issue related to retention. As well as provision of scholarship, financial assistance, vocational courses to be assured. In India where the 65 per cent of the people live below the bare subsistence-level here the educational system has to be directly linked with economic and social development. In this regard it is worth mentioning that Maharashtra and Gujarat adopted a policy of giving free education to girls up to college level it has to be replicated by other states too.
- Investment in female education is directly linked to the child and mother's health. Policy-makers should not ignore this while framing the necessary and emergency health packages for women.
- Policies may be devised accordingly for generating more and more employment opportunities.
- For empowering women we need to ensure equitable access and distribution of resources like land, credit etc.
- Effort needs to be geared for ensuring their participation in decision-making and planning process through reserving seats in Parliament and State Legislative Assemblies, so that, they can play crucial role in transforming the society.
- A large number of innovative schemes and programmes often launched, but actual implementation remains limited due to non-availability of funds. So, the fund must be earmarked.
- A large number of legal provisions exist, but when it comes to their enforcement which is often poor in nature. The need of the hour is strengthening the implementation mechanisms. At the same time, there is a need to review certain legislative measures considering the changing scenario in order to strengthen their provisions.
- To address the issue related to violence multi-pronged strategy like implementation of laws, awareness generation, strengthening support services etc. needed.
- Organizing women into SHG marks the beginning of a major process of empowering women by strengthening

their capacity for collective decision-making and entrepreneurship development.

- Sustained media campaign would be one of the most effective intervention strategy that can take place to address not only the issues of attitude and mind sets of men and women of the society but also of the functionaries of the Government—the bureaucracy, police and judiciary etc. A sustained campaign in the form of folk, print, electronic media is necessary to focus the attention of people on various issues such as health, nutrition, laws, value of the girl child, violence against women, right to adequate representation in politics etc.

References

Desai, N. and Thakkar, U., 2001, *Women in Indian Society*, New Delhi: National Book Trust.

Dhar, A., 2012, "Women and Child Health", *Yojana*. 56: 15-18.

Forbes, G.H., 1998, *Women in Modern India,* New York: Cambridge University Press.

Government of India, 2011, *Census of India*, New Delhi.

Kapur, P., 2001, *Empowering the Indian Women*, New Delhi: Ministry of Information and Broadcasting.

Tamang, A., 2012, "The Challenge of Ensuring Equal Access to Education for Women: A Critical Analysis", *Kurukshetra*, 16(11): 15-18.

www.ncrb.nic.in

www.iimb.ernet.in/research/sites/default/files/WP%20No.%20364.pdf

www.nfhsindia.org

www.genderbytes.wordpress.com

17

Contribution of National Rural Employment Guarantee Scheme (NREGS) in Community Development in India

With Reference to Women's Empowerment

Sekhar Sain and *Prasanta Kumar Ghosh*

Introduction

Community Development Experiments for Rural Development were initiated in India in 1920s. The Gurgaon Experiment by F.L. Brayne (1920), Marthandam Experiment of Spencer Hatch (1921), Rabindranath Tagore's Sriniketan Experiment in Rural Reconstruction in 1922, Gandhiji's Sevagram Project (1933), Baroda Experiment of V.T. Krishnamachari and Firka Development Scheme (1946) appeared chronologically in British ruled India. Among the above projects, Tagore's Sriniketan model was the pioneering and a unique one as it fostered the idea of total development of village and creation of self-reliant village society and development of personality. His cultural approach induced the Government in its community development movement. In Independent India the first initiative was Etawah Pilot Project of Albert Mayer in 1948. In free India, the reconstructed Grow More Food Campaign (GMFC) which was initiated in 1949, launched during First Plan headed by Sir V.T. Krishnamachari, recommended in 1950-51, the creation of an extension agency for more participatory and a co-ordinated effort of the people as the stakeholders for the development of themselves, which created the context of launching the Community Development Programme (CDP) on 2nd October, 1952 by the Government of India. Interestingly, the lessons of these experiments became the model for rural development in the country, especially the philosophy and approaches of Tagore and Gandhi influenced a lot in policy of the state.

As one flagship programme for poverty eradication and holistic development of the rural people, the Community Development Programme (CDP) was launched in 55 project areas over the whole country. Afterwards, in 1958 another enthusiastic scheme, National Extension Service (NES), landed for providing basic staff and fund support for commencing development work by way of self-help, converged with CDP in 1958. Then it was extended to all the rural areas in the country. It aimed at the development of the poor people adopting the theory and principles of community organization. As an essential requirement of the programme, Community Development Blocks were established in the rural areas for development and service delivery as the welfare activities were not initiated in the British regime. According to K. Singh, (2006), Community Development Programme as its programme orientation covered a range of activities, which included: (1) Agricultural and Allied Occupations, (2) Communication, (3) Education, (4) Health Care, (5) Skill Development (Training), (6) Social Welfare, (7) Employment, and (8) Housing.

As part of aims and objective of the programme, CDP augmented the objective to improve the lifestyle of rural poor by way of improving socio-economic and cultural conditions of the community, to develop cohesiveness through enhanced participation and integrating the rural poor in the development process of the nation. So, a holistic rural development concept and goal was manifested in the objective of the programme which surfaced subsequently in the consecutive plans in a series of poverty eradication and employment generation programmes.

The question is why Government of India took up a series of schemes and programmes for poverty alleviation and employment generation. The answer is not very complicated. The planners in the early period of planning found that a major part of the populace, about 77 per cent of the poor live in rural area (GoI data, 2010) and about 75 per cent were engaged in agriculture allied occupation. The engagement were purely temporary and full of uncertainty due to excessive dependence upon nature and climatic factors like temperature, rainfall etc. leading to natural calamity like flood or draught, which simultaneously pushes the farmer and the agricultural labourers into a very miserable condition. Hence, there is a grim situation of poverty and unemployment in the rural India. The poverty is mostly due to unemployment and similarly the unemployment is due to the part-time employment or the seasonal employment of rural landless labourer in agriculture. Since, inception of the planning, the planners emphasized upon employment generation and poverty eradication as a tool toward a comprehensive community development programme. A number of programmes, those were undertaken since beginning are as follows:

1. Community Development Programme, 1952.
2. Intensive Agricultural District Programme (IADP), 1960.
3. Marginal Farmers and Agriculural Labourers Scheme (MFAL), 1970-71.
4. Small Farmer Development Agency (SFDA), 1971-72.
5. Rural Works Programme (RWP), 1971-72.
6. Employment Guarantee Scheme (EGS), 1972-73.
7. Drought Prone Area Programme (DPAP), 1973-74.
8. Minimum Needs Programme (MNP), 1974-78.
9. Food For Work Programme (FFWP), 1977.
10. Desert Development Programme (DDP), 1977-78.
11. Integrated Rural Development Programme (IRDP), 1978-79.
12. Training of Rural Youth for Self-Employment (TRYSEM), 1979.
13. National Rural Employment Programme (NREP), 1980.
14. Development of Women and Children in Rural Areas (DWCRA), 1982.
15. Rural Landless Employment Guarantee Programme (RLEGP), 1983.
16. Jawahar Rojgar Yojana (JRY), 1989 (Merging NREP & RLEGP).

17. Indira Awas Yojana (IAY), 1989.
18. Employment Assurance Scheme (EAS), 1993.
19. National Social Assistance Programme (NSAP), 1995.
20. Swarnajayanti Gram Swarojgar Yojana (SGSY), 1999.
21. Annapurna Yojana (AY), 1999-2000.
22. Antyodaya Anna Yojana (AAY), 2000.
23. Sampoorna Grameen Rojgar Yojana (SGRY), 2001.
24. Pradhan Mantri Gramodaya Yojana (PMGY), 2000-01.

Emergence of National Rural Employment Guarantee Scheme, 2005

While adopting the Constitution of India on 26th January, 1950 the provisions of welfare and development of the rural people was given priority. In the 42nd Constitutional Amendment, 1976 the term 'Socialist Secular' was included in the Preamble to the Constitution. The word socialist affirms the intention of the state to construct a socialist economic order and commits to establish a welfare state. The Preamble also advocated the concept of social, economic and political justice for the people. Article 21 confers its citizens the Right to Protection of Life and Personal Liberty. In the chapter of Directive Principles of State Policy (Part iv) of the Constitution, the state strives to establish a just and equal society. Article 39(a) envisages, that "The state, in particular will direct its policy so as to secure for both men and woman equal right to adequate means of livelihood. Article 41 approaches for formulation of effective provision for securing right to work. Article 43 propagates the idea of securing for all its workers a living wage condition of work ensuring a decent standard of life" (Pylee, M.V., 2008). The Constitutional provisions, stated above, compelled the state, the Government to formulate a programme which will establish economic liberty, equality, secure the right to work, alleviate poverty and in the same time promote development. Thus, for utter compliance of the provisions envisaged in the Constitution, in 2005, NREGS was enacted as one of the most comprehensive scheme for community development.

Besides, not a single programme, mentioned earlier, was comprehensive and could prove itself effective in terms of its objective and achievements. In most of the cases, it was found that the unwillingness of the Government machinery and the absence of political will were the root causes of failure of the poverty alleviation programmes. So, it deserved a *compulsion* which could successfully implement the employment generation and poverty eradication programme in a full proof system. Hence, as being the latest version of employment generation programme, NREGS was introduced by the UPA Government in 2005 as one employment guarantee programme supported by National Rural Employment Guarantee Act (NREGS). It differed from the earlier schemes and programmes, in the way that, it had a 'right' component backed by the act which established the guarantee of having work on demand by any unemployed able bodied person up to 100 days in a financial year. So, this scheme provided the unemployed labourers a bargaining capacity in seeking employment. And from the part of the Government machinery, it compelled them to provide work on demand. As the 2nd component, the scheme aimed at creation of durable asset in the rural areas for improvement of rural infrastructure, which is the focus area of community development. Under NREGS, activities those are initiated include:

Major Field of Activity

(i) Water conservation and water harvesting;

(ii) Drought proofing (including afforestation and tree plantation);

(iii) Irrigation canals including micro and minor irrigation works;

(iv) Irrigation facility to land owned by SC, ST and IAY beneficiaries.

(v) Renovation of traditional water bodies including de-silting of tank;

(vi) Land development;

(vii) Flood control and protection works including drainage in waterlogged areas; and

(viii) Rural connectivity to provide all-weather access; and any other work which may be notified by the Central

Government in consultation with the State Government. (*Courtesy*: *NREGS: Operational Guideline* 2008, 3rd Edition, Ministry of Rural Development, Government of India.)

Conditions for Implementation

(i) The works taken-up under the scheme shall be in rural areas.
(ii) Labourer must be paid as per minimum wage as decided by the Government time-to-time.
(iii) The labourer shall get the wage working for seven hours.
(iv) No contractor should be engaged.
(v) Material component must not exceed 40 per cent. (*Courtesy*: *NREGS: Operational Guideline* 2008, 3rd Edition, Ministry of Rural Development, Government of India.)

Thus, Government thrives to secure development of the tangible assets of the community directly, along with a continual source of income through generation of employment, thereby assuring an enhanced standard of life with the enriched intangible components of development of the community like nutrition, health, education etc.

Theoritical Base

(a) NREGS as a Rights Based Approach

On part of the beneficiary it demonstrate right based 'bottom-up' approach and it provides right to get work on demand, right to minimum wages, right to get payment in due time, equal pay for equal work, gender-equity of payment etc. (Dreze, J. and Sen, A., 2013). Power, M. (2012) described the scheme as a 'right-based' scheme with 'bottom-up' enabling approach as the scheme at first confers the right to the rural poor to make their own plan, to take decision in regard to implementation and the right to participate. The scheme confers and confirms the right to self-determination and empowerment. During the course of empowerment, NREGS enables the stake holders to draw the plan, and take decision from the grassroot-level instead of implementing one ordinary programme by bureaucratic oppression from the top as happened in other 'top-down' schemes with 'trickle down' effect only.

(b) NREGS as a Strength-based Approach

On part of the Government it is a perfect show-piece of strength-based macro social work practice towards community development. As a right-based practice it provide 100 days of guaranteed work to the poor villagers, besides, it aims at creation of durable asset as part of physical development of the community. To reach this goal Government machinery facilitates the rural poor stakeholders to chalk out or draw the plan. This is simply the assessment of need (felt needs) in one side and at the same time exercise of their right to self-determination. Next to it, they prioritize the felt needs as part of decision-making followed by identifying the available resources or the strengths of the community. To conclude the cycle with social action, a specific scheme is selected from a huge 'shelf of scheme' towards implementation for a particular community in a given geographical area, by the stakeholders themselves, considering the regional balance condition, which justifies its principles with the 'Strength-Weakness-Opportunities (SWOT)—Threat' concept of strength-based macro-social work practice. It simultaneously detects the strength and in the same time utilizes the opportunity. But in practice all are not maintained, as all opportunities are not identified correctly, nor are they utilized properly, and some areas are over-utilized wasting public money while some important areas get less emphasis.

Impact of NREGS on Society

(a) Employment Generation

In the rural areas employment gained a powerful momentum after the scheme launched. Rural landless labourers are getting additional employment in the slack season of agriculture, when generally they used to sit idle at home earlier. In the last concluding financial year 2013-14 the MIS of NREGS website shows that the average persondays was, 45.96, i.e. each household was provided additional 46 days of manual work other than their engagement in private agricultural activity or in other unorganized sector. It is a great achievement although it is far away from the target of 100 days a year. In absolute term it is 219.83 crore person days in the whole country in the financial year 2013-14, which is also a gigantic figure. Table 17.1 shows the extent of achievement in terms of employment generation both in absolute figure and in average persondays for last three consecutive years.

Table 17.1: NREGS Physical Performance Report: INDIA

Financial Year	Total Person-days (cr.)	Total No. of H.H. Provided work (Cr.)	Average person days	H.H. completed 100 days work (Lakh)
2011-12	218.8	5.06	43.20	41.7
2012-13	230.5	4.99	46.20	51.7
2013-14	218.5	4.75	45.96	46.5

Source: www.nrega.nic.in

Although, the picture is not at all satisfactory, it is noteworthy that, in a country like India with poverty, unemployment, hunger and a huge population, the scheme was able to provide 45 days of subsistence support to a family in the existing economic framework. It provided complete 100 days of life support to 46.39 lakh families (GoI data, 2014). This is a great achievement for the Government and for the community as a whole, as the employment is directly related to livelihood, income generation, consumption, the living standard and the well-being of the members of the community. It also raises the other indicators of social development also.

(b) Durable Asset

This is the physical activity part of one development programme. NREGS, like other community development programmes, gives emphasis upon creation of durable asset which indirectly raises the living standard of the people and provides infrastructural support to other activities of the rural poor. As part of its asset creation the scheme developed rural roads (Rural connectivity), excavated and renovated rural water bodies for irrigation and domestic use and for development of culture fisheries. In individual benefit scheme mode (IBS) in SC, ST households or at IAY houses, land development work has been done (Operational Guideline, 2008) and in some places like Jharkhand wells have been constructed at individual owned land (Agarwal, A., *et al.,* 2012) and the water is being used for agriculture for the whole community. Government Irrigation Cannels have also been re-excavated and renovated through this scheme as part of asset creation for irrigation. For flood protection NREGS intervened in development and protection of river banks, etc. To protect the physical environment, this scheme has been implemented in social forestry, establishing fruit orchard, etc. Even in draught prone area it has intervened for creating contour trench, rift etc. and in establishing horticulture orchards, contour farming, etc., where the scheme allows people to combat with severe draught along with some life support to the poor people in the form of wage and the stake of the output (fruit, timber etc.) of the community asset. In Kerala, it has been mobilized for biodiversity management (Sebastian, M.K. and Azeez, P., 2014) towards plantation of various fruit trees, medicinal plants for conserving indigenous and traditional variety of rice seeds, cereal, millets and other edible plants.

(c) Income Source

NREGS is now providing the rural people a consistent source of income throughout the year. Earlier, the lower class landless labourers had to struggle, even to starve in the agricultural lean period. They are considering the scheme as one blessing (Jackimow, T., 2014). So, it is clear that the scheme is providing a formidable amount of income in addition to the wage income they earn from private engagement. The GoI data shows that on an average in the year completed on 31/03/2014 it provided 45.96 days of work to rural poor, i.e. a support income of Rs. $45.96 \times 151 =$ Rs. 6940 (approx.) to every Indian rural household possessing a job card. Besides, 46.39 lakh household completed 100 days, i.e. the income raised for these 46.39 lakh families in the financial year 2013-14 by an additional tune of Rs. 15,100.

It maintains clear consonance with the central theme of "Community Development" (as mentioned in the Dictionary of Social Work)—"Improve the quality of life of the members of the community of a designated area or a locality" (Pierson, J. and Thomas, M., 2010).

(d) Standard of Living

Studies and reports show that after implementation of NREGS the standard of living of the rural poor has changed formidably. The change has come in terms of their nutrition, health, education and other basic amenities. Agarwal, A. (2012) in a study of NREGS wells in Jharkhand had shown that, not only the project has raised their income by reducing cost of production providing easy and cheap source of irrigation to the community, but the families were eating well. The families admitted that they were producing nutritious vegetables, which are supplementing the nutrition source of the family members including the children (Panchayati Raj: Nov.-Dec., 2012). Sebastian, M.K. and Azeez, P. (2014) in a study in Kerala had mentioned the cultivation of fruits in community orchard maintained by SHG group members. They are getting the stake from the production which has helped in raising their income and at the same time giving nutrition support, which were earlier unaffordable for the poor families. In the same way the poor villages are getting fish from community cultured ponds excavated or re-excavated through NREGS. This in turn gives the poor villagers scope of better health care preventing diseases grown out of malnutrition. Besides, as their income increases, they are taking some responsive and remedial action against diseases and ailments. Recently one new concept has emerged,— the NREGS workers who have completed at least 15 days work in a financial year, are getting the facility of being enrolled under Rashtriya Swasthya Vima Yojana (RSVY), a subsidized health insurance scheme, under which they are getting free treatment up to Rs. 30,000 in the enlisted health care institutions for 5 members of one family on payment of just Rs. 30 per year. This is one giant leap towards better health care management and an example of social security from the state for the larger cause of the rural community.

On the education front also NREGS has left its footprints in the rural community. The rural households are saying that they are sending their children to school instead of forcefully sending them for work in agricultural field or other hazardous activity (Panchayati Raj: Nov.-Dec., 2012). Changes are evident in the daily life of the rural poor. More and more rural families are now using consumer goods like soap, hair oil, etc. which were even unimaginable to them. Some has bought TV and DVD sets and other consumer durable goods for their household comfort.

(e) Change in Social and Agrarian Relation

A vast change occurred in the social relation of the rural community. Now, the rural people have a different subject position from a submissive one to an independent one. Now, the system of untouchability and castism are history for the rural poor. NREGS provided the rural landless labourers a bargaining power, which in turn conferred the rural poor a sense of 'self-confidence' and 'Assertiveness'—two components of empowerment, which now compels the upper-class landlords to engage them in their farm with better working condition and above all, with dignity. The landlords now do not call the lower class people by their caste name (Jackimow, T., 2014).

In agrarian relation also there is a sea change from a strong domination by landholders, to an independent bargaining status possessed by the labour class. Now, they are getting better wage rate, much higher than the minimum wage and less working hours and less toil to do. Now, the landlord cannot force him to work more than 7 hours as it is the standard working hours according to NREGS (*NREGS: Operational Guideline 2008,* 3rd Edition, Ministry of Rural Development, Government of India).

(f) Impact on Economy

Economy had shown a mixed effect upon the society. The lower class people took it as a blessing as they are earning during the agricultural lean period. But for middle class farmers it is a curse as they cannot work under NREGS and they have to pay much higher rate of wage for their agricultural other allied occupations.

Again another thing is there, poverty started from ill-production in agriculture and NREGS pushed it to higher cost of production creating the same situation of worse agriculture and much unemployment following a vicious cycle. The rural poor are not getting the sweet fruits of the scheme as there enhanced purchasing power is getting neutralized by huge inflation due to increased cost of production (Dreze, J. and Sen, A., 2014; Jackimow, T., 2014). Above all, the other members of the whole society are paying the burden of inflated price of products of everyday use.

Impact of NREGS on Women

Another great contribution of NREGS towards the development of rural community lies in bringing about social equity by reducing social discrimination and discrimination on wage depending on gender. Both the issues of equality of status and wage existed constitutionally in black and white in our country, but in practice there was widespread difference in of both in rural Indian society. Stark inequalities existed between men and women in regard to opportunities for affording gainful employment and regarding wage rate. NREGS intervened to take serious action against both the evils in open-secret condition (Negi, R.S. and Kumar, A., ed., Beg, *et al.*, 2014). After NREGS came into being, the participation of women grew rapidly, as the scheme actually promoted maximized women inclusion, envisaged in its policy document, vide Schedule II(6), Schedule II(28), Schedule II(34). Table 17.2 shows the tune of women's participation in last two years:

Table 17.2: Tune of Women's Participation in 2013-14

Year	Persondays Generated (Crore)			Persons Provided Employment (Lakh)		
	Total	Women	Percentage	Total	Women	Percentage
2012-13	230.5	118.2	51.3 %	797.3	375.3	47 %
2013-14	218.5	116.1	53.1 %	733.3	351.4	48 %

Source: www.nrega.nic.in

Statistics shows a sharp rise in percentage share in individual participation of women in NREGS works from 47 per cent to 48 per cent and their contribution towards generating persondays rising from 51.3 to 53.1 per cent in two consecutive years, i.e. 2012-13 and 2013-14. This clearly indicates the rising participation of women in public works. This not only indicates the level of participation, it also ensures the equality of wage, both in Government and private occupational operations, which was out of reach for the rural poor so far and now affordable through the intervention of NREGS (Dreze, J. and Sen, A., 2014). Greater participation of women in public wage work in turn confers three advantages to the women as a whole: (i) a rise in tangible income for the household; (ii) greater financial inclusion of the women; and (iii) Gaining high esteem in the society for their formidable contribution to the society.

Cash income almost up to the same tune to the male counterpart of the family offered them a better and important position in the family and the much expected financial autonomy also. Financial autonomy of women is at the base of greater independence and esteem of women. They now have better financial control over the family also, as the wage, earned by them are directly paid to their bank account. As the women now afford the opportunity of their empowerment through their inclusion promoted by NREGS, they have now least susceptibility of being exploited by their in-laws, their male counterparts and even by the landlord also, as they have the confidence that, they can feed their children and can send them to school of their own income (Pellisary, S. and Jalan, S.K., 2011). They have now better control over their wage earning and they are spending independently towards sending their children to school, bearing medical expenses and repaying small debts (MORD, GoI, 2012). Moreover, they are now availing equal treatment in the family and in return they are doing justice also to their girl children at par with the boys.

So far their social status is concerned, the discursive practice against women in work sites disappeared as they exercise their confidence and assertiveness which frightened the landlord, male members of the family and other members of the society not to do anything against their dignity (Jackimow, T., 2014). The benefit of NREGS reached to the women in a two dimensional way, first by providing individual financial and social benefit and second by uplifting their status as community. As community they have gained some voice in the society as supervisor of the scheme, as member of social audit team (Panchayati Raj, Nov.-Dec., 2012), in the Gram Sabha while making the plan and in community meeting while taking decision about its execution (Vaishnaw, B.L., ed., Beg, *et al.*, 2014). This potential capability of NREGS affording women to exert their innate power and ability in the society opens another dimension of social development.

Future Prospects for NREGS and Women's Empowerment

Starting its journey in 2006 NREGS has already completed 8 financial years and experienced a lot of operational modifications to suit itself with the changing need of the community in changing socio-economic scenario. The political change-over both in the State and Panchayati Raj Institutions (PRIs) has also impacted on the mode of operation and implementation. Especially in selecting beneficiaries political affiliation and biasness continued to find a secured position, which is prevalent in other Government programmes and which is very unlikely in a Right-based scheme like NREGS. Besides, there are some other persisting problems in the scheme which inhibit it to prove itself a powerful welfare tool of the country. There is a number of unexplored area and some areas are over utilized, thereby diminishing the quality of delivery and denying its strength components. To improve the quality of the scheme the following components can be taken care of and can be recharged otherwise.

(a) Composite IBS Scheme

Individual Benefit Scheme (IBS) has been already in use in NREGS and proved to be very fruitful, as it directly benefits one individual curbing corruption. If the scheme is drawn and implemented in a composite way it will be productive also. As for example, an IBS scheme in an IAY beneficiary house at first can generate a number of person days and provide labour subsidy to the construction process and at the same time supply fund as wage to the beneficiary as job card holder. This benefit is improving the quality of the IAY house. After that, one IHHL (Individual Household Latrine) under Nirmal Bharat Abhiyan (NBA) toilet may be constructed to that house giving an additional infrastructure, providing wage and proper sanitation facility to the household ensuring better hygiene (Dhoot, V. and Rajsekhar, M., 2014). One small pond or ditch may be constructed at the backyard along with a kitchen garden (Sharma, R., 2014). The kitchen garden will ensure supply of nutrition supplement and the ditch will ensure continuous supply of water for irrigation to that kitchen garden and culture of weed fishes (like Koi, Magur, Singee etc.) which needs no care and management but are rich source of animal protein. Moreover, the ditch will conserve rain water ensuring better environmental balance and biodiversity management. This model may also be given to SCs, STs, small and marginal farmer families along with IAY beneficiaries. In the two cases mentioned above, the Central theme, i.e., health-hygiene and individual dignity are the main concern of the women member of the family, as the women are the main sufferer for want of a toilet so far the dignity is concerned other than its hygiene component. At the same time, it is the women member who is most concerned about the nutrition of other members. Hence, the women are to be mobilized first to make the scheme more successful. This model can be practiced in developing school grounds, cultivating in kitchen gardens for harvesting fresh vegetables to be used in the Mid-Day Meal of the same school ensuring supply of nutrition to the rural children.

(b) Community Assets

The scheme may be implemented to create community assets laden with collective responsibility. The initiative of micro-entrepreneurship development may be undertaken taking the women SHGs as the stakeholders. Micro-entrepreneurship like community fruit orchards, nursery, seed farms, fish farms, goatary, dairy, and poultry may be established in vest lands. For running of the projects, so created by NREGS, the scheme can be converged with National Rural Livelihood Mission (NRLM), The Horticulture Mission, Rashtriya Krishi Vikas Yojana (RKVY) or other programmes (Sharma, R., 2014). The assets will be best maintained by the women group members and the products will also be distributed among the community members itself. This will not only provide them wage and redistribute the products among the community members increasing their income level, but also will recharge the supply chain, curbing inflationary pressure upon the members of the society at larger scale.

(c) Agriculture and Allied Activities

NREGS may be better utilized in agriculture even in private land. It has already been experimented in Kerala and Karnataka as labour subsidy. In Kerala it has been practiced in private land for cultivating medicinal plants, cereals and millets, edible plants and for conservation of traditional variety of rice paddy, fruit orchards etc. and SHG members has also been mobilized for this purpose (Sebastian, M.K. and Azeez,.P., 2014). In Karnataka it has been implemented in private land of the beneficiaries of land reforms, i.e. to the tenant-turn-owners of land. NREGS provided labour subsidy to these marginal landowners, who earlier were forced to work on others' land deserting their own, due to their inability to chase the increasing investment towards various agricultural inputs including labour charge. Labour subsidy was provided not only to land reforms beneficiaries but also to the farmers owning land up to 5 acres (Pani, N. and Iyer, C., 2012). It reduces the production cost and in the same time recharges the supply chain thereby reducing inflation of food-product, benefitting the whole society to a certain degree. The newly formed Government in 2014 in its first budget has also proposed a change in NREGS in this line. They have proposed to realign it with agriculture and allied activities (*The Economic Times*: 11th July, 2014). The new form is targeted to create permanent asset in agricultural sector. This will also become a measure for restricting all sorts of leakage due to corruption if implemented in private land and towards creating community property with collective responsibility.

Conclusion

In spite of all the above virtues an army of vices are also there with the scheme. First of all, the scheme, after completion of 8 complete financial years, progressed only half-way of its target. It had managed to touch hardly 50 per cent of its first objective of generating 100 days of manual and unskilled employment. Secondly, it is criticized both by the educated persons and the beneficiaries of the scheme, that the asset so created are of poor quality and hardly provide any infrastructural base to provide livelihood support to rural poor. The shout of dissatisfaction is as loud as it was on the eve of passing of the bill to enact NREGA-2005 referring the chance of misuse of Government fund and the financial bankruptcy (Dreze and Sen, 2014). It is also criticized that, more useful and durable asset could have been created, had the fund of same corpus been used for the same purpose with other traditional scheme, although famous India-watcher and economist Jean Dreze, has opined the reverse (*The Hindu*, 23rd Aug., 2014). Thirdly, it is criticized on the same ground as the previous poverty eradication and employment generation programmes and that is corruption. Although, it is noticed that the extent of corruption is coming down, which was manifested heavily starting from inflated muster rolls to bulk payments by post offices or taking commissions during identification for payment from banks and post offices. Bank payment of wage, introduction of e-muster rolls placing muster rolls is public domain through dedicated website are considered as the panacea for bettering the situation (Dreze, J., 2014).

On the other hand, Dreze and Sen (2014) expressed their anxiety about the fate and future of the scheme. They suggested for some modification for its survival and expanding its scope. The new Government also footed in the same way. In the first budget of the Government in June 10, 2014 the Finance Minister had indicated same sort of re-orientation of the scheme. Government expressed its intention to realign it along with agriculture and allied activity (*The Economic Times*, 11th June, 2014). Government considers that for the development of the community it should be implemented for asset building in the field of agriculture, sanitation etc. This indicates a silver-line towards a better service and development of the rural community in convergence with National Rural Employment Guarantee Scheme (NREGS).

However, considering the objectives and methods of implementation of NREGS, inference can be drawn that, it has potential to improve socio-economic condition if focused on equal participation of women, bringing about equal wage for equal work, reduction of discrimination in wage and gender-bias while providing work etc. Orientation of NREGS with sanitation not only keeps good hygiene, it protects environment by restricting open defecation and at the same time a household toilet in each house is necessary for the dignity of women. As women are the worst sufferers in this regard, they can play the leading role in implementing this programme through NREGS. Women SHGs can be entrusted with the task of identifying the beneficiaries and supervising the whole scheme, replacing the old practice of engaging supervisors from the people having vested political interest that ultimately supersedes the goal of the scheme. Same process can be followed while implementing schemes targeted at biodiversity management like plantation, nursery rearing, establishing fruit orchards and medicinal plant gardens. Higher participation of women thus increases the accuracy of the scheme and at the same time curbs corruption. More participation directly benefits them by providing economic independence, which confers power of decision-making in the family and in bigger perspective of society thereby bringing about women empowerment. Moreover, it is evident that, NREGS not only witnessed increased women participation in it, but also it has catalyzed enhanced participation of women in other occupational operations and in diversified economic activity. This scheme has been effective and successful in withering the age-old notion and practices in our society that the female counterpart is meant for rearing offspring and managing household works. The scheme has finally taught our society a lesson that women can be utilized as an effective workforce along with the male counterpart for culminating an organized growth and development of the whole community.

References

Abraham, B.P., Chakraborty, B., Chattopadhyay, R. and Nath, S., 2013, *Journal of Rural Development*, 32(1): 19-31.

Agarwal, A., Gupta, A., and Kumar, A., 2012, "Evaluation of NREGS Wells in Jharkhand", *Economic and Political Weekly*, 47(35).

Dhoot, V. and Rajsekhar, M., 2014, "Sanitation Projects, Increasing Green Cover among Top Priorities for NREGS", *The Economic Times*, 22 July, 2014.

Drez, J. and Sen, A., 2013, *An Uncertain Glory: India and Its Contradictions*, New Delhi: Penguin Books.

Drez, J., 23rd August, 2014, Learning from NREGS, *The Hindu*.

Government of India, 2008, *NREGS: Operational Guideline 2008,* 3rd Edition, New Delhi: Ministry of Rural Development.

Government of India, 2005, *National Rural Employment Guarantee Act 2005*, New Delhi: Ministry of Law and Justice (Legislative Department).

Government of India, 2010, *Mid-Term Appraisal for Eleventh Five Year Plan,* (2007-12), New Delhi: Planning Commission.

Government of India, 2012, *MGNREGA Sameeksha—An Anthology of Research Studies on the Mahatma Gandhi National Rural Employment Guarantee Act,* 2005, New Delhi: Ministry of Rural Development.

Jakimow, T., 2014, "Breaking the Backbone of Farmers: Contestation in a Rural Employment Guarantee Scheme", *The Journal of Peasant Studies*, 41(2): 263-81.

Negi, R.S. and Kumar, A., 2014, "MGNREGA Empowering the Rural Women: A Comparative Study of Pauri and Beronkhal Block of District Garhwal", in Beg, M.A. (Ed.): *MGNREGA: Empowering Rural Poor through Wage Employment*, New Delhi: Kunal Books.

Pani, N. and Iyer, C., 2012, "National Strategies and Local Relative: The Greenfield Approach and NREGS in Karnataka", *India Review*, 2(1).

Pawar, M., 2012, "The Adaption of a Rights-based Approach to Welfare in India", *Journal of Comparative Social Welfare*, February.

Pellisary, S. and Jalan, S.K., 2011, "Towards Transformative Social Protection: A Gendered Analysis of Employment Guarantee Act of India (NREGS)", *Gender and Development*, 19(20).

Pierson, J. and Thomas, M., 2010, *Dictionary of Social Work,* New Delhi: Rawat Publications.

Pylee, M.V., 2008, *Indian Constitution*, New Delhi: S. Chand & Co.

Reddy, C.S., 2013, "Innovation Transparency and Governance: A Study of NREGS in Andhra Pradesh", *Journal of Rural Development*, 32 (2): 107- 20.

Sebastian, M.K., and Azez, P.A., 2014, "NREGS and Biodiversity Conservation", *Economic and Political Weekly*, 49(10).

Sharma, R., 2014, "For a Better NREGS", *Indian Express*, July 28.

Singh, K., 1986, *Rural Development: Principles, Policies and Management*, New Delhi: Sage.

Tice, C.J. Long, D.D. and John, D.M., 2006, *Macro Social Work Practice: A Strengths Perspective*, New Delhi: Thomson Brooks/Cole (now Cengage Learning).

Vaishnaw, B.L.A., 2014, "Employment Generation in Rural Areas through MGNREGA with Special Reference to Rajasthan", in Beg, M.A., (Ed.): *MGNREGA: Empowering Rural Poor through Wage Employment*, New Delhi: Kunal Books.

www.nregs.nic.in

18
Sustainable Development, Women and Environment

Tarun Bikash Sukai

In 1994 at the International Conference on Population Development (ICPD) in Cairo, 179 countries adopted a landmark 20-year Programme of Action, placing gender equality and women's empowerment and reproductive rights at the centre of population and sustainable development. In June 2012, the United Nations Conference on Sustainable Development, or Rio+20, convened more than 100 heads of state to begin development of Sustainable Development Goals (SGDs), which would reduce poverty while preserving the environment. Unfortunately, the conference missed a historic opportunity to affirm the critical link between investing in women and achieving sustainability goals. Regrettably, the Rio+20 organizers' omission of a strong focus on women and sustainability is not uncommon across the global community. Women support families through wage labour, preserve traditional knowledge, maintain biodiversity, and ensure household food security and nutrition. Despite these critical roles, women and young girls continue to suffer the effects of poor healthcare, education, and discriminatory policies. According to research by the UN Food and Agriculture Organization (FAO), women produce 50 per cent of agricultural output in Asia, and represent nearly 80 per cent of the agricultural labour force in parts of Africa. If women had the same access as men to agricultural resources, production would increase by 20-30 per cent, and has the potential to reduce the number of hungry people in the world by 12-17 per cent.

We all agree that progress in achieving sustainable development goals has been abysmally slow. In the 21st century, we are confronted with economic, environmental and social crises on a global scale. Advances in attaining gender equality have been equally sluggish. Is there a link between these two trends? The three pillars of sustainable development—economic, environment and social—are also relevant to discussions of gender equality. These dimensions have equal and interrelated importance as illustrated in some simple equations. Stressing the environmental and social dimensions of sustainable development in the absence of economics neglects the financial capital needed to pay for progress. Building up the economic and social pillars of sustainability while neglecting the environment degrades the natural capital needed for growth. Focusing on economics and the environment without attention to social factors can lead to green growth for a few. Given gender gaps worldwide, these few tend to be mostly men. An increasing number of studies indicate that gender inequalities are extracting high economic costs and leading to social inequities and environmental degradation around the world.

There is much debate over how to define the term Environmentally Sustainable Development (ESD) with many definitions emphasising some of the economic, political, social and ecological dimensions associated with the term. In recent years, there has been a marked shift from an emphasis on the notion of the 'sustainability' of socio-ecological systems to a focus on the notion of the 'resilience' of the ecosystem, and people's capacity to diversify their livelihoods to facilitate the ecosystem's recovery from shocks and stresses. Linkages between poverty and environmentally sustainable development are often dependent on how poverty is defined and the groups among the poor that are affected by environmental change/degradation in the context of uneven development. The causes of poverty and environmental degradation are structured by this uneven process of development operating *via* technologies, incentives and institutions and regulations which favour a few, not all. The broadening of conventional poverty measurements (income/consumption flows) to include other dimensions of poverty is changing the way linkages between poverty-environment are viewed.

Much of the mainstream literature on environmentally sustainable development has ignored the gender dimensions. In the instances where there has been specific attention to women, they have been viewed as naturally privileged managers of environmental resources with little attention paid to how gender relations systematically differentiate poor men and women. More recently, linkages between gender, poverty and the environment are increasingly discussed. A gender analysis is increasingly seen as important because the experiences of poverty and environmental change are gender-differentiated; environmental security is mediated by gender relations; and women and men have both conflicting and complementary interests and roles in environmental management. There are significant differences between women's and men's experience of poverty and environmental change because of gender inequalities in access to environmental resources (e.g., land and common property resources), command over labour (e.g., allocation of labour time), capacity to diversify livelihood strategies (e.g., accumulating savings and market oriented activities), and decision-making powers. This implies that there is a need to widen the range of choices available to poor men and women taking into consideration gendered differences in rights over land and resources to enhance environmentally sustainable development. This chapter has attempted to make a gender analysis of environmentally sustainable development and poverty. It has also highlighted the policy implications.

Environmentally Sustainable Development: Concept, Dimensions and Goals

There are numerous definitions of sustainable development, and much debate about what constitutes environmentally sustainable development. In the broadest sense, sustainability refers to the capacity of socio-ecological systems to persist unimpaired into the future (Raskin, *et al.,* 1996). "Environmental Sustainability" refers to the maintenance of the ecosystem and the natural resource base. Environmental degradation signifies failure in this regard. It takes three forms—depletion of resources; pollution, or overuse of the waste-absorbing capacity of the environment; and reduction in biodiversity—a loss of some types of resources. "Social Sustainability" is the term used to refer to the social conditions necessary to support environmental sustainability (Hardoy, *et al.*, 1992). This stresses the fact that natural resources are used within a social context and that it is the rules and values associated with this context that determine the distribution of resources within the present generation and the next. More recently, there has been more emphasis on the notion of '*resilience*'. Resilience is the time it takes to recover from shocks and stresses. It refers to the point at which the system can recover from stresses (Anderson, 1994). Ecologists have reached a better understanding both of the processes involved in the ecosystem's capacity to recover from shocks and stresses (such as drought) and of people's capacities to facilitate the recovery of the ecosystem and to diversify their livelihood activities from natural resource-based to money or market-based activities.

However, despite the multi-dimensional nature of ESD, the common goal is development which enhances rather than depletes environmental capital or assets. Hardoy, *et al.* (1992) point out that environmental capital can be divided into three broad types:

(i) the 'natural sink' capacity of local and global systems to absorb or break down organic wastes and absorb gases without adverse effects on climate or the stratospheric ozone layer;

(ii) the finite stock of non-renewable resources, e.g. *fossil fuels* and other minerals. Biological diversity, one key part of environmental capital, might also be considered a non-renewable resource; and

(iii) the renewable resources such as crops and trees which are renewable only within finite limits set by the ecosystem within which they grow. Fresh water resources are also finite; in the case of aquifers, human use often exceeds their natural rate of recharge and as such is unsustainable.

Box 1: Dimensions of Environmentally Sustainable Development

Economic Dimensions: economic needs such as adequate livelihood and productive assets, and systems, and how these interact with the environment.

Social and Cultural Dimensions: social and cultural needs and systems, e.g. health, education, shelter, equity, cultural institutions and norms, and their relationship with the environment.

Political Dimensions: political needs (ability to participate in decision-making processes) and systems, and how they influence the environment.

Ecological Dimensions: maintenance of ecosystems and the natural resource base.

Source: Raskin, *et al.* (1996); UNCHS (1996); WCED (1987); Hardoy, *et al.* (1992)

Poverty and Environmental Sustainability

The linkages between poverty and environmental issues are affected by how poverty is defined, by the type of environmental problem in question, and by which groups among the poor are affected. Research and policy has tended to focus on the relationship between poverty and environmental degradation in terms of pointing out that the poor are both victims and agents of environmental degradation: victims in that they are more likely to live in ecologically vulnerable areas; and agents in that they may have no option, but deplete environmental resources thus contributing to environmental degradation (Sida 1996; Leach and Mearns, 1991; UNEP, 1995). However, it is also acknowledged that the poor often have practices that conserve the environment. Great physical and spatial variability in natural resource endowments also seem to complicate the picture (Redclift and Skea, 1997).

In general terms, the underlying causes of both poverty and environmental degradation are structured by uneven processes of development operating *via* technologies, incentives, institutions and regulations which favour some social groups and some geographical areas over others (Leach and Mearns, 1991). The broadening of general poverty debates to include other measurements and dimensions of poverty (in addition to income/ consumption based flows) such as entitlements and vulnerability is evident in the literature looking at poverty-environment interactions. A recent development is the understanding that linkages between poverty and environmental change are determined by environmental entitlements as well as changes in resource availability. At the micro-level (individual, household, village), environmental entitlements are determined by a range of factors including natural resource tenure arrangements, labour mobilisation arrangements, social relations including gender, capital endowments and technology. At the macro-level (sub-national, national, global), wider processes operate *via* decisions on technologies, incentives, institutions and regulations (e.g., land rights) to favour some social groups and some geographical areas. These processes include demographic changes, environmental processes, macro-economic policies, markets and prices, donor and development agency approaches to poverty and environment, agricultural research, governance and political conflict (Leach and Mearns, 1991; Leach, Mearns and Scoones, 1997).

Gender and Environmentally Sustainable Development

Much of the mainstream literature on ESD has ignored gender relations. Where attention has been paid to women, thinking has been mainly influenced by the women in development (WID) approach (Joekes, *et al.,* 1996). Broadly, women, environment and Development (WED) thinking stresses the 'managerial' aspects of economic development. This seeks to minimise negative effects of the process of economic development by targeting women as recipients of environmental development assistance, simultaneously considering the effects of development on the environment—an approach propagated by many development agencies. A more philosophical stream of WED sees women's position as essentially closer than men's position to nature, because their work has always entailed a close relationship with nature. Women are depicted as naturally privileged managers of environmental resources. An economistic line of WED emphasises women's work: the sexual division of labour that has led to women's particular role in managing natural resources (Bradiotti and Wieringa, 1994).

Some critiques have pointed out that WED conceptualisations are flawed because of three main reasons:

(i) First, environment-friendly management practices by women can be explained in terms of rational short-term interests. For instance, women may only collect drywood for fuel because it is lighter and easier to carry, and certain tree species may be protected by custom or religious sanction rather than by women's motivation to conserve resources (Jackson, 1993).

(ii) Second, relations of women to the environment cannot be understood outside the context of gender relations in resource management and use. Women's relation to natural resources reflects socio-structural forces, within the framework of gender relations which systematically differentiate men and women in processes of production and reproduction. These forces relegate/confine women to environmentally-based activities by limiting their access to other types of livelihood activity.

(iii) Third, like the WID approach, the WED perspective completely focuses on women at the exclusion of men, and pays little attention to differences among women (Joekes, *et al.*, 1996).

In recent years, there has been an increasing focus on linkages between gender and the environment in development research, policy and practice. Gender-environmental relations are seen as integral to the social and economic organisation which mediates people's relationships with their particular environment. Gender is also viewed as a key dimension of social difference affecting people's experiences, concerns and capabilities in natural resource management. These analyses recognise that gender relations have a powerful influence on how environments are used and managed over time and the effects of this on patterns of ecological change (Leach, *et al.,* 1995).

Why is a gender perspective important? Environmentally sustainable development requires that livelihood activities be ecologically sound, socio-culturally acceptable, economically viable and equitable in terms of access to resources, benefits and decision-making processes. In this respect, a gender perspective is essential for achieving the goals of environmentally sustainable development because of three overlapping factors which, if ignored, can result in further depletion of environmental capital. These three factors are: (i) experiences of poverty and environmental change are gender-differentiated; (ii) environmental security is mediated by gender relations; and (iii) women and men have both conflicting and complementary interests and roles in environmental management. Environmental interventions need to take into account the relationships between environmental sustainability and gender equality. Other factors such as age, class and ethnicity, which also influence gendered experiences of poverty and environmental change, are equally important.

Gender, Poverty and Environmental Change

There are significant differences between women's and men's experiences of poverty and environmental change because of gender inequalities in ability to have command over environmental resource entitlements (e.g., land, trees), labour and income. These inequalities leave women with limited flexibility to respond to environmental changes in ways which maintain environmental resources. Some of the major factors affecting environmental change are discussed below:

(a) Command over Labour and Environmental Change

Women's heavier total workload constrains the allocation of their labour time, for example, forcing them more often than men to make trade-offs between environment conserving activities, socio-economic activities and health. For example, a woman who may have to combine food production with work on a husband's cash crops may have little time to invest in regenerating and sustaining the natural resource base. In parts of India, Nepal and other developing countries, women travel long distances to find fuel-wood due to deforestation. This reduces their inputs into agricultural production and environmental conservation (Leach and Mearns, 1991). These examples point to women's effective incapacity to make certain choices.

(b) Livelihood Strategies and Environmental Change

Generally, women's livelihood strategies are more limited than men's. Participation in distant labour markets is an extremely flexible strategy for minimising risks such as unpredictable variations in rainfall that result in natural crises. Men are more able than women to resort to migration as a longer-term strategy to reduce exposure to risk, whilst women may be thrust into greater dependency on the natural resource base. The widely held view that male out-migration makes women more vulnerable is questionable, because in some instances, male migration gives women greater decision-making powers, and opens up new livelihood possibilities (Redclift and Skea, 1997). Other livelihood strategies such as accumulating savings for harder times are not gender neutral. Gender disparities in access to income, combined with intra-household expenditure divisions and lesser rights in natural resource use, restrict women's ability to accumulate savings which could be a springboard to other rural non-farm activities. In general, the poorer the household, greater the dependence on the natural resource base and on customary rights of access to common resources, e.g., firewood for cooking, fodder for feeding livestock, wood for the construction of houses. Such access is particularly important to women. This access is also gender-differentiated. In parts of Sub-Saharan Africa, men's rights to trees and their products tend to be stronger than women's rights since men have full disposal rights while women have rights only for gathering fuel (Joekes, *et al.,* 1996).

Women's greater dependency on Common Property Resources (CPR) has been documented in India. Agarwal, (1994) shows that rural Indian women, depend more on employment in agriculture, on the natural resource base and common property resources than men. Women's share of labour force participation is 85 per cent in agriculture while male labour force participation is declining. This high dependence on CPR in India has policy implications for women, particularly as the productivity of India's CPR is falling drastically, and the acreage decreasing as a consequence of high population density, land privatisation, codification and titling etc. (Jodha, 1995, 1991). Access to CPR is being curtailed by changes in land tenure fuelled by privatisation and land grabbing (Sida, 1996). In addition, commercial pressures in many places are leading community institutions to re-interpret customary rights and obligations from collective use to individualised rights, a process which often disadvantages women (Woodhouse, 1997).

(c) Macro-economic Policies, Poverty and Environmental Change

Links between macro-economic policies, gender relations, poverty and the environment are not clear. Through, case studies from different Asian countries, Wee and Heyzer (1995), attempt to show how national and international economic policies that contribute to environmental degradation also fuel the feminisation of poverty. In these contexts, they suggest that women's resource loss and their increasing poverty has to be understood at three levels:

- (i) in terms of persisting gender inequities derived from the historical past, which have traditionally subordinated women;
- (ii) in terms of the reinforcement of existing inequities to serve the context of the present, such that women are excluded and disenfranchised from increasingly scarce resources; and
- (iii) in terms of new processes that have resulted in women's loss of livelihood resources (Wee and Heyzer, 1995).

However, the links between women's loss of livelihood resources and material impoverishment under environmental change are not clear. In Morocco, women are impoverished by environmental change in terms of increased energy demands and workloads, but there is no data on other measures of poverty (El Mdaghri, 1995). A study of some communities in Limbang district, Malaysia, highlighted variable community responses to declining resource availabilities in the face of deforestation and changes in Government policy (Heyzer, 1995). In terms of material indicators, women were better off than before. The lack of diversity in livelihood activities may have increased women's vulnerability, but not their actual standard of living. By contrast, in Kenya, anthropometric data shows that men's body weight fluctuates more inter-seasonally than women's (Oniango, 1995). Women's position in terms of relatively less access to resources, labour and decision-making powers to invest in managing natural resources translates into greater poverty depends on whether they can lay claim to other forms of support from households, kin, etc. when disaster strikes. This inevitably depends on the nature of gender relations in any given location.

(d) Impact of Environmentally Induced Population Displacements

The environmental impact of mass migrations and environmental change as a cause for migration are increasingly receiving attention (IOM, 1996). The concerns about the impact of migrants on the natural environment of host regions are relatively new. The environmental impact of mass migrations may be different for men and women. Pressure on firewood may be felt initially by women in terms of increased journey times. There was some concern that travelling long distances to fetch firewood made women more vulnerable to banditry and violence. Time spent on cooking may increase for women in cases of environmental changes such as deforestation. Women may have to resort to using green wood rather than dry wood.

Gender Relations and Environmental Security

"Environmental Security" means access to clean water, clean air and non-degraded land (Redclift and Skea, 1997). It is influenced by gender relations. Men and women in rural areas are primary resource users, but access to resources is socially constructed, so that men and women derive different benefits and uses from natural resources and in times of environmental shocks and crises may have fewer assets to fall back on, and limited diversification strategies. Some of the issues related to environmental security are discussed below:

1. Entitlements Analysis of Environmental Security

Entitlements analysis provides a framework to show how access to and control over resources is socially differentiated by focusing on following three elements:

(i) *Endowments*—the rights and resources that people have, e.g., land, labour, skills etc.;
(ii) *Environmental Entitlement*—the utilities derived from

Box 2: Entitlement Analysis of Access to and use of *Marantaceae* Plants, South Ghana.

Endowments—rights over the leaves—

- on Government reserved land, collection rights are acquired through a permit system.
- off-reserve, collection rights are acquired through membership or negotiation with the landholding family or household.

Entitlements—effective command over income from leaves (labour and marketing)—

- women may have to negotiate labour time to collect leaves.
- access to marketing is through village-based or visiting traders.

Capabilities—to satisfy needs—

- whether a woman can keep control of the income, and how it is used depends on intra-household bargaining arrangements.

environmental goods and services over which people have legitimate effective command such as direct uses in the form of commodities such as food, water, fuel or to environmental service functions, such as pollution sinks or properties of the hydrological cycle; and

(iii) *Capabilities*—what people can do or be with their entitlements, e.g., command over fuel resources derived from rights over trees (Leach, *et al.*, 1997).

2. Market-based Alternatives for Environmental Security

Because of nature of their responsibilities and direct dependence on land-based resources, women are the hardest hit by environmental degradation (UNEP, 1995), particularly in rural areas where women's livelihoods tend to be more resource-based rather than money-based (Wee and Heyzer, 1991). Poor women may become trapped into short-time horizons with respect to resources over which they have little control, because they lack assurances of future access to resources and because they lack other economic opportunities. To the extent that they are excluded from participation in the market economy, they also rely directly on non-market natural resources for their immediate survival (UNEP, 1995). Money or market-based activities are important fall-back options, when environmental security is threatened by variations in rainfall, desertification, soil and land degradation, flooding, etc. In general, men have more diversification strategies than women to limit environmental risks and vulnerability such as migration. Women have less access to productive assets and in cases where they do hold assets which tend to be consumption-based assets with low disposal value (Kabeer 1991).

3. Health and Environmental Security

An immediate environmental problem is ill-health caused by biological and chemical agents in water, food and the soil. While all people may be subject to parasitic infestations, women and children may be more likely to suffer from respiratory diseases caused or exacerbated by smoke and fumes from biomass and *fossil fuels* used for cooking due to their greater levels of exposure (Hardoy, *et al.*, 1992).

Gendered Interests and Incentives in Environmental Management

Women tend to have a greater involvement in environmentally sustainable activities and environmental management than men, but may incur certain costs or lack the required resources and decision-making powers to command control over resources.

1. Gender Differentials in Environmental Resource Management

Men's and women's interests in and incentives for environmental resource management differ in many situations, partly because of their socially constructed roles, and partly because of their lesser property rights and gendered interests. Women's socially constructed roles typically involve them in the management and use of environmental resources. A study of poor communities in three Latin American countries indicated that women make significantly larger contributions to managing or ameliorating the negative effects on family welfare of natural resource decline and environmental pollution, particularly among the poor (Paolisso and Gammage, 1996). The said study found that women's time and task allocations change in response to environmental degradation. Environmental tasks appear to impose additional burdens on women because their existing productive and reproductive activities are not easily transferred to other household members. This inability to substitute for female labour arises from high demographic dependency ratios, existing demands on household labour, and socio-cultural practices that determine the gender division of labour. Women's environmental tasks represent an important part of the household's first-line of defence against environmental degradation. Despite the time they spend mitigating the costs of environmental degradation, women and their families are still at risk of environmental health problems due to lack of public infrastructure and proper services, poverty and demographic constraints. They are also not aware about environmental health risks and dangers.

2. Tenure Rights, Ownership and Environmental Management

Other research shows that women's natural resource tenure rights and control over decisions rarely match their extensive environment-related work responsibilities. In Zaire, for example, men usually allocate securely-tenured household land to permanent tree crops such as coffee. Women's food crops are marginalised onto annually-rented steeply-sloped land with erosive soils, where they have little incentive to invest in soil conservation structures (Leach and Mearns, 1991).

3. Power Over Decision-making and Environmental Management

The many different ways in which water is used and managed often have distinct implications for men and women users. In Burkina Faso, women were in charge of rice production on the lowlands and men worked on higher value crops on the rainfed uplands. Development staff nevertheless deferred to the men for inputs on the design and management of new rice irrigation works, despite the fact that the men had limited knowledge of irrigated rice and that their interest was limited to land value (van Wijk *et al.,* 1996).

Policy Implications and Recommendations

1. Diversifying Livelihood Strategies

There is a need to widen the range of livelihood choices available to poor men and women by taking into consideration gendered differences in rights over land and resources. This implies a need for non-environment focused interventions such as market-based initiatives to enhance environmentally sustainable development (Leach and Mearns, 1991; Joekes *et al.,* 1996). Other poverty reduction focused measures are also a pre-requisite for environmentally sustainable development. Investments are required in both natural and human capital (UNEP, 1995).

2. *Natural Resources Management*

Alternative approaches are required which focus more on resource users rather than resources, recognising that women are key agents of change (Steady, 1993). Effective natural resources management requires a genuinely participatory approach that emphasises the different activities of household members to ensure that different uses and impacts of natural resources are recognised and accounted for in natural resource management (van Wijk, *et al.*, 1996). Where charges, e.g. for water, are involved, policies need to take account of the fact that women have lesser command over cash than men and that where men control household expenditure, they may not give proper weight to women's interests or priorities. Policy needs to recognise that men and women's interests in and incentives for environmental resource management differ in many situations. Furthermore, environmental management initiatives should give some consideration to women's time constraints and workload. Projects that rely heavily on women's inputs should pay for women's time and labour.

3. *Valuing Women's Work*

There is a need for greater attention to women's contributions to enhancing environmental capital. Both women and the environment are "shadow subsidies" that enable profits to be made, because both are taken as free goods. There is undervaluation of both environmental resources and of women's labour in managing and conserving these. Methods of valuing women's work as well as environmental goods need to be incorporated into approaches of environmentally sustainable development.

4. *Institutional Aspects of Environmental Change*

The institutional aspects of environmental change require some policy attention. There is widespread consensus within international development circles that environmentally sustainable development should be based on local-level solutions derived from community initiatives. But expectations often fall short because community approaches tend to ignore power and social difference. In terms of bargaining power, interests and needs, community-based organisations can like other institutions, reproduce relations of unequal power and authority (Leach, *et al.*, 1997). Policies aimed at environmental solutions through decentralisation, particularly the devolution of responsibility for natural resources to local communities need to consider social difference and gender relations.

5. *Property Rights*

In the wider context, attention to women's lesser property rights is required and the danger of further institutionalising gender disadvantage with moves towards individual ownership, unless counteracting measures are taken. Strengthening women's legal rights needs to be complemented by measures to improve women's bargaining power at local-level.

6. *Macro-Micro Policy Linkages*

There is a need for approaches that address both macro- and micro-problems. A recent approach to operationalising sustainable development within the development context has been Primary Environmental Care (PEC), promoted by NGOs. However, PEC deals only with environmental problems at local project or regional levels in the South. It does not address such poverty-inducing macro-economic processes like structural adjustment policies and austerity measures, which impose additional stress on local environments. Such policies necessitate people's increased reliance on local resources for their survival needs (Braidotti and Wieringa, 1994).

Effective natural resources management requires participatory approaches that take into account the different activities of household members, the impact of their different uses of natural resources on the environment, and the gendered interests and incentives for natural resource management. It is clear that more detailed research is required to establish the links between gender and environmental management in different contexts. This will include examination of the trade-offs faced by poor women between sustainable management of environmental resources, economic benefits and well-being. Use of pricing instruments in the management of environmental resources has gender differentiated effects (Joekes, *et al.,* 1996). The gender biases in community organisations and other forms of governance at the local level are a theme that warrants specific research.

References

Anderson, L., 1994, "Ecological Aspects of Drought Mitigation", *Insights for Policy-makers,* 12, Brighton: IDS.

Agarwal, B., 1994, *A Field of One's Own: Gender and Land Rights in South Asia*, Cambridge: Cambridge University Press.

Braidotti, R. and Wieringa, S., 1994. *Women, the Environment and Sustainable Development: Towards a Theoretical Synthesis*, London: Zed Books.

El Mdaghri, C., 1995, "Women, Environment and Population: A Moroccan Case Study", *IDS Bulletin: Gender Relations and Environmental Change*, 26 (1).

Hardoy, J., Mitlin, D. and Sattherthwaite, D., 1992, "Sustainable Development and Cities", in Hardoy, J., Mitlin, D., and Sattherthwaite, D. (Ed.): *Environmental Problems in Third World Cities*. London: Earthscan.

IOM, 1996, "Environmentally—Induced Population Displacements and Environmental Impacts Resulting from Mass Migrations", *International Symposium UNHCR*, IOM, RPG, April.

Jackson, C., 1993, "Doing What Comes Naturally? Women and Environment in Development", *World Development*, 21(12).

Jodha, N., 1991, *Rural Common Property Resources: A Growing Crisis*, International Institute for Environment and Development (IIED), Sustainable Agriculture Programme Series, No. 24, London: IIED

Jodha, N., 1995, "Common Property Resources and the Dynamics of Rural Poverty in India's Regions", *Unasylva: An International Journal of Forestry and Forest Industries*, 46 (180).

Joekes, S., Green, C. and Leach, M., 1996, "Integrating Gender into Environmental Research and Policy", *IDS Working Paper* 27, Brighton: IDS.

Joekes, S., Leach M. and Green, C., 1995, "Editorial: Environmental Change", *IDS Bulletin: Gender Relations and Environmental Change*, 26(1).

Kabeer, N., 1991, "Gender, Production and Well-Being: Rethinking the Household", *IDS Discussion Paper,* No. 288. Brighton: IDS.

Leach, M., 1992, "Gender and the Environment: Traps and Opportunities", *Development in Practice*, 2(1).

Leach, M. and Mearns, R., 1991, "Poverty and Environment in Developing Countries: An Overview Study", *Final Report to Economic and Social Research Council Society and Politics Group and Global Environmental Change Initiative Programme and Overseas Development Administration,* Brighton: IDS.

Leach, M., Mearns, R. and Scoones, I., 1997, "Environmental Entitlements: A Conceptual Framework for Understanding the Institutional Dynamics of Environmental Change", *IDS Discussion Paper*, No. 359, Brighton: IDS.

Oniango, R., 1995, "The Impact of Out-Migration on Household Livelihoods and on the Management of Natural Resources: A Kenyan Study", *IDS Bulletin: Gender Relations and Environmental Change*, 26 (1).

Paolisso, M. and Gammage, S., 1996, *Women's Responses to Environmental Degradation: Poverty and Demographic Constraints. Case studies from Latin America*, Washington: ICRW.

Raskin, R., Chadwick, M., Jackson, T. and Leach, G., 1996, *The Sustainability Transition: Beyond Conventional Development*. Stockholm: Stockholm Environment Institute.

Redclift, M. and Skea, J., 1997, "Environmental Security", *Insights* 21, Brighton: IDS.

Sida, 1995, *Promoting Sustainable Livelihoods: A Report from the Task Force on Poverty*, Stockholm: SIDA.

Steady, F., 1993, *Women and Children First: Environment, Poverty and Sustainable Development*, Vermont: Schenkman.

UNCHS, 1996, *Natural Resources Forum: A UN Journal*, *A Special Issue on Women and Natural Resources Management,* 20 (2).

UNEP, 1995, *Poverty and the Environment: Reconciling Short-term Needs with Long-term Sustainability Goals*. Nairobi: UNEP.

Wijk, C., de Lange, E. and Saunders, D., 1996, "Gender Aspects in the Management of Water", *Natural Resources Forum: A United Nations Journal*, 20 (2).

Wee, V. and Heyzer, N., 1995, *Gender, Poverty and Sustainable Development: Towards a Holistic Framework of Understanding and Action*, New York: ENGENDER, UNDP.

Woodhouse, P., 1997, "Land, Water, and Local Governance in Dry Land Africa", *Insights* 21, Brighton: IDS.

World Commission on Environment and Development (WCED), 1987, *Our Common Future*, Oxford: Oxford University Press.

19

Community, Cultural Practices and Reproductive Health of Women

Partha Sarathi De and *Amit Bhowmick*

Introduction

Indian society is very old, complex, plural and has a long history (Das, Chand, Jana, 2006). According to a popular estimate it has covered a span of five thousand years since the period of its first known civilization. During this long period several waves of immigrants, representing different ethnic strains and linguistic families, have merged into its population to contribute to its diversity, richness, and vitality (Dube, 1990). It is composed of different religious groups, racial groups and groups having cultural differences. In the long span of Indian history various groups from different parts of the world entered India with their own socio-cultural and racial features. The best example is Indus valley civilization (Das, Chand, Jana, 2006). Most of the major religions of the world—Hinduism, Islam, Christianity, and Buddhism—are found here, and in addition there is a bewildering variety of cults and sects with different orientations in belief and ritual (Dube, 1990). India has long been reckoned as the most stratified of all known societies in human history. The caste system with its myriad forms of super ordination and subordination, its many customs and taboos, is perhaps most responsible for conferring on India this dubious honour. Economically too India is highly stratified. As a people Indians have been deeply involved in moral and ethical questions regarding the caste system, cultural diversity and economic inequality (Gupta, 2004). Women can play an important role in determining the destiny of a nation. But history reveals that women have not been given their due status in the Indian society and precisely in the community sphere. They have been and still are the victim of various social taboos particularly in developing countries like India. The concept of equality is said to be the key word in the modern society but the attitude of discrimination against the second sex continues to exist. The root of inequality lies in the patriarchal nature of Indian society where subordination over the female folk continues to be dominant through the ages up to middle of the twentieth century. The role of community and its importance in Indian society was undeniable fact. Nobody can ignore the acquaintance of social living, because of its peculiar distinctiveness. Contextually, community is a self-conscious social unit and a focus of group identification. It also implies a certain identification of the inhabitants with the geographic are and with each other, a feeling of sharing common interests and goals, a certain amount of mutual cooperation, and awareness of the existence of the community in both its inhabitants and those in the surrounding area.

Cultural practices emanates from the community living and the rudiments of tradition that flows from generation after generation. As a concept culture is that complex whole which includes knowledge, beliefs, art, morals, law, custom, and any other capabilities and habits acquired by man as a member of society (Tylor, 1871). Therefore, it is the way of life of a social group. With the existence of village community, caste and joint family, three important pillars of Indian society, individuals have been sharing with the customs, folkways, mores, taboos with their fellows which are intermingled and deeply embedded in their minds that cannot be uprooted all of a sudden. Therefore, women, due to their subjugated position in the society, continue to pursue all the prevailing as well as emerging customary behavour without showing reasons whatsoever. The phases of reproductive health of women are the one such example of Indian society. Reproductive health is nothing, but the state of health during reproductive life in a total life span. In literary sense if the term—It is a state of complete physical, mental and social well-being and not merely the absence of disease or infirmity, in all matters relating to the reproductive system and to its functions and processes. Any attempt to improve in the sphere of reproductive health that has been motivated towards improvement of general health of female population. It is the basis for women's empowerment and healthy social and economic development of a country.

Indian Society, Inequality and Women

Indian society is mostly male dominated and the status of women is secondary in India (Bhatnagar, 1992). A woman has been a second rate citizen through ages (Raizada, 1992). They were increasingly dominated by social rigidities and historical events. The culture of a nation is judged by its behaviour and attitude towards women. When the Indians came in vital contact with the British in the latter half of the eighteenth century, the position of the Indian woman had reached the maximum degree of deterioration (Misra, 2007). Any assessment on the status of women has to start from social framework. Social structures, cultural norms and the value systems influence social expectations regarding the behaviour of both men and women, and determine women's role and her status in the society. They are culturally trained, through the process of socialization not to challenge discrimination, subordination, exploitation and subjugation within the social structure.

Women are an integral part of a society. They play an important role in determining the destiny of a nation. But history reveals that women have not been given their due status in the society. Women's suppression is rooted in the very fabric of Indian society. The patriarchal nature of the Indian society has always stood as an obstacle in the path of women's progress. Amartya Sen (1987) illustrated with examples, the different kinds of inequality between men and women that exist in most parts of the world. These are as below: mortality, inequality, natality inequality, basic facility inequality, special opportunity inequality, professional inequality, ownership inequality, and household inequality.

Health Status of Women

The concept of women's status and reproductive health does not only relate to health or fertility but is linked with the growing desire of women to be independent and equal in all spheres of human activity (Pati, 2002). Reproductive health implies that people are able to have a satisfying and safe sex for life and that they have the capacity to reproduce and the freedom of decision if, when and how often to do so. It is the right of men and women to be informed of and to have access to effective, affordable and acceptable methods of family planning of their choice, as well as other methods of their choice for regulation of fertility which are not against the law. The right of access to appropriate health care services that will enable women to go safely through pregnancy and childbirth and provide couples with a best chance of having a healthy infant.

In traditional societies people perceive health and sickness in their cultural terms. Healthy children possess better learning capacity, which translates into better earning capacity (Indian Human Development Report, 2011). Health is another indicator of women's status and empowerment in the society (Misra, 2007). A better health status plays a vital role in the enhancement of human capabilities in general and woman in particular (Sen, 1987). The health condition of Indian women is not good. Women eat after men; the diet of many Indian women is inadequate. A high proportion of women receive no medical treatment for illness and many use home remedies or traditional healers. Women's access to health care facilities has gradually been increasing through diverse initiatives of Government for the improvement of female education and employment opportunities. According to the Second National Family Health Survey, only 53 per cent of women in India are ever consulted on decisions about their own health when children fall sick, the possibility that medical help will be sought for boys than girls (NFHS-II). Women's nutrition, health and mortality are influenced by the nature of India's social environment (Sinha, 2007). The poor health of Indian women is a concern for women, family and ultimately for the nation. It is ascertained that the health of the future issues and children may be affected if mother's health is not sound enough for reproduction. It is the concern to a nation, like India, that how can it be possible for them to become an effective and productive next generation. Hence, there will definitely be a chance of reduction of productivity, both at the household level, as well as in different sectors of economy. The Government of India in its Ninth Plan period lunched the Reproductive and Child Health (RCH) programme in October 1997. It was an integrated and holistic approach that combines Child Survival and Safe Motherhood (CSSM) with a provision of family welfare and health care services.

Women and Cultural Practices

Although, science and technology has played an important role in this post-modern era, traditionalism is still present and people are as superstitious today as they have ever been. Superstitions, myths, beliefs, rituals, taboos, folkways, mores and customs have been and are still present in the daily life as they are part of our culture. They are often uncritically accepted automatically without much thought for their authenticity (Krajewsks, Kulak, Radziejwska, Lankau, Ortman, 2011). We understand the term 'superstition' as an irrational belief or practice, something, that is not based on knowledge or fact, an irrational fear of the unknown, or a blindly accepted belief. Essentially, it is based on fear and ignorance. Superstitions are a belief in a non-physical (i.e. supernatural) causality—that an event causes another without any physical process linking the two events. It is also commonly applied to beliefs and practices surrounding luck, prophecy and spiritual beings, particularly the belief that future events can be foretold by specific, unrelated prior events (http://en.wikipedia. org/wiki/ superstition). By and large superstitions take three forms which can be defined thus:

(i) The idea that if a certain action is taken then bad luck will be result.
(ii) The performing of a specified ritual which will bring about desired results.

(iii) The reading of omens by which a definite event, good or bad, will occur (Philippa Warning, 1998).

There are four species of superstitions:

(i) Improper worship of the true God
(ii) Idolatry
(iii) Divination
(iv) Vain observances, which include magic and occult arts.

It is a part of culture and varies from society to society. There are many superstitions in the world based on religion, old stories, legends and personal experience. Such superstitions may influence people's behaviour in various social situations. In many cultures, there are amulets that have the power to protect from disease and evil (Krajewsks, Kulak and others, 2011). Presently many people believe that precious stones and plants, especially root of the Mandrake, can bring safety, security, peace and happiness. Superstitious behaviour that arises through the incorrect assignment of cause and effect receives considerable attention in a psychology and medicine which typically frame superstitions as irrational mistakes in cognition (Vyse, 2000; Believing in Magic, The Psychology of Superstition). The process of a girl becoming a mother is not merely biological. It is a psycho-social matter. For this, a pregnant lady undergoes several social customs and religious rule. In most cases those are baseless and devoid of any scientific reason, yet a pregnant lady is forced to follow them. The customs are: in the period of pregnancy she has to tie the locks of her hair always, she has to return to her home before sunset, she has to keep herself always away from burning *ghat* and graveyard, she cannot visit a dead body, they are not allowed to taste prawn, mrigel, sheat-fish, they are not allowed to taste pineapple, orange etc., they are not allowed to wear deeply coloured sarees, they are not allowed to enjoy evening air, they are not allowed to give alms with unlock hair, they are not allowed to see a widow or infertile women, they are not allowed to eat twin fruit etc.

Food rituals are still popular today. Many religious taboos relating to foods are well-known in the West, but some are better known than others. In Western folklore, the apple is the symbol of love and fertility. A pregnant woman is subjected to different do's and do nots about her food. Generally, Women are not allowed to taste prawn, hilsa, sheat-fish, pineapple, mrigel, eel, orange, esculent root. The real contradiction lies in the fact that even the pregnant women themselves believe in such dictums. They believe that prawn would cause a child with curly hair. The mrigel fish would cause hysteria to her child. Eel fish would cause her child ill health. Hilsa fish may cause some blister on his body. Superstition has always claimed it is lucky to put on any item of clothing inside out, while it is unlucky to button anything wrongly (Waring, 1998). Women are advised not to wear sarees of deep and bright coloured. The belief goes that such attractive colours may attract supernatural and foul spirit on the lady; it may have bad effects on the child in her womb. During pregnancy the women must follow some regulations in the case of her movement. The pregnant woman must not go outside the room after evening especially on Tuesdays and Saturdays. It is the belief that if she goes outside the room, supernatural elements such as phantom, witch etc., can affect her and her unborn child. During pregnancy, she must not visit burning *ghats* and burial places; if she goes the unborn child may face premature death. A pregnant lady is subjected to different restrictions on her movement. Some of those could be: to return home before sunset, cannot go outside at noon or in the evening, not to go anywhere with unlocked hair, not to walk by the side of graveyard or burning *ghat*, not to enter in a labour room etc.

In Indian society, the family celebrates '*Sadh*' (function on pre-delivery of pregnant mothers) one or two months before delivery. The function is carried out by arranging varieties of food for the expected mothers in one hand and on the other hand it boosts up the morale of the pregnant mothers before delivery. The system being a traditional one every pregnant mother expects '*Sadh*' from their family as symbol of good sign for the offspring. For the sake of having a son the pregnant mother, sometimes herself or sometimes by pleasure, wear amulet and armlet on her hands. When a woman does not get a child in three or four years of gap after married life she is advised to do many things by other women. She is asked to go to some '*Devata*' or '*Mataji*' or swearing of not cutting the hair of her child for a certain period. In tribal societies it is seen that women pray for getting child, observe fast and take votives. There are so many unscientific and false notions running high among the village folks. One of them is the belief in the strength of spirit. They believe that the supernatural forces can play ominous role on the health of a pregnant and well being of her baby inside. During pregnancy a woman may have many physical problems. The village folk, most of the time believes that the magical effect of a village exorcist can cure the pregnant woman better than a doctor. Sometimes they take some preventive measures. They are: to keep an amulet at home from *Fakir*, to keep a piece of iron indoors, to keep a leather shoe inside the room, to keep an iron bar at the entrance of the room, and to keep match sticks on bed.

They think such materials may prevent the evil spirit from doing anything ominous. The door is the main entrance of the home, providing access to people, luck and evil spirits. Not surprisingly, superstition demands that this entrance be well protected. Hanging a horseshoe above the door provides good luck and protection. Ornaments, such as statues, are also used sometimes. A cross might be placed on the door to repel witches. The horseshoe is one of the best known lucky charms. It is believed to both avert evil and attract good luck. The power of the horseshoe superstition almost certainly developed because it was created in the sacred fire and made from sacred metal and iron. The pregnant ladies obey some restrictions regarding solar and lunar eclipse and the day of the new moon. They think that if they do not obey such restrictions their baby may be born disabled and crippled. A pregnant lady never gives alms with unlock hair. They fear that she may fall a victim to some satanic forces in such case. Like the pregnant ladies, the feeding ladies are also subjected to different restrictions and prohibitions regarding their intake of food. They are prohibited from having *hilsa* fish, prawn, dry fish, bringal, tamarind, mutton, duck-flesh, duck-egg, spicy soup, pineapple, *dal*, different leaves. The child may have breathing trouble if a feeding mother eats duck-flesh, duck-egg, and mutton. The other listed items may cause abdominal trouble to the baby. There may be some scientific reason in the selection of food but the feeding mother obeying such restrictions is only a matter of blind faith. A mother is very careful about the health and well-being of her child; even a little illness of her baby may become cause of her anxiety and concern. She is found to use amulet, armlet and charmed water. Another superstition is to keep a piece of iron in the child's bed. The mother thinks that by virtue of this piece of iron her child will remain harmless. So, there is the custom of using iron pieces even in the labour room. They think the iron can prevent spirit and ghost from doing any damage.

Woman's perception about reproductive health is closely related to the local customs, beliefs and tradition of the groups. Human behaviour occurs always in a cultural milieu and that the judgement of that behaviour is always culturally relative. There exists some important links between cultural pressure and values on the one hand and behavioural practice on the other. Patterns of behaviour may be seen as a product of social and cultural conditioning because they may be experienced and enacted naturally in social contents within which they appear relevant (Sharma, 2007). A variety of socio-economic and cultural factors shape the individual's reproductive aspirations and behaviour.

Most of the respondents are having more than 4 members in their family. Hence, crowding families have a considerable influence over the reproductive mothers' health and as a matter of fact, as the total number of members increase the problems of supply of nutritious food decreases. It has been surprisingly discern from a study that women of rural Bengal still prefer their place of delivery at home rather than the modern facilities available at the institutional setup. This may cause high mortality rate. A significant number of deliveries made with the assistance of untrained *Dai* in rural Bengal (40.69%). Therefore, lack of doctors, nurse and trained *Dai* is held responsible for the mothers' health to a large extent. The number of children, interval between the children and non-preference of female issue are important factors which determine largely the health of mothers. Birth of a son in a family is a permanent and strong support for the family. Regarding birth of a child, mostly the women of rural India are superstitious and blind about the scientific reasons. In this society, there are prohibitions and restrictions imposed by society on pregnant women and forbidden to act differently. Therefore, most of the women avoid defecating at places where ghosts and spirits prevail, avoid visiting cremation grounds, avoid talking to woman having menstrual difficulties and of them avoid watching sacrifice of animal.

In Indian society, particularly in rural areas there exist some magico-religious beliefs amongst the pregnant women. These beliefs are traditional in nature since time immemorial. All these beliefs stand in the way of securing good health of pregnant mothers as because these beliefs have no scientific base. '*Jhad-Phook*' and 'Amulet' from *Fakir* cannot bring the birth of a child in the family. As a result, the expecting mothers ultimately suffer both physically and mentally which in turn affects their health adversely. Most of the rural people believe in the existence of malevolent spirit. The fear of malevolent spirit leads them to act accordingly depending upon the situation. This sort of social practices is found to prevail in our society. All these practices and beliefs make their mind unscientific which is an important obstacle for getting scientific treatment for their ill health.

Conclusion

Education has been regarded as a significant instrument to bring about the social change and development towards desired goal. In order to properly bring up women, it is not only essential for them but also imperative for making up of family and the advancement of nation as a whole. It is not possible to change the condition of women only through law and legislation. In every sphere of social life, women are denied of their rights and privileges and chances of enrichment. Mother and pregnant women both are equally facing compulsion to practice taboos and customs unequivocally. Those have no justification in the modern times because of the scientific advancement in the field of health and medicine.

The influence of community in our daily lives is so pervasive that cannot be ignored all of a sudden by the members, but the initiatives are on from the concerned corners of our society to educate people about the logic and underlying principles behind any miraculous activities happening simultaneously here and there and within and outside the residence of the members. It is the plea of the society that not to follow and practice any such illogical customs and actions that impede other members of the community directly of indirectly. Though cultural activities are embedded with the community living that should perform without hampering the personal life any more. But they must aware about the consequences of the illogical or irrational activities upon the neighbours. Sometimes that might end of a precious life of fellow members. Everybody should uphold 'fellow-feeling' and 'we-feeling' to a great extent. It is very much expected that our illogical imposition may make vulnerable to the life of both pregnant women and women after child birth. It requires sympathetic attitude to extend all sorts of possible cooperation as a social being.

References

Bhatnagar, U., 1992, "Women in Family and Society", in L. Mishra (Ed.): *Women's Issue—An Indian Perspective*, New Delhi: Northern Book Centre.

Das, M., Chand, S. and Jana, K., 2006, *Indian Society and Culture*, New Delhi: Kalyani Publishers.

Dube, S.C., 1990, *Indian Society*, New Delhi: National Book Trust, India.

Government of India, 2011, *Indian Human Development Report,* 2011, New Delhi: Institute of Applied Manpower Research.

IIPS, 1999, *National Family Health Survey –II, India.* Mumbai: IIPS.

Krajewska, Kulak, E., Kulak, W., Radziejwska, P., Radziejwska, E., Lankau, A., Kowalewska, B., Kandzior, D., Szysko Perlowska, A., Krajewska-Fersishah, K., Ortman, E., Moczydlowska, A., 2011, "Current View of the Traditional Superstitioins in General Population of Podlaskie Province: Preliminary Study", *Prog. Health Science*, 1(2): 76-83.

Misra, P., 2007, *Domestic Violence against Women*, New Delhi: Deep & Deep Publications Pvt. Ltd.

Mohanty, B., 2002, "RCH—A Perspective", in R.N. Pati (Ed.): *Reproductive Child Health*, New Delhi: APH Publishing Corporation.

Pati, R.N., 2002, 'Introduction', in R.N. Pati (Ed.): *Reproductive Child Health*. New Delhi: APH Publishing Corporation.

Raizada, S., 1992, "Social Status of Women in India", in L. Mishra (Ed): *Women's Issue – An Indian Perspective*, New Delhi: Northern Book Centre.

Sen, A., 1992, *Inequality Reexamined*, New York: Russell Sage Foundation.

Sen, A., 2011. *Peace and Democratic Society*, England: Open Book Publishers.

Sharma, V., 2007, "Womens Reproductive Health and Values", in Pandya, R. (Ed.): *Women in India—Issues, Perspective and Solutions,* New Delhi: New Century Publications.

Sinha, A., 2007, "Women Reproductive Health: Status and Challenges". in Pandya, R. (Ed.): *Women in India—Issues, Perspective and Solution*, New Delhi: New Century Publications.

Tylor, E. B., 1871, *Primitive Culture,* Vol. I, London: John Murray.

Vyse, S.A., 2000, "Believing in Magic", *The Psychology of Superstition* Oxford, UK: Oxford University Press.

Warning, P., 1998, *A Dictionary of Women and Superstitions*, London: Souvenir Press Ltd.

www.en.wikipedia. org/wiki/superstition

20

Review of the Scheme of Family Counselling Centre

A Platform to Resolve Marital Disputes

Swapan Shaw

Conceptual Understanding of Terminologies

Family

Family is an oldest institution that has helped the human kind to survive all these centuries. It is united by the ties of marriage, the members interacting and communicating with each other in their respective roles of husband and wife, mother and father, son and daughters etc. It provides an environment of love, belongingness security to its members, which guarantees them marital peace, fulfilment and growth. But today, the scenario is fast changing and the family, a very precious unit of the society is being threatened by many factors. In fact, it has been seen across the country that powerlessness among women is directly proportional to the intensity to violence experienced by women. In the face of widespread prevalence, domestic violence is not acknowledged and has remained invisible from the public domain. Silence is maintained around this issue and it is construed as an issue unworthy of legal or political attention. Phenomenon of domestic violence is recognized as private affair and is kept under wraps because of concerns of guilt, shame and secrecy. Interference into domestic privacy has traditionally been seen as a greater evil than actual violence inflicted upon a woman.

Marriage

Marriage is regarded as a sacrament, as a tie which once tied cannot be untied. The Hindu notion of sacramental marriage differs from that of others. Derrett puts it succinctly thus: the intention of the sacrament is to make the husband and wife one, for physical and spiritual purposes, for this life and for after lives.

Domestic Violence

Domestic Violence Act, 2005 defines domestic violence as abuse or threat of abuse that is physical, sexual, verbal, emotional and economic. Harassment by way of unlawful dowry demands to the woman or her relatives has also been covered under this definition.

Reasons for Family Disputes

A few reasons for family disputes are as follows: (i) the wife, as such, may not consider the husband as the sole provider, protector or philosopher who will direct and control major or even minor family decisions; (ii) when provocations and hurting each other by taunts, sarcasms and abuses become a repetitive pattern of behaviour of spouses; (iii) wife battering, dowry, bride burning; (iv) violent behaviour of either spouse more often than not the husbands; (v) another factor is education, particularly when the wife is more educated than the husband and the husband does not have regular or steady work; (vi) use of alcohol and drug abuse are also important factors; (vii) some women consider sex dirty and find it difficult to enjoy it with their partners, the husband or the wife or both may be anxiety prone; (viii) in many parts of India the question of dowry or promised dowry becomes a bone of contention and a point of wrangling between the spouses and thus the situation may be further worsened or aggravated by needless interference from in-laws; (ix) extra marital relations by either spouse or promiscuity; (x) doubting the integrity/character of spouse (by either spouse); and (xi) there are highly competent wives who may make the husband feel small. They are indiscriminate, insensitive and do not exercise caution in hurting fragile male vanity. The husband may retaliate to cover-up feelings of inferiority by showing his physical power and aggression.

In India, in the wake of increased family disputes, divorces, family violence, and dowry harassment and family maladjustments, some support systems came into existence to help the victims and the aggrieved parties. This gave rise to introduction of family courts and the concept of Family Counselling Centres.

The Family Courts

Family courts are a specialized type of courts entrusted with the disposal of cases concerning disputes relating to the family. In brief, these courts deal with litigation concerning marriage and divorce, maintenance, guardianship and the property of spouses. They are established under the Family Courts Act, 1984.

The object of family courts (as stated by the legislature) is to promote conciliation and secure speedy settlement of disputes relating to marriage and family affairs. Besides this, the idea underlying the movement for family courts is that ordinary courts with their conservative atmosphere, setting and procedure, cannot appropriately deal with family disputes in the proper spirit. There is also the feeling that all matters concerning a family should be settled speedily in one court.

A Family Court may consist of one Judge, or may consist of more than one Judge. The Judges are appointed by the State Government with the concurrence of the High Court. Where it consists of more than one Judge, the State Government, with the concurrence of the High Court, may appoint a Principal Judge and an Additional Principal Judge.

The State Government, in consultation with the High Court, determines the number and categories of counsellors, officers and other employees required to assist a Family Court. The educational background of these counsellors should be graduate with a law degree. They are appointed on contractual basis for the initial period of six months and further, extended based on their success and performance. These family counsellors discuss the case with both the parties and try to come up with acceptable solution/compromise accepted to both the parties then again these case files are sent back to the Additional District Judge for final decision.

Counselling

The term counselling denotes a wide variety of procedures for helping individuals to achieve adjustment, such as giving help in finding solution to problems and therapeutic discussion. It aims at making individual self-sufficient, self-directed and to adjust themselves efficiently to the demands of a better and meaningful life.

According to Rogers, an effective counselling consists of a definitely structure permissive relationship which allows the client to gain an understanding of himself to a degree which enables him to take positive steps in the light of his new orientation.

The term counselling is used in a number of ways. It is viewed as a special kind of helping relationship, or as a set of activities and methods or as defining an area in which services are provided.

The Family Counselling Centres as a Scheme

The concept of family counselling was conceptualized by the Central Social Welfare Board (CSWB) in 1980s when there was a spate of dowry deaths. The Board spearheaded the campaign by setting up Voluntary Action Bureaus, which subsequently took the shape of Family Counselling Centres.

The objective of the Family Counselling Centres is to provide preventive and rehabilitative services to women and families who are victims of atrocities and family mal-adjustments through crisis intervention and systematic counselling. The centres also create awareness and mobilize public opinion on social issues affecting status of women. The scheme of Family Counselling Centres (FCCs) was launched by Government of India in 1983 and it is being implemented by CSWB through voluntary organizations across the country. At present, approximately 800 Family

Counselling Centres are functioning in different states. The centres also create awareness and mobilize public opinion on social issues affecting status of women. The FCCs work in close collaboration with the local administration, police, courts, free legal aid cells, medical and psychiatric institutions, vocational training centres, short stay homes etc.

A grant of rupees one lakh ninety-two thousand per annum was given to voluntary organizations for running the centres on an 80:20 matching basis. The budget includes honorarium of two counsellors and other recurring expenditures. Family Counselling Centres (FCCs) have also been set-up for special interventions in different set-ups. These are given below:

FCCs at Police Headquarters

Family Counselling Centres are being run in some Police Headquarters premises under the administrative control of the State Social Welfare Boards. These FCCs were established with the objective of providing speedy crisis intervention to those women whose cases were registered in Police Stations. Such FCCs attempt to arrive at out of court settlement of family discord cases.

FCCs in Mahila Jails

Twenty-three FCCs have been set-up in Mahila Jails in Bihar, Chandigarh, Delhi, Gujarat, Karnataka, Maharashtra, Madhya Pradesh, Orissa, Punjab, Tamil Nadu, Uttar Pradesh and West Bengal.

Pre-marital Counselling Centres

This new initiative is being implemented in Women Development Centres at various colleges in Delhi. They lay special emphasis on pre-marital counselling and deal with other areas of psycho-social crises management for young women.

Centres for Devadasis/Red Light Areas

At present there are two FCCs working for the welfare of *Devadasi* and sex-workers and their children one each in Mumbai (Maharashtra) and Belgaun (Karnataka). The Centres are set-up with the objective of providing preventive services through awareness campaigns on STD, AIDs and other health and legal matters and also rehabilitative measures for children of prostitutes.

However, the FCCs were set-up for reuniting the families and helping the clients to resolve their disputes through a process of dialogue. It was over a quarter century ago the FCCs were established and are still being run all across the country today, contributing in family reintegration and meeting the expectations of aggrieved parties and settling down their disputes as envisaged in the Scheme.

Conclusion

In a country where in every six hours a young married women is burned alive, beaten to death or driven to commit suicide, 37 per cent married women in the country are victims of physical or sexual abuse by their husbands coupled with insensitive judiciary and Police the usefulness or relevance of the scheme of FCC is a foregone conclusion. Further, the responses of innumerable clients who felt after coming to FCC that they came to a 'right place' is reason enough to say that the services provided at FCC are invaluable. The clients not only got psychological support, legal advice, self-reliance but also the FCCs exerted pressure on the Police to register cases where the victims were denied their rights. At places FCCs with the help of media opened up otherwise closed criminal cases to provide support to victims of dowry and domestic violence. The above mentioned facts prove that the scheme is no doubt very useful in providing support to victims of domestic violence and offering a level playing ground to aggrieved parties to settle their disputes to save families from breaking up. There were a number of families which were at logger heads on flimsy grounds and had snapped communication were brought to a common platform to sort out difference by FCCs.

References

Ahuja, R., 1987, *Crime against Women*, Jaipur: Rawat Publications.

Bengtson, *et al.* (Ed.), 2005, *Sourcebook of Family Theory and Research*. New Delhi: Sage Publications.

Bhattacharya, R., 2004, *Behind Closed Doors' Domestic Violence in India*, New Delhi: Sage Publications.

Kant, A., 1997, *Women and the Law*, New Delhi: APH Publishing Corporation.

Kishwar, M.P., 2008, *Zealous Reformers, Deadly Laws: Battling Stereotypes*, New Delhi: Sage Publications.

Mishra, O.P., 2003, *Law Relating to Women and Child*, Allahabad: Central Law Agency.

Namita, A., 2002, *Women and Law in India*, Delhi: New Century Publications.

Nelson, R.J., 2008, *Basic Counselling Skills, (A Helper's Manual)*, New Delhi: Sage Publications.

NIPCCD, 2006, *Counselling Services for Child Survivors of Trafficking: Manual for Counsellors*, New Delhi: Ministry of Women and Child Development.

NIPCCD, 2011, *Family Counselling Centre: A Study*, New Delhi.

Patri, V.R., 2001, *Counselling Psychology*, New Delhi: Authors Press.

Sehgal, M. and Sherjung, N., 1997, *Marital Disputes and Counselling* (Vol. I), New Delhi: APH Publishing Corporation.

Sehgal, M. and Sherjung, N., 1997, *Marital Disputes and Counselling* (Vol. II), New Delhi: APH Publishing Corporation.

Sehgal, M. and Sherjung, N., 1997, *Marital Disputes and Counselling* (Vol. III), New Delhi: APH Publishing Corporation.

Sharma, B.R., 1997, *Women: Marriage, Family Violence and Divorce*, Jaipur: Mangal Deep Publications.

Sinha, P.C., 2000, *Global Sourcebook on Human Rights* (Part II), New Delhi: Kanishka Publishers.

Sinha, S., 1984, *Women's Rights: Myth and Reality*, Jaipur: Print Wells Publications.

Tanwar, R., (ed.), 1998. *Women: Human Rights, Religion and Violence*, Kurukshetra: Nirmal Book Agency.

Index